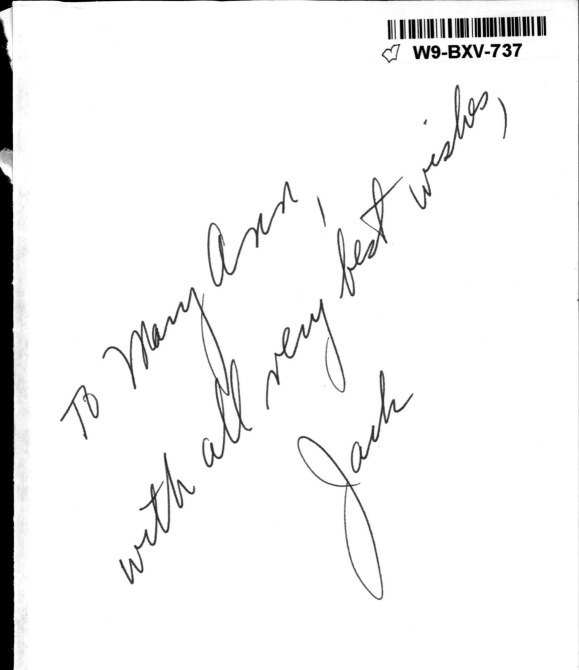

To Mary Ann,
with all very best wishes)

Jack

Defense Conversion

Board of Trustees of the Twentieth Century Fund

Defense Conversion

Transforming the Arsenal of Democracy

Jacques S. Gansler

A Twentieth Century Fund Book
The MIT Press
Cambridge, Massachusetts
London, England

This book was set in Sabon by Graphic Composition, Inc. and was printed and bound in the United States of America.

Library of Congress Cataloging-in-Publication Data
Gansler, Jacques S.
  Defense conversion : transforming the arsenal of democracy / Jacques S. Gansler.
    p. cm.
  Includes bibliographical references and index.
  ISBN 0-262-07166-5
  1. Economic conversion—United States.   2. Defense industries—United States.   I. Title.
HC110.D4G35   1995
338.4 76233 0973—dc20   95-2228
                                                                    CIP

For Leah

Contents

Foreword

For most of U.S. history, defense conversion had a certain similarity to the experience of St. Paul on the road to Damascus: it was sudden and complete. Blessed by domestic tranquillity and buffered by two immense oceans, Americans returned, after each of the nation's early wars, to a level of military spending that was by international standards astonishingly low. The dislocations caused by returning war veterans and cancellation of arms contracts were largely and roughly "solved" by time and the business cycle. Only during and immediately after World War II did policymakers devote serious attention and resources to planning for and coping with the resumption of a peacetime economy. Even that experience turned out to be unusual, for it was premised on the assumption that the United States would be able to demobilize for the foreseeable future— as long as it maintained sufficient nuclear power.

By the late 1940s, the military and budgetary demands of the cold war began to take shape. They proved persistent, if not uniform. Even apart from the massive bulges caused by Korea and Vietnam, there were lesser peaks and valleys caused by changes in the level of tension, in the perception of threat, and in the domestic political climate. Yet, the "minimum" security needs of the nation for more than forty years provided a solid floor of support for the defense industrial base. In this sense, the end of the cold war involved a qualitative, as well as quantitative, change in the sorts of issues that confront those concerned with defense conversion. The choices are complicated not only by the absence of cold war certainties, but also by the enormous cost of most effective weapons.

For several years, as the Soviet threat receded and then seemed to fade dramatically, there have been intense discussions of just how far reductions in the defense budget could and should go. Base closings became a hot-button political issue in virtually every state. During the period 1989 to 1995, the services themselves were reduced by about 250,000 active-duty military personnel. And layoffs in defense industries over roughly the same period amounted to nearly 2 million. The overall defense budget dropped by 8 percent, procurement by 25 percent. As of this writing, additional restraints on federal spending seem certain. Obviously, a new threat to the nation's security could change the situation overnight, but without the broad and deep public consensus that characterized public opinion during the cold war, one must assume that the defense sector is likely to lose ground in the furious competition for national revenues.

There is nothing particularly novel about a significant decline in the output of any industry. Economic theory and generations of experience tell us much about the likely consequences for investors, workers, and communities affected by the change. The costs to them can be very great, but the overall economy may well benefit in the long run by this aspect of dynamic capitalism at work. Two things, at least, make the defense case special: the "consumer's" preferences are determined by an uneven alchemy of politics and perceived international threats, and, perhaps even more extraordinarily, there remains a strong desire for the producer to continue to invest in and improve the product. Indeed, with regard to the latter preference, Americans actually want something more than continued development of the world's most advanced weapons; they also insist on a military force that clearly is the best on the planet. It is also worth noting that, despite the heavy emphasis on reducing global tensions, the U.S. lead in weapons quality contributes to its $600 million trade surplus in armaments sales.

The ideal scenario involves a shift to technologies that cut across civilian and military lines, which would enable the government to save money while maintaining a strong defense base and preserving jobs. Concurrently, tough choices would have to be made about the extent to which restrictions on overseas sales of weapons manufactured in the United States might be eased. The possibility of subsidizing defense plants that may not be needed now to keep them available for future demands also needs to be weighed.

Jacques S. Gansler, senior vice president and director of an applied information technology company, TASC, former deputy assistant secretary of defense, and author of two highly acclaimed books on the defense industry, has a clear vision for converting the military sector in the context of today's unprecedented challenges. He argues that defense companies, encouraged by the federal government through a variety of means, should realign their established manufacturing processes to produce products valued in civilian markets while maintaining their defense capabilities. Gansler includes a wide range of specific examples to demonstrate how the industry could become more efficient and flexible.

Those who will disagree with Gansler's prescription are likely to argue that defense companies will inevitably fail in civilian markets that differ from the unique military sector, which has only a single customer that behaves far differently from private consumers. But Gansler shows how many defense firms have, in fact, succeeded when they branched out into civilian products. A transition of the scope Gansler envisions will not work, however, unless the government overhauls its procurement rules and other overly restrictive policies.

This project bridges two of the Twentieth Century Fund's priorities: developing new directions for American foreign policy and strengthening the U.S. economy and work force. Other Fund books related to the future of the American military include *Small Wars, Big Defense: Paying for the Military After the Cold War* by Murray Weidenbaum, *The Politics of National Security: Congress and U.S. Defense Policy* by Barry M. Blechman, and *The Defense Procurement Mess* by William H. Gregory. We thank Jack Gansler for adding clarity and vision to a timely debate.

Richard C. Leone, President
The Twentieth Century Fund
January 1995

Preface

Defense budgets in the United States and most other countries around the world have plummeted in the post–cold war era. The nation's challenge is to maintain its military strength—including technological superiority and a strong industrial base—with a greatly reduced resource budget. At the same time, these defense dollars must enhance (rather than reduce) the nation's international economic competitiveness. The hypothesis advanced here is that the solution to this challenge does not rest in maintaining the current U.S. defense industrial structure or in converting all U.S. defense firms into solely commercial corporations. Rather, the answer lies in a dramatic transformation of the nation's industry into a largely integrated (civil/military) structure.

This book explains why a total transformation is required, describes what such a transformation would entail, and provides details on how to achieve it. The book presents specific "lessons learned" from prior industrial diversification/conversion efforts and offers considerable guidance as to how future efforts can have higher probabilities of success. Clearly, the major efforts in transforming the U.S. defense industry must be made by individual firm and plant managers; however, the book emphasizes that the government has a considerable role in facilitating this transformation. Thus specific guidance for public policy is also provided. To achieve a strong, twenty-first-century defense industrial and military posture at a greatly reduced budget level, the nation has only a few years to initiate and bring about the required transformation. This book is both a plea and a set of guidelines for appropriate action. Without it, the nation's future security and its economic growth will be at risk.

Unfortunately it is not possible to acknowledge all of the many friends and associates, on both sides of the so-called military-industrial complex, who have helped and influenced my thinking during the past forty years. I would like to specifically acknowledge the ideas, advice and, in some cases, the specific chapter reviews of: Bill Perry, Bob Hermann, Norm Augustine, Lew Branscomb, Colleen Preston, Leon Reed, Brian Dickson, Lois Lembo, David Leech, Nevzer Stacey, and Debbie van Opstal. In addition, I would like to thank my associates at TASC for their understanding and encouragement of my work—specifically Art Gelb, Harry Silverman, Joe Kasputys, and Jack Holt. Also, special thanks are due to Mary Shover, without whose dedication this whole manuscript would not have been possible. Naturally, I would also like to acknowledge my appreciation of the Twentieth Century Fund for its sponsorship of this effort. Finally, and most important, I would like to acknowledge the love and support that I have received from my family: Gillian, Douglas, Christine, Jenna, Samuel, and, especially, Leah.

1
The Challenge

The 1980s witnessed the greatest peacetime buildup in military expenditures that the world has ever known. The cold war confrontation caused nations on both sides of the iron curtain to dramatically increase their nuclear and conventional military capabilities in preparation for, and/or in an attempt to prevent, the apocalypse—World War III. Defense budgets were doubled; millions of men and women were in the armed forces, constantly training for the high-tech demands of modern warfare; thousands of nuclear-tipped missiles and nuclear-stocked bombers were kept in constant readiness for instantaneous launch; massive tank battalions and fighter plane squadrons were poised on both sides of the central European dividing line, waiting for the conflict to begin; and defense industries pressed ahead, turning out still greater quantities of even more advanced weapons.

Then, unexpectedly, in 1989 peace broke out. The Berlin Wall fell; and after more than four decades of cold war that began with the Berlin blockade in 1948 and climaxed with the Reagan defense buildup in the 1980s, the world suddenly witnessed the disintegration of not only the Warsaw Pact but of the Soviet Union as well. American and Russian disarmament commenced with a vengeance; 1,846 Russian and 846 U.S. ballistic missiles were literally sawed apart. The defense budgets of both superpowers plummeted. And the political and economic structures of the countries of the former Soviet Union came undone.

At the same time, American public concern began to shift rapidly toward domestic affairs. Economic and social needs took on new importance. Japan overwhelmingly replaced Russia as the biggest perceived threat to the nation. A 1989 public opinion poll found that by a three to one margin, Japan's economic challenge was seen as the greatest threat to America's security.[1] Signaling the breakdown of the nation's historic separation between security and economics, the Commerce Department was added to the National Security Council for the first time. The dramatic transformation that took place in global economic competitiveness during the 1980s fueled the growing concern with what became known as "economic security." America's international position shifted from that of the dominant world economic power to a nation with a huge and growing national debt and a growing trade imbalance. In only two years, the world's greatest source of capital became the world's greatest debtor nation; and annual interest payments on the debt exceeded expenditures on national security.

With the end of the cold war, Americans expected that the hundreds of billions of dollars being spent annually on defense could be redirected to solving the nation's economic problems—the hoped-for "peace dividend." Unfortunately, however, the end of the cold war did not bring peace and stability to the world. Rather, the removal of the bipolar nuclear umbrellas the superpowers provided for over four decades unleashed regional, ethnic, religious, and nationalist conflicts on an accelerating worldwide scale. In 1993 alone, there were some 118 movements for self-determination, many involving armed conflict.[2] The dissolution of the Soviet Union created fifteen independent nations, few of which are economically or politically viable and all of which must contend with volatile ethnic problems. Many of these new nations are extremely well armed. Four nations of the former Soviet Union, for example, were left with a total of around 30,000 nuclear weapons.

In addition, many developing nations, often with dictatorial rulers, have large military forces equipped with modern high-technology weapons. These nations continue to build up their forces and buy the best equipment from around the world, which is now being offered at bargain prices. Table 1.1 clearly indicates the proliferation of weapons of mass destruction. The proliferation of advanced conventional weapons is even greater.

These national military threats are matched at the other end of the spectrum by a large number of terrorist groups—many state-supported; most have modern weapons, sophisticated intelligence capability, and a

Table 1.1
Proliferation of advanced weapons capabilities in the developing world's weapons programs[1]

	Nuclear	Chemical	Biological	Missile[2]
Middle East				
Egypt		X		X
Ethiopia		X		
Iran	X	X		
Iraq[3]	X	X	X	X
Israel	X	X		X
Libya	X	X	X	X
Saudi Arabia				X
Syria		X	X	X
South and East Asia				
Myanmar		X		
China	X	X	X	X
India	X	X		X
Korea, North	X	X	X	X
Korea, South		X		
Pakistan	X	X		X
Taiwan	X	X	X	
Vietnam		X		
Other regions				
Argentina	X[4]			
Brazil	X[4]			X
South Africa	X[4]			X

Sources: For nuclear programs, Leonard S. Spector, "Nuclear Proliferation in the 1990s," Aspen Strategy Group, *New Threats: Responding to the Proliferation of Nuclear, Chemical, and Delivery Capabilities in the Third World* (Lanham, MD: University Press of America, 1990), pp. 35–59; for chemical and biological programs, Elisa D. Harris, "Towards a Comprehensive Strategy for Halting Chemical and Biological Weapons Proliferation," *Arms Control*, vol. 12, no. 2, 1992; for missile programs, C. Aaron Karp, "Ballistic Missile Proliferation, *SIPRI Yearbook 1991* (Oxford: Oxford University Press, 1991), pp. 337–343.
Notes: (1) deployed or under development; (2) with ranges in excess of 300 km; (3) Iraq's programs are being eliminated in accordance with UN Security Council Resolution 687 (3 April 1991); (4) recently signed or acceded to agreements forgoing development of nuclear weapons [Ivo Daalder, "The Future of Arms Control," *Survival*, Spring 1992, p. 61].

means of achieving mass destruction. Traditional deterrence threats are often as ineffective against the fanatical national ruler as against the terrorist. Thus one can conclude that peace and stability are not the dominant conditions in the world today, nor are they likely to be in the coming decades.

America's challenge in the post–cold war era is to reduce its military forces and restructure its defense industry while ensuring its national security and economic growth for the twenty-first century. This book addresses itself to meeting this challenge.

Economic Trends

The poor economic condition of the United States in the immediate post–cold war period was caused partially by the huge increase in defense expenditures during the Reagan era, matched by a simultaneous reduction in taxes. In addition, the problem was greatly aggravated by adverse trends in American industrial productivity[3] at a time when there was growing industrial strength in other nations, especially Japan and Germany. As America was building up a large negative trade balance, its citizens' standard of living was declining. Trade in high-technology products declined to negative levels in 1985; and by 1990, real hourly wages for Americans had fallen to below the levels of the mid-1960s (from a peak in 1978).[4]

The post–cold war defense employment cutbacks compounded these problems. Although the initial drawdowns were gradual, by 1995 there were two million fewer jobs than in 1985. When indirect employment effects on local suppliers and services are included, at a minimum these numbers must be doubled.[5] Senator David Pryor (D-Ark.) estimated that between 1992 and 1997, 1,000 Americans would lose their defense-dependent jobs every day.

As shown in figure 1.1, the percentage declines were far greater in the industrial sector than they were in the government (civilian and military)—a reflection of the fact that weapons' procurement budgets were being cut even faster than the overall defense budget. For example, by 1993 defense outlays had been cut by 30 percent—or $100 billion below the Reagan peak—while weapons procurement budgets had been cut by

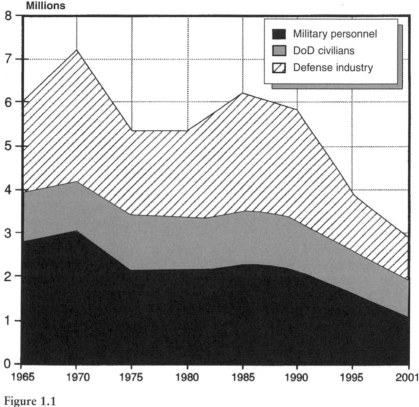

Figure 1.1
Defense employment levels 1965–2001
Source: Office of Technology Assessment (1992).

over 50 percent. At this point, defense industry capacity utilization was already down to only 35 percent—in comparison to an efficient level of around 85 percent; and it was rapidly declining even further. The military services, believing that their forces were adequately equipped for any near-term conflict needs, were attempting to preserve their manpower dollars. As a result, the greatest impact of the defense budget cuts was being felt by defense industry workers. Nonetheless, the defense budget continued plummeting—with only an occasional congressional or presidential bailout to save jobs.

By 1998, defense spending would represent less than 3 percent of the gross domestic product (GDP)—a level not seen since before World War

II.[6] At these low levels of GDP percentages, the overall macroeconomic effects of the defense budget cuts would be far less significant than in past downturns; however, at the local (city and plant) and human levels, the effects could be devastating. McDonnell-Douglas alone laid off 10,000 workers in eighteen months. General Dynamics, General Electric, Grumman, Hughes, Lockheed, LTV, Northrop, Raytheon, and other major defense contractors continue to announce layoffs in the thousands.

The fact that the defense cutbacks were occurring when the U.S. economy was weak exacerbated the consequences of the layoffs. Leading commercial firms in high-tech civilian sectors (e.g., aircraft and computers), where the employee skills most directly overlap with those of the defense sector, were facing severe economic problems: IBM lost $5 billion in 1992 and more than $8 billion in 1993. It reduced its work force by over 180,000 between 1986 and 1994;[7] Boeing eliminated 10,000 jobs in 1992 and 28,000 in 1993.

Significant restructuring throughout American industry was necessary to achieve international industrial competitiveness. For example, the auto industry (especially General Motors) was making large layoffs to adjust to new production and management methods being used by the Japanese. The changes resulted in far greater efficiencies with far fewer middle managers and administrative workers—again, areas with large employee skill overlaps with the defense industry. In addition, the United States was rapidly losing its technological leadership position in many critical areas. A 1990 study by the Commerce Department of twelve "emerging critical technologies" concluded that Japan already led the United States in five of them and was fast gaining ground in five more. A 1992 National Science Foundation study found the United States to be behind Japan in advanced materials, advanced semiconductor devices, digital imaging technology, high-density data storage, and optoelectronics—all essential future technologies for the military and for the nation's economic growth.[8] In many cases, the foreign lead was in deployed technologies (items that had reached the market sooner), but in some it was even in research.

In response to these adverse conditions, many Americans were blaming "unfair" foreign trade practices, such as dumping of foreign-made products in the American market and restricting imports of U.S.-made products into foreign markets. These factors exacerbated but did not cause the decline of U.S. economic competitiveness. In reality, the problems existed within the American economy, at both the macro- and micro-economic levels. It was time for a new economic and industrial paradigm in America. The required restructuring of the defense sector brought about by the end of the cold war is simply a subset of the overall problem—but a very important subset, where an appropriate solution is critical.

Historical Perspective

It is important to put the current defense downsizing in historic perspective. As shown by figure 1.2, the cold war period exhibited unusually high levels of military expenditures for over four decades. However, there were periods of significant downturns (post–Korean War, post–Vietnam War, and, of course, immediately after World War II). Although each of these periods has important lessons for us today, it is worth noting that there are significant differences among them. The best way to see this is to briefly review each of the prior three cycles.[9]

World War II represented a total mobilization of the U.S. economy. But from the beginning, the Roosevelt administration undertook comprehensive planning for the postwar demobilization of military personnel, defense workers, and defense plants. Policies and laws were adapted to enable plants to return quickly to civilian production, to ease the returning veterans' reentry into the labor force, and to give consumers and industry the resources they needed to rapidly rebuild the postwar economy. As a result, the demobilization went remarkably well, especially considering its vast scale. Industrial plants were reconverted to their civilian prewar uses. Commercial demand, which had been significantly restrained during the war, was extremely high for new goods and services, enabling the demobilized work force to be rapidly employed in new commercial production activities.

So thorough was the demobilization after World War II that only five years later the nation required a substantial remobilization to meet the new crisis in Korea, albeit on a much smaller scale. After the war, only a portion of the defense production needed to be reconverted to civilian

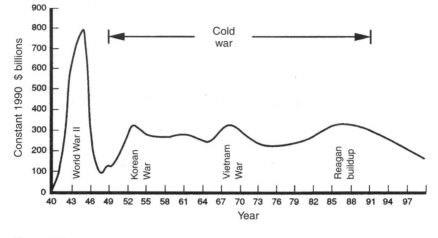

Figure 1.2
Defense expenditures versus time

pursuits. A large standing army was maintained, and the government continued to pay for the development and procurement of increasingly sophisticated weaponry. Partly as a result of the lack of need, and partly because of the Eisenhower administration's noninterventionist economic philosophy, there was an absence of any significant transition assistance after the Korean conflict. The only program provided, a generous GI Bill package of benefits, encouraged many veterans to go to school rather than to return immediately to the labor force.

There were far more similarities between the Vietnam War drawdown and that of today. As the cutbacks began after the war, it was clear that defense production had become more specialized and distinct from normal commercial production. Defense firms found it much more difficult—and in many cases, impossible—to convert their capabilities to meet civilian demands (for reasons discussed in detail in chapter 5). In addition, during the course of the drawdown, the economy went into recession in 1970 and again in 1974, following the 1973 oil price shock. Because of these adverse conditions, many assistance programs were put in place to aid displaced defense workers, companies, and communities affected by military base closings or defense plant cutbacks. By the early 1970s, over two dozen federally funded programs were available to help displaced defense workers and veterans.[10] Veterans also received a new GI Bill, albeit one less generous than its previous counterparts.

The one obvious difference between the Vietnam drawdown and that of the end of the cold war is that, in the former case, defense firms could simply opt to retrench and wait for the next defense buildup. The Soviet threat was still there and the Warsaw Pact arms buildup continued unabated.[11] The next buildup cycle was inevitable and, as expected, it began in the late 1970s.

Today we are not experiencing a cyclical defense budget decline but, more likely, a permanent one. Therefore, efficient and effective defense industry restructuring is even more critical. However, it must be based not just on economic considerations but, first and foremost, on the likely national security needs of the United States in the twenty-first century.

National Security

America designs and builds the best weapons in the world. These weapons, however, cost far too much (especially in the small quantities likely to be bought in the future), take too long to develop and produce, and are often unreliable and prohibitively expensive to operate and support.

The Department of Defense (DoD) achieved its goal of gaining technological superiority over the Soviet Union or any other potential adversary. In the future, although America will still require technological superiority (including many new and different state-of-the-art weapons), there will be an added requirement—that this be achieved at a dramatically lower cost. The challenge is to maintain military superiority (adequate quantities of advanced weapon systems and well-trained troops) with far fewer dollars.

Unfortunately, historic defense trends are adverse to these needs. Weapons performance has been improving from generation to generation but at increasingly greater costs.[12] Weapons that used to cost in the thousands of dollars each now cost in the millions. Bombers (in very small quantities) cost around $1 billion each; ships are in the $3 billion to $5 billion range. As we strive for increased performance in the next generation of weapon systems, with a reduced defense budget the nation obviously cannot afford to allow this trend to continue.

Other high-cost elements of the cold war defense posture must also be dramatically changed. For example, the focus on strategic nuclear forces and the expected war in central Europe demanded enormous U.S. commitments to large numbers of expensive weapons and large military force structures, which are no longer needed or affordable. Similarly, the historic focus on a large defense industrial base, geared to a long-duration, high-intensity central European conflict (including the possibility of resupply and repair of equipment for a conflict that would last many years), is no longer required. Accordingly, many significant changes are in order; the subsidization of the defense industry must be drastically reduced; many of the government-owned repair depots, arsenals, laboratories, and so on must be shrunk or eliminated to match future needs. Future military requirements are likely to be based on short-duration, low-attrition, decisive regional conflicts—all of which will require very different force structures than in the past.

Perhaps the greatest shift is the change from the concept of attrition warfare (large, heavy forces wearing each other down) to information-based warfare[13] (with real-time, all-weather intelligence; dramatically improved command and control; unmanned, precision-guided, brilliant weapons; and nullification of the enemy's information systems). Constant development and deployment of new breakthrough technologies will be needed to stay ahead. Thus there has to be not only a continued focus on technological superiority and funding for research and development (R & D), but also a dramatic change in defense procurement practices. The average cycle time, from concept to first production, for U.S. weapons in the early 1990s was an incredibly long 16.5 years.[14] This is totally incompatible with the pace of change in modern information technology where, for example, a new electronics line is obsolete in six to eighteen months.

To better understand this new "information-based warfare" world, one must recognize what the United States achieved in Operation Desert Storm.[15] Here, reconnaissance satellites and advanced aircraft intelligence systems were used for full support of the ground, air, and sea forces. They continuously monitored enemy air and ground movements and pinpointed all enemy targets. The U.S. forces also made extensive use of night-vision devices to turn night into day and used the satellite-based global positioning system to precisely locate their position in the desert. Thus U.S. troops knew exactly where both they and the enemy were located at all times. Then, to assure that the enemy would not have a similar capability, very early in the conflict the coalition forces destroyed the Iraqi command, control, communication, and intelligence systems, along with their air defense systems. This was done using precision-guided weapons. It was a clear demonstration of their effectiveness over the unguided weapons of the past. In fact, it was the integrated effect of these advanced systems that suggested the likely form of conflict in the future. Today only the United States possesses this full spectrum of capabilities, but many others are rushing to acquire it.

In addition to dealing with the shift from attrition warfare to information-based warfare, the national security establishment will have to counter the proliferation of advanced weapons throughout the world. For example, Desert Storm also showed that in the future, it will be necessary to have antiballistic missile capability to detect and then destroy, as early as possible, both long- and short-range ballistic missiles.

In World War II, the air force estimates that it took about 9,000 bombs to destroy a target. In Vietnam, the number declined to about 300 bombs. In Desert Storm, it took about two precision-guided munitions to destroy a target.[16] Of course, to do the job you have to have enough of these and also be able to get them rapidly to the target. Therefore the Defense Department doctrine now says that the objective is to make sure that American troops "are able to reach trouble spots quickly and with overwhelming power, in order to detect and, if needed, defeat aggression, with the help of allies and friends."[17] This is truly a different focus from that of the prior forty years of the cold war. The emphasis is now on mobility, overwhelming power, and coalition forces.

Another major change is that the concept of warfare itself is shifting from all-or-nothing to limited objectives.[18] A significant driver here has been televised coverage of warfare—the so-called CNN factor. It means human losses or the capture of military personnel must be greatly minimized. It also means that wars must be short because Americans will not tolerate body bags or hostage parades on TV for any length of time.

Significant shifts in each of the military services' operations will be necessary. For the navy, it means antisubmarine operations near shore versus on the open sea. It means a smaller role for aircraft carriers, because they are extremely expensive to deploy and equally expensive to defend. (Instead, ground-based, long-range aircraft and missiles can often be used.) Major roles for the navy will involve sea-lift of the army, limited missile attacks (both conventional and nuclear) from submarines, and ballistic missile defense of a foreign land site from an offshore ship. Similar dramatic changes will be required of the army and air force.

Finally, warfare will likely require all military services, and probably several nations, to fight together. To have total force effectiveness, it will be necessary to have interoperable information and communications, as well as interoperable supplies (fuel and bullets) and logistics support.

These new roles and missions of the services will require very different equipment from what the United States purchased during the cold war. Then, the equipment was geared to either the strategic nuclear confrontation with the Soviet Union or to the large land conflicts projected between NATO and the Warsaw Pact in central Europe. Now, especially after Operation Desert Storm, it is clear that new defense needs include:

• all-weather, day and night, global surveillance;
• antiballistic missile capability;
• all-weather, precision-guided weapons;
• location and destruction of mobile targets;
• real-time intelligence and command management;
• active countering of enemy target-acquisition systems (electronic counter measures and stealth);
• rapid response, with extended holding power for force projection onto foreign lands;
• lightweight, high firepower, minimally manned, survivable forces;
• twenty-four-hour-a-day warfighting operations against enemies with night sights and night-vision goggles; and
• war fighting simulations ("virtual reality") for troop training and new weapons and tactics developments.

The military force of the twenty-first century, although much smaller, will still be very expensive, even after design and production efficiencies are achieved. The all-volunteer service will have to be highly skilled, extremely well trained, and provided with rapid lift, air cover, high-tech weapons, and exceptional intelligence data. As the dollars shrink, a clear and critical balance must be maintained between force size and equipment modernization. A continuation of the preference for force size (manpower) over equipment modernization means that future U.S. forces will be fighting with old, and often obsolete, weapons.[19] That result must be prevented.

One way to address the defense budget crunch is to take advantage of changing geopolitical and military conditions. Areas of enormous potential defense savings include: reductions in nuclear arms (weapons, missiles, long-range bombers, submarines); reductions in the number of aircraft carriers and their defending and support ships, as well as their aircraft; and reductions in the number of heavy army divisions (tanks and armored vehicles). The potential savings of *tens of billions of dollars per year* in each major area are not just in equipment but in facilities, manpower, operations (e.g., fuel), and maintenance.

Strategic deterrence will continue to receive funds, but it will be for antiballistic missile capability and chemical/biological defense equipment, rather than for large numbers of nuclear weapons and their delivery systems. Most dollars will go for information-intensive systems—a distinct shift from the historic weapons' budget focus on ships, planes, and tanks, and an area of significant potential cost savings.

The other major way to address the defense budget crisis—especially for the procurement of the next generation of weapons after the year 2000—is to design these weapons so that they can be produced at dramatically lower costs. This represents a significant cultural change as well as a change in the defense industrial structure.

These dramatic shifts in the missions of the services and the impact of new technology will be fiercely resisted by the military establishments, as will the needed changes in the procurement process and the industrial structure. Despite the lessons of history, it is highly probable that implementing these needed changes will be extremely difficult and will take many years.[20] This only serves to emphasize the importance of beginning now. America essentially has a ten-year window of opportunity before the next round of weapons modernization will be absolutely required.

Arms Proliferation

Perhaps the single greatest threat to stability in the post–cold war era is the worldwide proliferation of nuclear and sophisticated conventional arms. Historically, the Defense Department's position with regard to arms control has been analogous to the resistance that the police had for many years to gun control. Today the police recognize that the nation needs both a strong police force *and* strong gun control laws; for a long time, the police failed to see that the proliferation of guns increased the likelihood of crimes and also the dangers to the police force itself. Instead, they argued the position held by the National Rifle Association on the "right to bear arms." Many in the military still do not actively support arms control as an important national security initiative. They do not recognize that the nation needs both a strong U.S. military posture and arms proliferation control, and must arrive at an integrated strategy that combines these two aspects of national security.

Any such effort must begin in the nuclear arena. A single nuclear weapon can do incredible harm; yet literally thousands exist around the world (in the United States, Russia, Ukraine, Kazakhstan, Belarus, France, China, Britain; likely in Israel, India, Pakistan; and, possibly in the future, in North Korea, Iraq, Iran, South Africa, and Libya). In the former Soviet Union nations alone, Russia has 7,213 strategic nuclear warheads, Ukraine 1,400, Belarus 80, and Kazakhstan 1,360.[21]

Arms control concerns, however, cannot be limited to the nuclear arena. Worldwide proliferation of conventional arms, driven by an excess of existing weapons and surplus defense industry capacity, dramatically compounds future security problems and represents a significant threat— perhaps the greatest and most likely one—to global security.

In 1992, the Iranians agreed to pay $600 million to the United Admiralty Sudomekh shipyard in St. Petersburg for two Kilo-class Russian submarines, with an option to buy a third. U.S. analysts fear that the exceptionally quiet Russian diesel-electric submarines, whose stealthy characteristics will be enhanced by the complex sonar conditions of the Persian Gulf, would be difficult to locate and destroy. The Kilo can operate underwater at its quietest (on battery power alone) for more than six days and can carry food and provisions for up to sixty days. Furthermore, in May 1993, Iran took delivery of eight supersonic, land-launched cruise missiles from Ukraine.[22] These could destroy a ship passing through the Strait of Hormuz about seventeen seconds after they were launched. The combination of the submarines and cruise missiles constitutes a real military concern, since the DoD's contingency plans to reinforce the Arabian peninsula in the event of war require hundreds of unarmed cargo ships to pass through the Strait of Hormuz. In the worst-case scenario, according to an American admiral, that lifeline could be cut off for the two months it might take to exhaust the submarines' supplies.[23] And that was before Iran began to purchase the cruise missiles!

With the end of the cold war, the Russians have 1,600 surplus military aircraft and some 10,000 tanks just waiting to be sold. A large part of the former Soviet navy, including the $3 billion aircraft carrier *Varyag* (under construction in Ukraine), is also on the block. Industrial conversion was supposed to refashion the former Soviet Union's 1,100 defense enterprises and 900 research institutes into commercial concerns; "the only problem," said Michael D. Maley, Russian president Yeltsin's conversion adviser, "was that no one ever said where the [conversion] money would come from." To raise the conversion dollars, Moscow is testing world arms markets to determine which plants can produce marketable goods. Those that can will have hard currency to design and make even better weapons. Whether this will eventually lead to conversion is still a question.

China spent $1.2 billion in cash and barter goods for twenty-four Su-27 Russian fighters and continues to scour the former Soviet Union for more aircraft, missiles, and technical know-how. Western sources say Iran is spending over $2.2 billion for 110 planes, including Tu22M3 Russian bombers and the highly regarded MiG-29 and MiG-31 Russian jet fighters. An American firm, FMC Corporation, planned to sell 500 state-of-the-art Bradley armored fighting vehicles to the United Arab Emirates when Russia offered its BMP armored personnel carrier for a third of the Bradley's $1.5 million price.[24] In fact, Russia has been offering arms for food and shelter. At the same time, its nuclear scientists are being offered huge salaries by countries such as Iran and Libya to develop their own nuclear weapons capabilities.

Similarly, as China becomes increasingly dependent on oil imports, it is expected that it will need to increase its exports of ballistic and cruise missiles, advanced weapons, and nuclear technology to generate revenue.[25] But Russian and Chinese sales of advanced and conventional equipment notwithstanding, the United States is by far the world's leading supplier of arms. By 1993, its foreign arms sales had reached an annual level of $38 billion and it had captured over 70 percent of the total[26] of the world's arms market. Indeed, with government budget cutbacks, the U.S. defense industry was aggressively selling weapons. Even the U.S. Army was offering to sell older M-60 tanks to get money to buy newer M-1 tanks. And rather than return weapons stored in Europe to the United States, the DoD was willing to sell them to their Mediterranean allies for only the transportation costs. In fact, both Congress and the White House see foreign arms sales as creating defense jobs—and, therefore, votes—even if the sales have obviously destabilizing security implications.

While many western countries are dramatically shrinking their defense budgets, many developing countries, particularly in Asia, are continuing to increase theirs. Between 1990 and 1993 China doubled its defense spending.[27] Myanmar, with its bank balance quite full from the sale of heroin, recently offered to buy $1 billion worth of arms from China, twenty helicopters from Poland, and guns from Yugoslavia. It has 230,000 men in its armed forces—forces that are respected, even feared, by the Thais.[28]

Controlling proliferation will require collective multinational action, as will many other national security issues in the post–cold war era. Yet as the sole superpower, and the leading arms export nation, the United States must take the lead. At the same time it must continue funding for arms control verification including, but not limited to, on-site inspections. In FY93, $505 million was provided from DoD's budget for nuclear arms control, plus $254 million from the Department of Energy's budget for verification support.

With the end of the cold war, the dominant factor influencing the level of intensity and the potential damage that can be caused by regional conflicts, or even individual acts of terrorism, is likely to be the level of weapons proliferation. The highest priority is to limit weapons of mass destruction—that is, nuclear, chemical, and biological—with the control of sophisticated conventional weapons close behind.

The Future Need

A restructuring of the U.S. defense industry must satisfy three essential criteria:

1. Effective national security—with far fewer dollars.

2. An efficient, responsive, innovative defense industrial base that requires far less DoD subsidization and does not need to rely on worldwide proliferation of weapons to create revenue.

3. Generation of more domestic economic growth and industrial competitiveness from the tens of billions of defense R & D and procurement dollars spent annually.

The interrelationship among these three criteria is critical to ensuring the nation's future security.

Gradually, institutional inertia has been removing America's greatest historic asset, its innovativeness and flexibility.[29] As the sociologist Thorstein Veblen observed, societies decline as they lose their capacity to adapt.

The end of the cold war represents a qualitative change in many aspects of American life, particularly in the international and defense arenas. This is not just another cyclical downturn of the defense budget. Yet history has shown, and current conditions confirm, that Plato's projection will remain true—that "only the dead will see no more war." Therefore we must continue to be prepared for, and/or be capable of deterring, future conflicts—but with far fewer dollars.

2

The Cold War Defense Industry

Known as the "arsenal of democracy" during World War II, the mobilized U.S. defense industry produced 296,000 aircraft, 1,201 naval vessels, 65,546 landing craft, and 86,333 tanks for the allied powers. This output made a significant difference in the war's outcome. Although almost totally demobilized immediately after the war, this industry was reactivated for the Korean War and operated thereafter on a virtual wartime basis for the duration of the cold war. The current efforts at defense industry downsizing and restructuring (for the post–cold war era) begin from this basis.

This industry is characterized by its enormous size and complexity. The Department of Defense spends over $100 billion every year in about 15 million separate contract actions—or approximately two contract actions per second. These actions are carried out by more than 150,000 government acquisition personnel and another 300,000 supporting government personnel, using 30,000 pages of regulations issued by seventy-nine different offices. The process is overseen by twenty-nine congressional committees with fifty-five subcommittees and 28,000 congressional staff members.[1] In one recent year, the Pentagon was required to respond to 120,000 written requests for information from Congress plus 600,000 telephone inquiries from Capitol Hill. During the same period, it supplied 1,300 witnesses who gave 1,500 hours of testimony at 450 hearings, much of it relating to the procurement process. This activity is monitored in minute detail by 26,000 government auditors who are assisted by numerous public-interest groups and newspaper reporters. On the industrial side, millions of people employed in firms both large and small, public and private, operate within this Byzantine maze of regulations and oversight that make up the unique way in which business is conducted in the defense arena.

President Dwight D. Eisenhower, in his famous farewell address in which he coined the phrase "military-industrial complex," first warned of the potentially adverse impact that the defense industry could have on the U.S. economy. He then described the critical importance of this industry to the nation. Similarly, as America restructures its defense industry for the twenty-first century, it is essential to consider both the potential dangers and benefits of any new structure.

Unless one had been a resident of another planet for the past few decades, it would have been impossible not to have read about the inefficiencies associated with the U.S. defense industry, usually headlined in articles highlighting "waste, fraud, and abuse." It would have been equally impossible, however, not to be aware of the major contributions of the defense industry to U.S. economic growth: high-wage, high-skill jobs, advanced research and development, and contributions to the balance of payments (via large exports)—all this in addition to providing weapons for the nation's security.

On a relative expenditure level, the defense industry plays a larger role in the U.S. economy than the auto industry and almost as large a one as the residential and commercial construction sector.[2] Even at the reduced current and planned levels, the defense industry remains an important part of the U.S. economy. It has far greater reach than its 3 to 4 percent share of GNP would suggest; for example, it has supported approximately 25 percent of all U.S. engineers, around 20 percent of all U.S. manufacturing, and 50 percent of all university computer science research. It has also created many of America's leading commercial high-tech industries, such as communication and navigation satellites, supercomputers, jet engines and aircraft, numerically controlled machine tools, and the Internet or "information superhighway."

The tens of billions of annual defense R & D and procurement dollars are clearly a positive factor in America's economy. From both a security and an economic perspective, the defense industry is a "strategic"[3] sector.

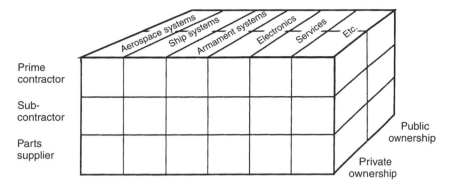

Figure 2.1
The defense industry

Structure

The structure of the U.S. defense industry (figure 2.1) includes aerospace contractors as well as producers of small electronic microchips and manufacturers of tanks as well as engineering services contractors hired for the independent testing and evaluation of advanced weapon systems. Thus any overall understanding of the industry—and any policy decisions made with regard to its restructuring—must recognize the critical differences among these various sectors.

Similarly, there are very great differences between the large "prime" contractors and the so-called lower tiers of the defense industry (figure 2.1). The former primarily assemble and test weapon systems, while the latter supply the subsystems and parts that go into them. Although there may be only a single prime contractor, there may be tens or even hundreds of thousands of smaller suppliers who feed into the system. In many ways the U.S. defense industry can best be described as a "dual economy"[4] where the large contractors deal directly with the government (on major weapon systems), while the industry's lower tiers act much more like typical commercial industrial suppliers—except that they are greatly burdened by unique defense requirements such as procurement laws, military specifications, and accounting practices.

In addition, the defense industry is a mix of public and private ownership. In some areas, such as the munitions plants, the sector is largely under public ownership. In others, such as aircraft plants, there is mixed ownership; the government owns much of the capital equipment and plants, but they are operated by the private sector. And the overhaul and repair of military aircraft is done in both government-owned depots as well as in private firms. (The question of how much mixed ownership should exist in the restructured U.S. defense industry will be dealt with in chapter 7.)

Approximately 3.2 million people were employed in the private sector of the U.S. defense industry in 1991; this number is expected to be less than 2.3 million by 1997.[5] Public sector employment, which includes a majority of the one million DoD civilian employees and a significant number of military personnel in government depots, arsenals, laboratories, and contractors' plants, is also quite large. In addition, there are tens of thousands of employees in the quasi-government activities known as the federally funded research and development centers (FFRDCs). These include nuclear weapons laboratories run by the Department of Energy for the Department of Defense, systems engineering companies supporting the air force, and other similar nonprofit, government-funded, noncompetitive activities directly supporting defense-related operations.

The defense industry work force is exceptionally well paid. The average worker at the Northrop Corporation's B-2 Stealth bomber plant in Pico Rivera, California, had a salary of about $50,000 a year when the plant was closed in 1993.[6] The high salaries are partly due to the cyclical nature of the defense business, as well as to the lack of sensitivity to price in a sole-source environment, that is, no one else builds the B-2. These factors result in the average worker receiving around 20 percent more than a worker in an equivalent commercial job.[7] Mainly, however, the pay differential is due to the heavy share of research and development and the associated concentration of jobs in areas such as engineering, computer research, sciences, high-skill labor, management, and administration. In fiscal year 1994, the DoD budget requested $38.6 billion for R & D, only slightly less than the $45.5 billion requested for production. Such a ratio is extremely rare in any other industry.

One characteristic of the defense industry is the extreme concentration of a few firms by type of weapon, geography, and employment. Supplier firms may number in the tens, or even hundreds of thousands, but there is extreme concentration at the top of each sector. In 1991, only twenty-five companies received 46 percent of the value of all DoD prime contract awards;[8] the seven largest defense-dependent companies accounted for nearly 25 percent of all prime contracts (General Dynamics, Grumman, Lockheed, McDonnell-Douglas, Martin Marietta, Northrop, and Raytheon).[9] And there is even more concentration at the subsystem level. In the large jet engine business, for example, there are only two suppliers, Pratt-Whitney and General Electric. One of the major dangers is that downsizing will result in only one or, in some cases, no firm left in a particular sector.

In the same way, there is extreme geographic concentration. Six states have 45 percent of the defense business: California 18.5 percent, Texas 6.6 percent, New York 6.3 percent, Massachusetts 4.7 percent, Virginia 4.5 percent, and Ohio 4.2 percent. Finally, there is a heavy concentration of employment within these few large firms. Specifically, 95 percent of the defense industry workers are employed by companies with over 4,000 employees each.[10]

This situation has a number of obvious disadvantages in terms of normal free-market behavior. Attempts at oligopoly, or even monopoly, pricing practices are common. Because so few firms are involved, however, it also offers the opportunity for significant government-driven restructuring. And because so much of the defense budget is concentrated in only a few weapon systems, it makes restructuring more amenable to achievement through individual government R & D and procurement actions.

Barriers to restructuring clearly exist, however. During the forty years of the cold war, a body of laws, regulations, and practices has developed that control the many daily procurement actions between the DoD and its suppliers.[11] Although each of these may have a valid historic rationale, the result is that there are only a few firms skilled in conducting defense business, and they may be totally isolated from, and uncompetitive with, their commercial counterparts. Even firms that operate in both the military and commercial worlds are forced to separate the two parts of their operations. For example, Motorola maintains its obsolete (but conforming to DoD requirements) defense electronics plant literally on the other side of town (Phoenix, Arizona) from its world-class commercial electronics plant (which does not satisfy DoD laws and regulations). Other commercial firms (e.g., Hewlett Packard) simply refuse to accept R & D contracts from the DoD because of their specialized rules. Thus any restructuring plans for the defense industry must directly confront these barriers.

Government's Role

It would be proper to simply allow the market to operate to achieve the required efficiency and effectiveness if the defense marketplace was a truly free market, with numerous suppliers and buyers free to act in their own best self-interests. This is not an arena, however, in which it is even relevant to ask whether the government should be involved. As the only buyer, the regulator of all market activities, the specifier of the goods to be purchased, the banker (through progress payments), and even the court of claims (for any improper procurement actions), the government is already fully involved. In addition, in most sectors of the industry, the government relies on either a single (monopoly) supplier or, at best, a few (oligopoly) suppliers. Thus the unique nature of the defense industry makes it as far removed as possible from that considered characteristic of a free market. And yet in the past, the government has argued that "free market forces would achieve the desired performance" [12]—even though it was obvious that free-market forces were not present.

What then should be the government's responsibility? Its primary role is to set the proper macroeconomic policies for the nation (debt, interest, employment) and to create a strong, growing economic environment. Further, it can use procurement laws, regulations, specifications, trade and tax policies, and its purchasing power to aid in moving the defense industry in the desired direction for the post–cold war era. Finally, the government can selectively invest in the critical defense, dual-use, and even civilian technologies in which widespread public benefits greatly exceed narrow corporate benefits to any individual firm. These investment areas and the anticipated benefits must be extremely well defined, or the decisions will be subject to extensive political pressures from special interests.

There is significant difference between government stimulation of a strategic industrial sector for its transformation and growth into a dual-use enterprise and the subsidization of an industry simply to prevent its shrinkage or to defer the loss of jobs in that sector. The former action can be very positive, offering long-term benefits for the economy. The latter is a short-term holding action that will not expedite diversification and will only result in further purchases of unneeded goods or services.

Significantly, the United States is the only country whose government shows so little concern about the health of its defense industry. For example, France, Japan, Sweden, Israel, Germany, and China[13] explicitly attempt to guide the structure of this strategic sector. In the future, government leadership will also be required in the United States in order to achieve the requisite downsizing. It must create incentives and use specific defense investments to realize the desired results; it should not, however, get into detailed (firm-level) management.

While preaching the principle of no government involvement with industry, the United States has always had de facto industrial policies, not only in the defense sector—which it totally controls—but also in medicine, agriculture, housing, and in selected threatened industries such as automobiles and steel. For example, annual government subsidies to the agriculture and housing industries are around $25 billion each,[14] but individual firms still have their outcomes decided through market competition.

The United States often does not make its industrial policy explicit, but it makes it nonetheless. In the critical $200 billion high-technology telecommunication sector, Congress and the executive branch allowed Judge Harold Green's legal rulings on the deregulation of AT&T to become national policy. This legalistic approach is in keeping with the American tradition, where historically the United States has been a "rule-driven" economy.[15] Economists, and particularly lawyers, play a key role in defining and interpreting the rules. In this model, government and industry are basically adversaries. By contrast, Japan, with its "plan-driven" economy, stresses results and is therefore driven more by engineers and business people (both in and out of government) who work together to achieve common economic objectives. Yet within the local economy firms compete fiercely, and free-market forces determine the winners and losers.

It is important to observe that the U.S. government's involvement in research and development in such areas as agriculture, health, and aerospace has been extremely successful. These three sectors of the economy have remained strong and internationally competitive.

To determine how the government can play a significant future role in transforming the current defense industry into a diversified—civil and military—dual-use industry, it is instructive to see how it has done so in the past. First, the aircraft industry: The National Advisory Committee on Aeronautics, better known as NACA, was established in 1915 to provide a national stimulant in early aircraft research. Despite having invented the airplane, the United States was lagging behind several European countries in the development of an aircraft industry.[16] Fearing the negative consequences of this situation for both the commercial and strategic interests of the United States, the Congress and the president created NACA.

Its mission was to achieve world leadership for the U.S. aircraft industry. NACA was directed to conduct research jointly with industry, to assist industry in commercialization of new technology, and to create a business environment conducive to investment in the aircraft industry. The first research facility was quickly established in Langley, Virginia (and is still in operation). The NACA did the ground-breaking work on early propeller technology and, in many cases, placed initial orders for new equipment in an effort to achieve production volumes sufficient to enable low-cost production. The United States has continued to support the aircraft industry through both defense and NASA expenditures on R & D and procurement of aircraft and jet engines, and this sector remains the single largest export industry of the United States.

Government support of the transistor industry is another example of a targeted policy. Largely through the Army Signal Corps of the Department of Defense, the government sponsored research, subsidized engineering development, funded the planning for production, became the initial guaranteed buyer, standardized practices, and disseminated the work. The army's programs increased the pace of transistor development to such an extent that the industry actually experienced a sizable overcapacity by 1955.[17]

The manufacturing area and, specifically, the revolution in numerically controlled machine tools is a third example of the government's role in a dual-use sector of the American economy, again using Defense Department sponsorship. During the 1950s, the U.S. Air Force created a market by purchasing, installing, and maintaining over one hundred numerically controlled machines in factories of its prime contractors. It also paid aircraft manufacturers and various parts suppliers to learn how to use the technology. Not surprisingly, machine tool builders got into the action, and research and development expenditures in the industry multiplied eightfold between 1951 and 1957.[18] Thus the military inaugurated and sheltered one of the most important manufacturing technologies of the twentieth century during its initial phases.

These are just a few of the examples that could be listed for critical industries. Others include the initial DoD purchases of computers to stimulate the industry—including the supercomputers of today—and the original navy/RCA joint government/industry effort to support the communications industry. The tools used to stimulate these industries included R & D (NACA); buying power (computers and semiconductors); and patent control (RCA and communications). In every case the objective was not only to dramatically influence both civil and defense markets but to help establish and/or maintain U.S. leadership in these strategic sectors.

Today the defense industry is what the economists term a "sick" industry, and it is getting worse. The current congressional and executive bailouts—through extension of old, unneeded production—and the simultaneous increase of government regulation and oversight are only making the inevitable changes more difficult. The required restructuring of the U.S. defense industrial base can only come about with active government involvement—in a positive direction. In the process, there are likely to be business failures in many sectors of the defense industry. The dominance of market forces should be used to determine the outcome of the restructuring, on a firm-by-firm basis. But the government must set the long-term structural objectives for the defense industry as a whole.

Industrial Vulnerability

Whether an individual firm or plant is particularly vulnerable to defense budget cutbacks is a function of a number of variables, specifically: (1) the particular industrial sector to which it belongs, and the sector's dependence on defense versus commercial business; (2) the size of the firm, and its available resources to aid in the conversion effort and to withstand the significant time period that the conversion process will take; (3) the management culture—particularly its willingness and enthusiasm for change; and (4) the individual plant's product and process technologies, and the degree to which these are applicable in commercial areas.

As previously noted, there are enormous differences, from sector to sector, within the defense industry. One of the major differences is the degree of dependency of a particular industrial sector on defense business. The data in table 2.1 clearly show this for a selected set of industries. The spread becomes even more extreme at the subsector level. For example, if the category of shipbuilding and repair were split between new ship construction and repair work, it would be clear that almost 100 percent of new ship construction in the United States is now done for the Department of Defense. In the overall U.S. shipbuilding area (for 1987), ship repair (including conversions) accounted for approximately 50 percent of the work; and as the defense drawdown progresses it will be an increasing share. Firms that undertake maintenance work in the private sector can easily shift their activities from new ship construction to maintenance. However, if the maintenance work is given to the public yards—which do not produce new ships—the private sector will be much more severely affected by the drawdown, perhaps causing some or all of the private shipyards to close. The Shipbuilders Council of America estimated that employment in the private shipyards will fall from a level of around 130,000 in 1990 to 30,000 by 1998. It predicted that "if the government doesn't do anything there may not be a shipyard open in the U.S. by the year 2000." [19]

This prognosis raises a very difficult question: Is DoD wise to budget billions of dollars for the building of additional ships simply to keep a shipyard open, rather than taking the chance that closed yards could be reopened or new ones built some time in the future when new ships are

Table 2.1
Defense and nondefense sales for selected industries

Industry	Estimated sales (percent)	
	Defense	Nondefense
Shipbuilding and repair	80	20
Ammunition, except small arms	84	16
Aircraft	55	45
Radio and TV communication equipment	51	49
Semiconductors	34	66
Electronic computing equipment	10	90

required? Or should DoD search for some more attractive alternative approach, such as the initiation of R & D work on a next-generation ship in order to keep a yard open? The costs of any of these choices are very significant; for example, to build an extra nuclear submarine simply to keep a submarine shipbuilding yard open (as President Clinton did in 1993) costs around $3 billion for each submarine. An analysis of this sector also raises the difficult issue of the choice between doing maintenance work on ships in public or private shipyards (see chapter 7).

Besides the overall sector variations, the vulnerability of individual corporations to defense cutbacks will depend on their total sales devoted to defense. Table 2.2 groups the top twenty-five defense firms (in 1991) by their exposure to defense budget reductions. It also shows their individual defense and commercial corporate sales. Large firms that are the least dependent on defense contracts are in the best shape[20]—even though an individual plant within that firm may be 100 percent dependent on defense and be quite vulnerable.

It is at the plant level itself, which is the most important area as far as individual employees are concerned, that surprisingly little information is available. The Commerce Department data do not separate out defense-unique operations. The danger of the lack of visibility into individual plants is that, as the defense budget shrinks, a single remaining source for a critical or unique weapon system part may be forced out of business, leaving the DoD with no alternative supplier. This happened, for example, when the Avtex Fibers plant, the nation's only defense-qualified source of rayon, closed on November 3, 1988. This resin-impregnated

Table 2.2
Top DoD prime contractors

Company	1991 Revenues ($ millions)			
	Defense/space	Total	Percent	Category
Alliant Techsystems	1,187	1,187	100.0	Extremely exposed
Grumman	3,597	3,963	90.8	
Northrop	5,100	5,694	89.6	
Martin Marietta	5,200	6,075	85.6	
Lockheed	8,340	9,809	85.0	
General Dynamics	7,400	8,751	84.6	
Loral Corp.	2,170	2,882	75.3	
McDonnell-Douglas	10,150	18,432	55.1	Highly exposed
Raytheon	5,000	9,274	53.9	
Hughes	5,900	11,700	49.6	
Litton Industries	2,450	5,219	46.9	
Textron	3,423	7,822	43.8	
Rockwell	5,200	11,927	43.6	
TRW	3,111	7,913	39.3	
FMC Corp.	1,172	3,899	30.1	
Texas Instruments	1,890	6,784	27.9	Moderately exposed
Unisys	2,350	8,696	27.0	
United Technologies	5,500	21,262	25.9	
Westinghouse	3,245	12,794	25.4	
Boeing Company	5,846	29,314	19.9	
Allied Signal	2,213	11,831	18.7	
General Electric	7,300	59,379	12.3	
ITT Corp.	1,201	20,421	5.9	Minimally exposed
General Motors	6,800	122,081	5.6	
GTE	1,000	19,621	5.1	
Total	106,645	426,730	25.0	

Source: DRI/McGraw-Hill.
Note: Revenue data pertain to calendar year. Contained in "The Impact of Reduced Defense Spending on U.S. Defense Contractors," Annex D to "Adjusting to the Drawdown," report of the Defense Conversion Commission, February 1993, Washington, D.C., p. 8.

base fiber cloth is used in the production of rocket nozzles for the space shuttle, the first and second stages of the MX strategic ballistic missile, the Trident 2 submarine-launched ballistic missile, and other military rocket systems. It cost the government over $18 million, in that case, to keep Avtex open until an alternative could be found; but the low volume demand for the product, plus environmental and safety considerations, made it simply an economically undesirable operation.

Reliance on a single defense-unique plant will result in a large drain on the Defense Department's budget in the future if the plant can only be salvaged through subsidies. A far better solution clearly needs to be found.

It must be emphasized that the vulnerability problems are most severe, and growing worse most rapidly, at the lower tiers of the defense industry. Here the traditional suppliers are being influenced by four effects at once. In addition to the budget cuts, the primary weapons contractors are compounding the problem by reversing many of their purchase decisions and bringing more work in-house. Also, the prime contractors are protected by the "Buy American" Act, but the lower-tier suppliers have no protection and are being increasingly replaced by superior performance, lower-cost foreign sources. Finally, many prime contractors are greatly limiting their suppliers to only a few high-quality sources. This latter action is extremely desirable from a competitiveness perspective; however, it results in a dramatic downsizing of the number of supplier firms (especially when combined with the other three effects). Fortunately, it is among these firms that the most obvious commonality of product and process technologies exists between the commercial and military worlds. Thus if the current barriers to integration can be removed, there is hope that firms at this level can make the transition to dual use.

Overall, the Department of Defense and the nation face two important issues in the downsizing and vulnerability area: first, how to achieve an efficient and effective reduction among firms in sectors where there are too many; and second, how to create or maintain at least one or two operations in each important sector where there may be too few. In the first case, allowing each firm to shrink to inefficient levels and still remain in business is not an acceptable solution. But the Defense Department (the monopsony buyer) must be careful not to favor individual firms.

Rather, the government must assure that if a given industrial sector can be efficiently maintained at a level of, say, three plants, it is not being artificially and inefficiently maintained at its current level (of seven or eight plants). This can be achieved through the use of the DoD budget and procurement process—allowing market forces to achieve the desired downsizing and firm selection. Second, at the opposite end of the spectrum, there is the problem of too few plants, or none at all, in a given sector. Here it is essential to consider maintenance of both engineering and manufacturing capabilities. Also, wherever possible an attempt should be made to maintain competition within at least the design arena. Competition creates incentives to drive down costs and improve product quality. It may often be possible to have an existing equipment source compete against a next-generation supplier. In cases where it would be inefficient to maintain more than one source, it is essential to assure that technology is being adequately advanced and that the prices are not based on monopoly considerations. Foreign sourcing might be an alternative to this sole-source condition. In some cases, direct DoD subsidization may be required to maintain the critical suppliers—but obviously this should be minimized.

Perhaps the most difficult part of the defense drawdown is the problem created by the politics of the situation. Some of the defense plants, particularly some of the public sector operations, are major employers in a particular geographic region. Clearly, no congressional representative or senator wants layoffs in his or her district or state. Thus it may be necessary to take an approach similar to that of the Base Closure Commission, which overcame much of the political resistance it encountered by bypassing the political system with an all-or-nothing voting process.[21]

Four Examples of Restructuring

To see how an individual sector might evolve from its current largely defense-unique operations to more of a dual-use structure—one that integrates the military and civilian portions of the industry—it is useful to take a brief look at four representative sectors: tanks, aircraft, electronics, and services. They consist of one sector that is almost exclusively military (tanks); one (aircraft) that is about 50 percent military and 50 percent civilian; and two (electronics and services) that are critically important to defense and yet are dominated by the civilian economy—here, one is manufacturing oriented (electronics) and the other is labor intensive (services).

Tanks   At the prime contractor level, the tank industry essentially consists of one firm (General Dynamics) running two tank plants that are largely government owned and where the production equipment is primarily government supplied. It is significant that when the army decided to establish the second tank plant, it chose not to have a different firm running it. Therefore, instead of creating competition in the tank industry, the army discouraged it by simply having one portion of the tank built in one of the General Dynamics plants and the other built at the second General Dynamics plant. This approach represents the traditional arsenal model that has been common practice throughout the history of the army's industrial base. Under monopoly conditions of this sort, however, there is very little incentive for the continuous price reduction and/or the technological innovations that would come from normal market competition. Similarly, there is very little incentive for introducing commercial products, or even any other military products, into these facilities, because they are considered "tank arsenals." Obviously there is no commercial application for a tank; however, much of the production process for building a tank is similar to that associated with other heavy metal equipment, such as railroad cars. In fact, during the cold war the Russians built tanks and railroad cars in the same plant for just this reason.

By the mid-1990s, budget cutbacks forced the U.S. Army to plan to not buy any tanks. Their hope was that foreign sales of U.S. tanks could at least keep one of the tank plants in production, until subsequent funds could be allocated to either buy more M-1 tanks or to buy the next-generation tank. The army did plan to upgrade the existing tanks and of course to perform normal maintenance on those that needed overhaul or repair; however, the army has traditionally done this maintenance and upgrade work in a separate government depot, rather than in the tank plant. Obvious redundancies result from performing a minimum level of activities in both the tank production plant and the separate overhaul-and-upgrade tank facilities—an issue we will return to later.

on the next-generation military fighter aircraft. Even when the products are similar, and manufacturing is done by the same firm, they are done in separate facilities. Boeing and McDonnell-Douglas have both split their commercial and military transport aircraft operations to keep the burdens imposed by the DoD's unique business practices from harming their commercial businesses. Thus neither the U.S. commercial industry nor the DoD benefit from the potential synergisms. As the combined markets shrink, and it becomes increasingly clear that the U.S. aircraft industry has far too many suppliers and enormous excess capacity, downsizing becomes absolutely essential. The question is how to do it efficiently and effectively. The choices are very similar to those in the tank sector. Here, however, the interrelationship with the civilian economy is even more obvious.

Historically, the government (both the DoD and NASA) has played an important role in establishing the U.S. leadership position in the aircraft and jet engine businesses. The links between the KC-135 military tanker and the 747 transport (both Boeing airplanes) have been well accepted, as has the linkage between the jet engines designed for military aircraft that were subsequently used in commercial aircraft. Similarly, wide credit is given for the early research on aerodynamics, aircraft experimentation, and advanced propulsion to NASA (and its predecessor NACA). In recent years, much of this historic synergism has been lost.

By contrast, in Europe there has been an integrated multinational, government-supported focus involving Germany, France, and the United Kingdom on commercial aircraft developments. This has placed Airbus as the number-two supplier in the world, ahead of McDonnell-Douglas. Similarly, in Japan the government (specifically MITI) has declared the aircraft industry an area of national focus. Here the four major companies in the aircraft and jet engine business have received significant funding from the Japanese Defense Agency to modernize their factories in order to build both the advanced fighter of the Japanese air force (the FSX) and the major structural elements of the 777 Boeing commercial transports—on the same machines, in the same factories. Each of these suppliers is 75 to 85 percent dependent on the military for its current funding, but each is simultaneously focusing on future commercial business. Even now, they have basically replaced American companies such as

Northrop and LTV as the major suppliers to the U.S. commercial transport industry.[23]

No similar integrated approaches have been undertaken in the United States. Not only have military expenditures for aircraft been made independent of any commercial aircraft strategy, they have even been independent of a military aircraft strategy. By viewing each military program as a separate decision unto itself, an enormous excess capacity has been created. As Laura D'Andrea Tyson, President Clinton's chair of the Economic Advisory Council, has stated,[24] an "industrial policy is surely needed to guide the American aircraft industry through the difficult days of conversion, restructuring, and intensified foreign competition that lie ahead." She went on to say that "the real error of American policy has been that of a haphazard defense industrial policy" in the aircraft industry.

Surprisingly, the suppliers of jet engines—the critical subsystem for the aircraft industry—are relatively integrated. And General Electric and Pratt-Whitney, the two dominant jet engine suppliers for both the commercial and military arena, are in continuous competition. Historically, the Defense Department has played a very significant role in assisting the jet engine industry through continuous funding for product improvements. Even with the declining defense budget, the need remains to press forward with the technology in this area. The danger is that without careful government attention and support, the industry will dwindle down to a single supplier and the benefits of competition will be lost.

It is also important to recognize that, as with the tank sector, the aircraft and jet engine industries have a large public sector in direct (but often informal) competition with the private sector. Both the air force and the navy maintain significant maintenance, overhaul, and upgrade facilities for aircraft and engines that compete for similar work with private sector firms. Again, this is a difficult political issue (see chapter 7).

Electronics More than 50 percent of the DoD's budget for research and development, as well as for production and upgrade of military equipment, is now being supplied by the defense electronics industry. Essentially, the DoD is moving from a platform-based strategy—that is, ships, planes, and tanks—to one that is much more information based—

involving sensors, computers, intelligence data, communications, and simulations. Nonetheless, the U.S. electronics industry is clearly dominated by the growing information age in the commercial arena. Computers, personal communication equipment, office automation, and factory automation have put the commercial world significantly ahead of the defense world in electronics, and the gap is widening.

Semiconductors produced for the commercial sector now more than meet the environmental demands of the military. For example, a semiconductor chip hard-mounted to the engine block of a car now meets or exceeds all military requirements. In fact, it exceeds the military temperature range requirement by 10 degrees. Yet the commercial products cost far less than their military equivalents, have higher reliability (in both cases because of the high-volume of commercial production), and are two to three years more advanced in performance (because the commercial development and procurement processes are much more accelerated than those in the defense world). The problem is that the government has mandated specialized specifications, standards, procurement and accounting practices, etc., forcing its electronic supplier plants to be totally isolated from the company's commercial operations. As a result, five of the top ten U.S. semiconductor producers have stated that they "refuse defense business because of the burdens and special requirements the government imposes."[25] Thus the military pays high prices for small quantities of electronics equipment that are often using obsolete processes, parts, and software. Clearly, this area is crying out for a change in the way that defense does business.

Services   The government has tended to maintain its focus on hardware as the central issue of procurement and has established all of its buying practices on that assumption. The reality is that services are increasingly the dominant sector not only in defense procurement but also in the general economy.

A breakdown of the government's federal procurement data system for 1993 identifies $103 billion spent on services by the federal government,[26] which includes $62 billion for the DoD. Although many so-called service items could probably be listed elsewhere, many items under hardware also contain large elements of services. For example, the cost of much electronics equipment is now devoted to software programming, which is clearly a labor-intensive service item.

Although some of these procured services are of the relatively unskilled type and can be purchased at the lowest hourly rate, it is important to recognize how large a share of this is high-skilled labor, particularly engineering and computer sciences. Thus the traditional government procurement practice of source selection based on the concept of "technically acceptable, low-bid wins" has resulted in some very perverse procurements of high-skill services by the government. For example, during the mid-1980s the navy was actually procuring degreed-engineering services at $6.50 an hour, with contract awards based solely on the lowest hourly rate bid. Certainly no commercial organization would buy its engineers based on the fact that they had an engineering certificate and a temperature of 98.6 degrees. For high-skilled services, the proper evaluation must be made on the basis of best value for the money. In this case, the services of one smart engineer at a higher hourly rate might well be worth ten low-cost engineers—in terms of the new ideas and technical designs that he or she could contribute. Again, many of the expenditures made by the Defense Department for these high-skilled services, for example in advanced information technology, could easily be used in the commercial world, if it were not for the specialized set of practices developed in the defense market.

Finally, any future defense industrial strategy in the services area must choose between the public and private sector. In this case, there is considerable overlap between both the Defense Department and the Department of Energy (DoE) laboratories and the engineering services provided by private sector firms. There is also redundancy between the quasi-governmental federally funded research and development centers (FFRDCs) doing systems engineering work for the DoD and the private sector firms performing similar work. These FFRDCs (such as the Aerospace and Mitre Corporations) were established at a time when there were few, if any, private sector firms doing equivalent professional services work. They receive their funding without competition and pay no federal taxes. Yet today, thousands of people in these FFRDCs are doing work that is identical to that done by private sector firms for other parts of the federal government as well as for industry. In the private sector, the services industry is extremely competitive. In fact, many firms compete for every award, and there is no shortage of potential firms that have extremely high technical competence. Again, downsizing will present a politically difficult choice.

There has been a dramatic change in the role of government in the service sector in recent years. In the past, the government was the provider of services—the retail deliverer through federal agencies and workers. Today it is largely a wholesaler of services, contracting work out to private contractors, nonprofit organizations, and even state and local governments. In this new role the federal government acts as financier, arranger, and overseer rather than as the direct provider.[27] These changed responsibilities require a different set of skills and perspectives for government workers that actually gives them greater management responsibility. This change has not been well understood, and government workers have often not been hired for, or compensated for, this new role.

Drawdown Issues

From these four cases—that is, tanks, aircraft, electronics, and services—it can be seen that the development of a defense industrial strategy by individual sectors is difficult but necessary. And the transformation of individual firms and plants to either dual-use or commercial operations is similarly essential. This transformation has received much attention and government funding under the heading of "defense conversion," yet its definition has been left, perhaps intentionally, extremely vague. In fact, the term has become so all-encompassing that it has included:

- community economic adjustment to defense cutbacks and downsizing;
- industrial defense plant conversion/diversification to civil sector work;
- retraining of laid-off defense workers;
- training in modern manufacturing technology to redundant defense firms—usually at the lower-tier supplier level;
- transferring defense technology to nondefense businesses;
- transformation of the isolated defense industry into an integrated civil/ military industrial base; and

• shifting defense R & D investments to focus on dual-use product and process technologies.

This list spans an extremely wide spectrum, suggesting that all the recent attention to defense conversion has not produced a consensus on what should be done.

The purpose of this book is to develop a plan around which a consensus can be built. One essential factor to consider in this connection is the growing international character of the U.S. defense industry.

3

Growing Foreign Involvement

Many of the critical components of almost every U.S. weapon system are provided from suppliers outside of the United States.[1] Yet self-sufficiency has always been a basic tenet of national security policy. In 1791 Alexander Hamilton, in his influential "Report on Manufacturers," recommended the development of a domestic industrial base to avoid excessive reliance on foreign suppliers. In 1933, the United States implemented the "Buy American" Act, which still exists and which states that all weapon systems bought by the Department of Defense must be produced domestically. Since subcontractors and parts suppliers, however, are not specifically mentioned in this act, they are exempt.

Even though today's global economy has made autarky virtually impossible, the issue of dependency cannot simply be ignored by assuming that the free market will satisfy a country's needs. An individual corporation trying to optimize its own short-term profit may sell to the "wrong" country (from a national security perspective), while a foreign company may offer goods that are more attractive in performance and/or in cost than those of its American counterpart. As a result, the issues of foreign dependency and technology export controls have been moving up on the national security agenda, especially since foreign companies began to acquire critical firms in the lower tiers of the U.S. defense industry (and even a few offers were made for prime contractors).

Shintaro Ishihara, a best-selling novelist in Japan and a member of the Diet, wrote a book (together with industrialist Akio Morita) called *The Japan That Can Say No*. In it, Ishihara claimed that Japan could bring the United Sates to its knees within six months, simply by withholding semiconductors.[2] Demonstration of this threat occurred when the Japa-

nese Ministry of International Trade and Industry (MITI), under antinu-
clear pressure from Socialist members of the Diet, forced Dexcel, the
American subsidiary of Kyocera, to withhold its advanced ceramic technology from the U.S. Tomahawk cruise missile program. During the war
in the Persian Gulf, newspaper headlines acknowledged that a significant
number of critical parts for deployed U.S. weapons were supplied from
offshore. When spare parts appeared to be a potential problem, DoD representatives were sent scurrying around the world begging for special arrangements to expedite the sale of these needed foreign parts. Thus the
internationalization of the defense industry is no longer an issue that the
United States can afford to ignore.

Vulnerability

In reality, the United States has always been dependent on support from
foreign countries. Certainly, in areas such as critical raw materials, this is
a problem that will exist no matter what policies the government pursues,
and this has been acknowledged in our operations. For example, the
United States has long had strategic stockpiles of critical raw materials
that it could only obtain offshore, so that the nation could not be held
hostage to suppliers. But as we consider various states of processed
goods, including final equipment for military weapons and the prospect
of rapid obsolescence, the concept of stockpiling becomes less and less
practical. Nonetheless, the threat of cutting off supplies is real. The
Reagan administration used it when it ordered the European subsidiaries
of Dresser Industries and General Electric to cancel their contracts to supply technology for the Soviet gas pipeline.

The threat today is that political leverage will be used on suppliers by
their home country to cut off sources of critical equipment for U.S. military weapons. The issue, however, is less one of foreign sourcing than
vulnerability. The objective is to ensure enough alternative sources of supply to preempt loss of control to a foreign monopolist.

Diversification and multiplication of the companies and locales upon
which a nation can draw offer the most dependable method for minimizing the threat of foreign control.[3] Once the threat is understood to be
foreign control arising from external concentration in key industries, it

can be assessed on a common basis by national security analysts and economists alike. It should be possible to establish quantitative measures of vulnerability and determine whether actions are required,[4] and if so, what those actions should be. The important point is to recognize that the issue is vulnerability—not foreign dependency—so that any impulse toward autarky is misplaced.

Foreign Ownership

In 1991, when Thompson-CSF, a French government-owned company, attempted to buy the U.S. defense divisions of LTV, the issue of foreign ownership of defense firms reached headline proportions. After much public pressure was brought to bear on the case, the intended acquisition was dropped, but the awareness of foreign ownership remained alive. Americans read that the French company Matra had purchased the Fairchild Space and Defense Company in 1988, and many other lower-tier sales of the defense industry (parts and subsystems) have similarly been concluded in recent years: Cardior Electronics to Germany's Siemans; Reflective to British Aerospace; Cincinnati Electronics to Britain's General Electric; Gould Inc. to Japan's Nippon Mining Company; Singer's Military Simulation operation to CAE of Canada; Singer's (LINK) Motor Products to Ryobi of Japan; Singer's Electronic Systems to Plessey of the United Kingdom; and Singer's American Meter Division to Rhurgas AG of Germany.

These examples parallel a growing trend in foreign ownership of U.S. commercial sector plants. Overall, foreign ownership of U.S. assets rose from around $250 billion in 1976 to over $2.2 trillion in 1990.[5] In some cases these were purchases of the sole remaining U.S. supplier; and, often, these were dual-use, critical supplier firms. In 1990, Nippon Sanso purchased Semi-Gas, the only American manufacturer of the rarefied gases needed to produce semiconductors. In late 1988, the last two United States commercial makers of silicon, the basic building block of most electronics, were sold to a German and a Japanese company.[6] In a period of ten years, 100 computer companies, 45 semiconductor companies, 35 advanced materials companies, and 20 aerospace companies were purchased by foreign firms from U.S. owners.

To understand what is causing this phenomenon, consider that a modern semiconductor chip factory costs between $250 million and $1 billion. U.S. firms have a great deal of difficulty getting long-term financing at home for these very high-cost investments and are often forced to look abroad for capital. The same applies when a U.S. owner decides to sell a division or a whole company. In Europe and Japan, however, where financing is more long-term oriented, companies are more readily able to acquire money to make a strategic investment. Thus, even when a U.S. firm wants to find an American purchaser, it frequently is forced to go offshore to secure financing.[7] By the year 2000, more than 1 million Americans are expected to be working for Japanese-owned companies in the United States.[8]

Adding to the foreign ownership issue is the astute nature of the investments foreigners are making in the United States. For example, NEC will produce four-megabit chips not only in Kumamoto, Japan, but also at a plant outside Sacramento, California. Increasing U.S. dependency on Japanese technology is reversing the trend of the last thirty years. Silicon Valley executives looking for state-of-the-art parts shops end up in Japan. Then, as demand builds, the Japanese build a plant in the United States.

In 1988, the U.S. Congress passed the Exon-Florio Amendment (Title VII, Section 720) to the Defense Production Act of 1980 to address the defense firm foreign ownership issue. The act was initially established to provide broad presidential economic powers to help maintain a strong defense industrial base. The amendment established a Committee on Foreign Investment in the United States (CFIUS) and authorized the president to conduct investigations to determine the effects on national security of corporate mergers, acquisitions, or takeovers that could result in foreign control of firms doing business in the United States. If national security—broadly defined—is found to be impaired, the president can suspend or prohibit the transactions in question. If the transactions have already been completed, the president may seek divestment as a means of enforcement.

The responsibility for implementing this bill was given to the Treasury Department. Since the Treasury is very keen to encourage foreign investment in America, and since it has traditionally been a strong advocate of free and open markets, the department's review (under CFIUS) of foreign purchases between 1988 and 1992 produced little opposition. Seven hundred cases were reviewed and only one was rejected—a Chinese government agency that sought to acquire a Boeing supplier, but was suspected of being a front for spies. Each time an individual case is reviewed, it is treated as a "special case." Since there is no stated policy as to the desired overall objective for the defense industry, there is usually some valid rationale for accepting the foreign offer. The act is considered a paper tiger.

To properly address this issue, then, foreign ownership must be made an explicit part of a coherent U.S. defense industrial strategy. On the whole, foreign investments are extremely desirable, bringing money, jobs, and advanced technology to the United States. The critical determinants are simply U.S. vulnerability and the transfer of critical technologies to potential adversaries.

Technology Transfer Control

During the cold war, America had a policy of openly sharing military technology with our allies in Europe, Japan, and elsewhere, withholding it only from potential military adversaries, particularly the communist countries. Today, by placing economic competition on an equal or greater footing than military security, it becomes necessary to reassess the question of technology transfer because our principal military allies are also our principal economic competitors. The United States must continue to advocate free markets, and—when reciprocity is present—everyone gains. Since our economic competitors have managed markets in many high-tech areas, however, it is important to consider the U.S. position.

In the past, it was relatively easy to control the transfer of defense technologies because it was relatively easy to distinguish militarily relevant technology from that which was exclusively commercial. In addition, military technologies clearly represented the state of the art. Today, neither of these conditions is typical. One frequently finds a critical technology used both in the commercial and military fields, and the civilian technology is often more advanced. A classic case of this occurred when, prior to the Gulf War, Saddam Hussein's brother-in-law bought a high-tech U.S. machine-tool company in Ohio (Matrix Churchill, Inc.) through a London-based parent firm. The Commerce Department approved the shipment of this equipment to Iraq for "building a fiberglass factory for the Iraqi oil industry." Ironically, it could also be used to build missile casings.

The FSX (advanced fighter aircraft) case in 1989 was a highly publicized example of a military technology transfer issue. The United States and Japan agreed on the development of a joint military fighter program, based on the U.S. F-16 fighter technology, with General Dynamics as subcontractor to Japan's Mitsubishi Heavy Industries. In this case, the American rationale was based partly on helping a military ally, partly on the dollars that would flow to the U.S. firms (since Japan was funding the effort), and partly on the hope that the United States would acquire some advanced military technology (electronics and structural materials) from Japan—all in exchange for the release of U.S. fighter aircraft technology. The controversy arose over the fact that aircraft technology has obvious civil and military applicability, and MITI has consistently announced that the development of a world-class domestic aircraft industry—focused particularly on the commercial transport business—is a long-term Japanese objective. Prior to the FSX, Japan had pursued this objective through the combination of licensing older military subsystems and systems from American defense firms and acquiring major subcontracts to U.S. commercial companies: Boeing for airframe parts; Pratt-Whitney and General Electric for engine technology; and numerous U.S. firms for avionics technology. The FSX was to be the first overall aircraft development. The controversy rested on the recognition that the Japanese primary weakness in developing a competitive commercial aircraft industry has been in the overall design, systems engineering, and integration requirements for an advanced aircraft, some of which they might acquire through the FSX.

In view of the critical role aircraft play in the U.S. military and, particularly, since aircraft exports are the single largest positive trade area of any U.S. business, this was obviously a critical technology-transfer question. Yet in the negotiations, the United States lacked a coordinated position among the Commerce, Defense, and State Departments; and it went into the international negotiations with the U.S. supplier firms openly competing against each other—and they were often not in agreement with their government. The Japanese, on the other hand, exhibit a cooperative position between their major industrial suppliers and their government.

Clearly, under such conditions the United States is not in the stronger position.[9]

Joint international ventures are becoming far more prevalent, which is compounding the technology control issue. These ventures can be advantageous to the United States if foreign know-how is transferred to America; they also have the potential to exploit U.S. technology if there is no reciprocity. A few recent examples of such joint ventures include:[10]

· Advanced Micro Devices Inc. (U.S.) in a $700 million deal with Fujitsu Ltd. (one of Japan's largest electronics companies);
· IBM (U.S.), Toshiba (Japan), and Siemans (Germany) to develop a memory chip that would be the foundation of next-generation computers;
· Boeing (U.S.) and Mitsubishi Heavy Industries (Japan) to develop a new commercial aircraft;
· Hitachi (Japan) and Texas Instruments (U.S.) to develop next-generation electronics; and
· NEC Corp. (Japan) and AT&T Co. (U.S.) to develop advanced microchip technology.[11]

One unresolved question is whether foreign companies should be allowed to participate in U.S. government-sponsored research activities. To date, there are no guidelines. Decisions have been largely ad hoc, with each individual government research manager making his or her own determinations. In some cases, these have contradicted each other, and in others, they have not been in the nation's long-term interest. This problem becomes particularly acute as large research institutions are being set up by foreign firms within the United States, typically near U.S. research universities, and are primarily intended to tap the talents of top U.S. scientists. In 1990, the giant Japanese electronics company NEC set up a $32 million research center at Princeton University. Hitachi, Toshiba, and Sony have followed suit. At a time when U.S. companies are cutting back on research, the Japanese are using this foreign investment approach to overcome their long-standing weakness in basic research. The American scientists employed by these centers, or working in U.S. research universities supported by the Japanese (MIT is a big recipient), state that they are trying not to be just a channel for transferring American technology back to Japan. Only time will tell. Kojio Kobayashi, former chairman of NEC, "credits access to MIT research for much of NEC's success in computers." [12] At the same time, MIT is one of the major U.S. research universities receiving large R & D contracts from the Department of Defense for state-of-the-art, often dual-use, technology development.

The physical location of the critical engineering and initial manufacturing is a key issue in the debate over the internationalization of the defense industry. Advocates argue that U.S. R & D projects should be open to foreign-owned firms that make a substantial contribution to U.S. GDP by being located in the United States. This position was also taken by an expert group from the National Academy of Engineering,[13] which argued that many U.S.-based foreign-owned corporations help improve the quality of the U.S. work force; often introduce advanced technologies and management techniques; and contribute directly to U.S. economic growth and its standard of living. They maintain that the benefits of foreign participation outweigh the potential costs and risks.

The question of whether foreign ownership and technology transfer is good does not require yes-or-no answers. But the United States does need to set up terms and conditions sector by sector. In many cases, the easiest and best solution may involve a strategy of reciprocity depending on what other countries are doing in the areas of technology transfer and foreign participation vis-à-vis the United States. For example, if it is necessary for a U.S. firm to form a joint venture with a Japanese firm to enter their market, then America could mandate the same. Or, if a country insists on procurement offsets when purchasing military equipment from the United States, the United States should request the same.

Primarily, the United States needs consistency between policy decisions in this critical area and the overall vision of the defense industrial base transformation that will evolve in the coming decade.

4

Initial Post–Cold War Developments

The defense budget began to fall in the second half of the 1980s; but equipment deliveries did not begin to plummet until the early 1990s. The delay was due to the large backlog of past orders and the long production cycles for major weapons. Between 1982 and 1992, U.S. defense industry sales actually more than doubled. In the aerospace industry alone, sales increased from around $70 billion to over $140 billion per year. But with the post-1989 geopolitical changes and the resultant budget cuts, defense contraction was inevitable. By the end of 1992, with utilization rates of defense plants averaging only 35 percent (and falling rapidly), overhead costs were skyrocketing. All infrastructure—facilities, equipment, managers, and administrators—had to be amortized across a much smaller volume of business. Thus weapons costs increased further, causing volume to decline even more and prompting additional cost increases. The industry was in a serious downward spiral.

The widespread drawdown affected all areas, but it was by no means uniform for every sector. Between fiscal years 1985 and 1990, DoD contract obligations fell 55 percent in armor, 49 percent in aircraft engines, 49 percent in ammunition, 47 percent in aircraft, 39 percent in electronics, 34 percent in missiles, 32 percent in communications equipment, and 29 percent in ships.[1] Then, in the early 1990s, some sectors were hit even harder; for example, by 1994 spending on munitions had fallen almost 80 percent.[2] Some defense firms would have to close down, and almost all would have to shrink.

The job of corporate management is to adjust to the dramatic quantitative and qualitative changes taking place in the American economy. In the defense industry, however, which was totally dependent on the DoD, it was surprising that both the Reagan and the Bush administrations argued strongly that the government should not establish any guidelines to help industry leaders, and this policy continued even after the fall of the Berlin Wall and the subsequent collapse of the Soviet Union. In addition, critical policy actions and resource allocation decisions were being taken on a largely random basis, resulting in increases in inefficiency, chaos, and waste.

Various Contraction Models

From the perspective of an individual defense contractor, five broad options exist for dealing with the downsizing.[3]

Stick with Defense A corporation may choose to remain in the defense market and adapt to the permanent drawdown in military spending by consolidating its defense operations and, in some cases, even buying the defense operations of other firms. This option involves cutting costs, reducing company-funded R & D and capital spending, and, in particular, downsizing its work force and eliminating jobs, while preserving core capabilities and key operations in defense R & D and production. It also often involves bringing work in-house that was previously subcontracted out. By concentrating on niche markets or increasing market share, a defense firm can attempt to capture a larger percentage of a shrinking defense market.

Sell Overseas Defense companies may seek to balance reductions in the U.S. defense market by increasing military sales to foreign markets and by gaining new international access via increased cooperative arrangements (on military programs) with foreign firms. Initially, U.S. firms may simply attempt to sell more current military products overseas, either off-the-shelf or involving offsetting counter-purchases (known as "offsets").[4] In time, however, companies may also attempt a more ambitious approach involving joint development and production of weapon systems, or simply merging operations with defense-related firms in other countries. This strategy is closely related to the stick-with-defense option.

Sell to Other Government Markets A defense firm may elect to diversify by increasing sales to the nondefense government market. Certain civilian government agencies—the National Aeronautics and Space Administration (NASA), the Federal Aviation Administration (FAA), the Department of Energy (DoE), the Environmental Protection Agency (EPA), and the Department of Transportation (DoT)—all have requirements for the type of high-technology, high-quality products that defense manufacturers usually produce. Additionally, there is a great deal of crossover, in terms of applications, between civil and military government space programs; for example, the NASA space station *Freedom* was frequently cited as a replacement program for displaced defense aerospace workers. By sticking to familiar government markets, this strategy is clearly a mild form of the broader diversification strategy.

Diversify Firms may choose to remain in defense, with a reduced dependency on defense purchases, by diversifying into commercial products and markets. To gain access to new markets, a defense firm may attempt to acquire or merge with companies already manufacturing and selling commercial products. Alternatively, it may decide to diversify through developing (in-house) new nondefense products. The firms could convert their defense assembly lines and work force to produce for commercial markets if necessary, but they would have a much easier transition if dual-use production processes were already in place.

Get Out of Defense Finally, a viable alternative is simply to pull out of the defense market. A firm may divest itself of defense production assets or discontinue defense-related operations. Many of the big corporations, for which defense divisions do not make up a large share of their total business, have chosen this route.

Given the heterogeneous nature of the defense industry, no single adjustment strategy is best for the entire defense industrial base, or even for a given industry sector. As would be expected, however, there appears to be a strong relationship between such factors as a firm's size and degree of defense dependency and the selection and implementation of a particular adjustment strategy.

General Dynamics, a corporation heavily dependent on defense, chose the stick-with-defense option and, as enunciated by then chairman and CEO William Anders, argued that rationalizing the defense industry would require dramatic consolidations. He said that General Dynamics had tried to buy other firms' defense operations, but in every case the sellers had held out. Therefore he sold off his operations one by one— missile operations to Hughes; aircraft operations (once the heart of the company) to Lockheed; and space launch vehicle operations to Martin Marietta; while the remaining tank and submarine operations were still up for sale. In the process, he downsized the company by over 50,000 employees in just a few years.[5]

Loral, a defense electronics firm, aggressively went out and acquired other defense firms to get a larger share of a shrinking market. Others buying up defense firms include Martin Marietta, which purchased General Electric's aerospace operations, and Lockheed, which bought General Dynamics' aircraft operations. In each case, after the firm rationalized the combined structures and laid off many employees, stock prices soared. In addition to these buying and selling activities, many defense firms have been attempting diversification/conversion efforts:

• Westinghouse's defense electronic systems operation has moved into home and commercial security gear, airport and weather radar, airline reservation systems, mail-sorting equipment, systems for tracking mass transit and commercial vehicle fleets, and power systems for electric cars.
• Hughes Aircraft now manufactures avionics and video systems for airliners, plus high-tech arcade games. It is also designing electric-car power systems, advanced car phones, and direct-broadcast TV technology.
• TRW's space and defense sector is involved in developing air traffic control systems, airport security equipment, and tax-processing equipment for the Internal Revenue Service, and planning ways of disposing nuclear waste for the Energy Department.
• Martin Marietta now makes commercial aircraft components and mail-sorting systems for the U.S. Postal Service. It also manages computer systems for the Housing and Urban Development Department and research labs for the Energy Department.
• Lockheed does contract maintenance for commercial airlines, handles the collection of parking fines for the city of Los Angeles, and dismantles nuclear weapons.[6] It also designs small satellites for cellular phone networks.

In spite of these initial success stories, diversification or conversion—other than through selling off defense activities or buying commercial operations—has proven to be very difficult and time consuming. In fact, it is fraught with danger. Nonetheless, it is the most attractive option in the long run. Thus it is unfortunate that the government has perversely created significant barriers not only to diversification but even to effective and efficient defense industry downsizing.

Barriers to Effective Downsizing

The cancellation of a few major programs and the closing of a few major facilities, whether private or public, would result in the required budget reductions. Unfortunately, this approach would also have a devastating impact on employment in the region of the plants affected unless there were a specific government-sponsored conversion effort. Government support for base closures has been quite successful in converting former military bases to commercial activities, but the transition takes time, and the problem is the initial unemployment.

In any case, this solution is far from what the politics of the situation will allow. Instead, each of the military services argues strongly for the need to maintain its individual program, even if at much lower volumes. They also advocate the need to maintain the industrial base in their particular product area. This lobbying effort is enhanced by a coalition of industry management and labor leaders backed by their congressional delegations.

By arguing for the combination of security and employment benefits, the Congress has been extremely successful even in maintaining weapons programs that the Department of Defense was willing to terminate. In FY92, Congress added over $8 billion worth of programs to the defense budget; in each case, the justification was "to keep the production lines open."[7] In FY93, Congress found money[8] to buy four more of Northrop Corporation's B-2 Stealth bombers (at a price of $4 billion) and provided $300 million to begin fixing flaws in the fleet of B-1 bombers. President Bush proposed a shutdown of General Dynamics' line of tanks, fighter planes, and submarines (for which even the generals and admirals admitted there was little military requirement), but Congress, asserting the need to "preserve the defense industrial base," provided funds to keep all three lines open. Also, with a big push from Virginia's congressional delegation, Tenneco's Newport News shipyard won initial funding for a new $5 billion aircraft carrier. This appropriation was made despite a continuing dispute among military planners on whether a new carrier was really needed. Ingalls, another winner among the navy shipbuilders, won appropriations for two new destroyers to be built at its yard in Pascagoula,

Mississippi, in order to match the two destroyers authorized for its rival's shipyard in Bath, Maine. Finally, while members of Congress were fighting fiercely to maintain private sector industrial employment in their districts and states, they were battling equally hard to maintain local public sector facilities. In many cases, these government operations were duplicating private sector efforts. Clearly neither national security nor program efficiency was a consideration in making these decisions.

The long-term view is an extremely difficult perspective during a period of budget cutbacks. From an industry viewpoint, shareholders are looking at quarterly returns and, from Congress's viewpoint, the issue is votes in the next election. A rational position would be to expect some quid pro quo for short-term actions through long-term initiatives. For example, a requirement that some short-term corporate profits be reinvested toward gradual conversion and some congressionally awarded funds be used for long-term plant conversion could be considered. During the initial phase of the post–cold war period, very few of these long-term actions were undertaken.

One obvious method of achieving greater savings is merging two or more companies that are inefficiently operating in the same business. The Justice Department and the Federal Trade Commission (FTC), acting on the general principles of competition and not driven by concerns for efficient or effective downsizing, have been aggressively blocking many such consolidations. For example, ignoring the advice of the Pentagon, the FTC moved to block a merger between the two remaining suppliers of army tank ammunition. The FTC asked U.S. District Court Judge Louis Oberdorfer to prohibit the sale of Olin Corporation's ordnance division (in St. Petersburg, Florida) to its only rival in the tank ammunition business, Alliant Techsystems Inc., of Minnesota. The army and its two suppliers had argued that there was only enough business to support one supplier: forcing two suppliers to remain in operation would increase costs to the taxpayer. In a similar case involving the merger of two suppliers of night-vision equipment to the army, the FTC position (against consolidation) was upheld on appeal by the U.S. District Court in Washington, D.C.[9]

The defense industry, along with a number of lawyers and economists, has argued that, in general, it is folly to apply traditional antitrust criteria to such transactions because the Pentagon is both the market regulator and the only customer for most defense products. Thus rules made for free market conditions should not apply to defense market operations. To date, the courts have been guided by antitrust laws, which, in this context, need to be revised.

Normal rules regarding antitrust concentrations and mergers cannot apply to this highly concentrated industry where the single buyer (DoD) actually encourages collaboration among suppliers. In addition, the issue is greatly compounded by the difficulty of defining the market itself; for example, is it aerospace, or missiles, or air-to-air missiles, or even a more narrow definition such as radar-guided, long-range, air-to-air missiles?[10] As industry downsizing takes place, firms will be forced to go into complementary business areas—initially within the defense sector itself. Therefore, since the definition of the relevant market will be expanding, it will be necessary for the antitrust rules to be more loosely interpreted. Similarly, as the defense market continues to become more international, the antitrust policymakers must recognize that, as long as there is an overseas alternative to many of these products, a single remaining U.S. firm will still be operating in a competitive market and will be unable to get away with monopoly profits.

The costs and consequences of environmental cleanup are another major barrier to the downsizing of the defense industrial structure. The cost for the disposal of nuclear waste alone is estimated to be in excess of $180 billion; the cost is considerably more for non-nuclear waste. Remediation will take years, but putting it off will only make the downsizing problems worse and increase the environmental damage.

The large amount of underappreciated defense-unique capital equipment and other assets that were built up during the Reagan era are additional obstacles to restructuring. This excess now makes the defense plants very uncompetitive for other business, since these equipment costs must be depreciated against new business. It also makes it difficult to justify further investments in modern, far more efficient, manufacturing equipment. Tax laws and defense accounting rules would have to be modified to allow the needed rapid writeoffs, and there is always the political question of whether it is fair to give preferential tax treatment to defense firms over other firms suffering from general adverse economic conditions. There are no easy answers.

Other barriers include specialized government procurement practices, military specifications and standards, and unique cost accounting requirements. Under the circumstances, many defense firms say "forget it" to long-term diversification/conversion and look for short-term profits instead.

Short-Term Profits

A December 10, 1992, headline read "Wall Street Hails Defense Consolidation: General Dynamics' and Lockheed's Stocks Up." This was the reaction to General Dynamics' sale of its aircraft business to Lockheed. During 1991 and 1992 General Dynamics' stock had gone from $20 to over $100 per share. Investors looking for short-term gains clearly were pleased with the gradual liquidation of assets. Through extra dividends, stock repurchases, and debt repayment, the firm had returned hundreds of millions of dollars to the stockholders. As a reward, Bill Anders, chairman and CEO, received $20.85 million in compensation in 1992. Many, however, criticized General Dynamics' decision not to reinvest the money back into the company. And tens of thousands of laid-off workers did not appreciate the corporate strategy.

Partly in recognition of the historic difficulty of defense firms in achieving successful conversion and partly in response to stockholders' demands for increasing profits, many defense firms dramatically cut back on their long-term investments in diversification, as well as in capital equipment and R & D. Thus they were neither modernizing their facilities nor pursuing new product development. In 1990 alone, defense firms experienced a 22 percent drop in overall capital investments and an 11 percent drop in R & D.[11]

To be successful, firms often have to act contrary to the short-term perspective of the investment community. When Norm Augustine, the president of Martin Marietta, said the company planned to invest heavily in R & D to realize the company's full technological potential, the company's stock fell eleven and one-half points in five days—but six years later the investments have paid off well for Martin Marietta.[12]

In the early 1990s, defense firms were enormous cash cows. They were earning sole-source awards on traditionally profitable businesses such as follow-on production of current programs, maintenance on prior deliveries, and foreign military sales. Also, due to layoffs, cutbacks in R & D, and little capital investment, costs were falling faster than revenues. Finally, these firms were generating huge piles of cash through the sales of many of their operations, and their equity value was skyrocketing on Wall Street.[13]

Firms had four choices for using their newfound wealth: (1) buy defense competitors, and further concentrate; (2) buy nondefense operations for diversification; (3) give the cash to their stockholders—directly or by buying back company stock; and/or (4) invest in the company's long-term future—other than through acquisitions. From some of the examples cited above, it can be seen that different firms chose different options. The stock market, however, was clearly rewarding the short-term options, including acquisitions—despite the overwhelming evidence regarding long-term problems associated with mergers and acquisitions.[14]

Unfortunately, as downsizing continued, the decreasing volume of business caused most defense activities to become less and less efficient. As a result, firms were increasingly forced to isolate their defense plants to keep them from pulling down their commercial operations, although this is contrary to what is necessary for diversification. In addition, work that had previously been subcontracted out to other firms was being brought in-house in an attempt to utilize the available work force and facilities. Again, this is contrary to the policy being pursued by world-class commercial firms that are outsourcing work to gain greater efficiencies.

As can be seen, the steps taken by defense contractors are perpetuating a vicious cycle: there is little long-term investment in R & D or new capital equipment, and the increasing separation of defense and commercial business is making defense business still less efficient. These trends bode poorly for any long-term restructuring—yet such restructuring is clearly required.

Increasing foreign military sales seems to be the one action that can address all of the defense firms's short-term needs. Here current production lines can be maintained; no significant new investments are required; and management can even argue that this is only a short-term fix and that the profits from these foreign military sales will be reinvested in future conversion efforts.

Foreign Military Sales

From 1987 to 1993, America's foreign military sales (FMS) grew from $6.5 billion to $32 billion. Additional out-year sales were assured when, during the 1992 presidential campaign, President Bush approved F-16 fighter plane sales to Taiwan, F-15 fighters to Saudi Arabia, and M1-A1 tanks to Kuwait and the United Arab Emirates.

Such foreign military sales receive support from defense companies, labor unions, Congress, the State Department, the Commerce Department, and the military, which feel it maintains the defense industrial base and helps lower the cost of its own weapons. In fact, the DoD often is actively involved in FMS efforts. Pentagon officials have said that U.S. military booths, aircraft displays, and aerial demonstrations at the Paris and Singapore air shows alone cost the public around $1 million annually. In addition, a $30.2 million marine corps jet crashed while returning to its base from the Singapore show.[15]

In 1987 the United States and the Soviet Union were the major arms exporters, with 33 percent and 35 percent of the market, respectively; France had 10 percent, Britain 5 percent, West Germany 4 percent, and all others a total of 13 percent. With the collapse of the Soviet Union and the problems of its former nations, however, the United States began to totally dominate the FMS market, capturing a 60 percent share by 1992 and growing to 70 percent by 1993.[16]

Defense budget reductions in Europe have caused shrinkages to their defense industries as well, and a clamor, similar to that in the United States, for FMS; especially since defense budgets in Asia and the Middle East are still growing, with nations there acquiring first-line equipment.

Arms sales to one country often necessitate sales to another country in the same region, in an effort to return the balance of forces and provide stability. For example, in 1992 the United States supplied $650 million in Apache and Black Hawk helicopters and Harpoon antiship missiles to Israel as compensation for the sales of $9 billion worth of F-15 warplanes to Saudi Arabia (announced three weeks before).[17] Even approval of co-production of weapon systems, such as the M1-A1 Abrams tanks in Egypt and in South Korea was justified by Congress to sustain the U.S. defense industrial base.

After the Gulf War, President Bush vowed that the United States would lead the world in achieving arms control in the Middle East. But in less than a year he had approved $13 billion of arms sales to the region—making the United States the biggest supplier to that highly volatile region. In the two years following the Gulf War, the United States contributed roughly half of the $45 billion flow of arms into the Middle East.[18]

In spite of the short-term desirability of foreign military sales to help defense firms weather the storm, one is forced to ask the obvious question about the longer-term desirability of spreading modern weapons around the world. Americans seemed to be shocked to find that in the five years preceding the Gulf War, the United States approved sales of $1.5 billion in advanced technology and products to Iraq, including a sale of $695,000 in advanced data-transmission devices just one day before Iraq invaded Kuwait.[19]

Yet even this revelation was not enough to encourage a slowdown in the frantic search for foreign military sales. Most companies in most countries were willing to make extremely attractive offers to almost any buyer. Increasingly, firms are required to provide very significant (often over 100 percent) offsets for the equipment sales. For example, in the Boeing AWACS sale to Britain, Boeing was forced to agree to spend $1.30 in Britain on parts and labor for every $1.00 in revenue from the AWACS sale. They later struck a similar deal with France.[20] In such cases, Boeing, the prime U.S. contractor, is basically giving away large sales of future business by U.S. parts and subsystem suppliers. They argue that they could not have gotten the sale without such offsets. Unfortunately, the overall, long-term impact to the U.S. economy is often far less clear, as is the impact on global security.

Controlling sales of advanced conventional weapons requires multinational cooperation—as has been shown in the nuclear nonproliferation arena. The United States, Russia, and France are currently the major independent designers, producers, and exporters of state-of-the-art military combat aircraft; the United States, the United Kingdom, France, Germany, Russia, and China account for 99.3 percent of all exported tanks in service today.[21] Therefore, with so few countries involved, if it becomes U.S. policy to do so, it is conceivable that future multinational controls can be placed on many forms of foreign military sales. However, this means that a defense industry restructuring strategy must be developed that can maintain a viable defense industry without counting on such sales. Unfortunately, this was not the initial focus of the U.S. government in the early years of the post–cold war era.

Initial Governmental Actions

It must be emphasized that the end of the cold war, the collapse of the Soviet Union, the accompanying decline of the U.S. defense budget, and the immediate need for defense industry conversion occurred during a period in which the nation had a Republican administration and a Democratically controlled Congress. Getting agreement on an overall strategy and direction would have been difficult, even under the best of conditions. The administration was convinced that the only way to achieve conversion and/or stimulation of the U.S. economy was through passive use of normal free-market forces. When it was pointed out that in the defense sector a free market does not exist, the administration's position was "we do not pick winners and losers," or "if the government gets involved, it will only make things worse." Early in the Bush administration, to demonstrate the commitment to an inactive role, two senior administration officials (Deputy Secretary of Commerce Tom Murrin and the Director of the Defense Advanced Research Projects Agency Craig Fields) were actually forced out because they were advocating some small steps toward government involvement in trying to stimulate critical U.S. industrial sectors.

The result of this strongly laissez-faire position was, as expected, essentially a random set of actions by various government agencies. Yet the argument for objecting to a defense industrial strategy was clearly fallacious, since DoD annually spends approximately $38 billion on research and development and over $50 billion on procurement, and, in doing so, decides which technologies—and therefore which industrial sectors—are stimulated and which are not. Thus there was a de facto defense industrial policy in existence. The real issue for the administration in the post–cold war era was how best to use this policy leverage to meet the nation's security needs while assisting its economic growth.

In contrast to the passiveness of the administration, the Congress during the late 1980s and early 1990s became increasingly concerned about defense industry unemployment and instituted various actions under the heading of "defense conversion." As expected, the first and least effective of the congressional steps involved extensions of existing defense production programs and even bailouts of firms in trouble. In addition, there was considerable "conversion" funding authorized, but without any prior analysis of how it could be most effectively used. Allocated in time for the 1992 election, Congress was spending over a billion dollars in an effort to show that it was "doing something."[22]

Fortunately, some members of the House and Senate gradually began to take a long-term perspective of the needs of the nation—in terms of an overall conversion effort and an economic stimulation of selected critical technology areas. These legislators focused on four areas: civilian R & D, dual-use R & D, technology transfer, and consortia.[23]

Senator Jeff Bingaman's (D-N.M.) Critical Technology and Industrial Base Initiatives, contained in the Senate Armed Services Authorization Act of FY89, is an example of growing congressional concern. Another is the Defense Production Act, which was revised to shift its policy emphasis toward dual-use military and economic programs. Then Congress began to increase the budgets for dual-use R & D. Examples of DoD-funded projects included:

• $650 million (over seven years) for R & D on very high speed integrated circuits (VHSIC);
• $200 million per year on manufacturing technology;
• $600 million (over six years) for semiconductor advanced manufacturing technology ("Sematech");
• $150 million (over three years) for superconductivity research; and
• $250 million (over three years) for gallium arsenide integrated circuit devices ("MIMIC").

The Commerce Department, getting pressure from Congress and recognizing that there clearly had to be some initiatives taken in the civilian R & D area by the administration—but, maintaining a strong desire to have the initiatives industry-led and based on market preferences rather than government selection of critical technologies—in 1991 announced

$9 million in grants aimed at helping companies bring promising new civilian technologies to the market. Although modest, it was the first R & D money for industry from the Commerce Department. The funds were used in such fields as computerized reading of handwriting, electronic control of machine tools, and thin display panels for computers. Known as the Advanced Technology Program, it required the funding to be matched dollar-for-dollar by the recipient companies. It also encouraged proposal submissions by consortia, not only among industrial firms but also between industry and universities.

"What we're trying to do is speed up the commercialization process by applying funding fairly early in the process," said John W. Lyons, then director of the Department's National Institute of Standards and Technology (NIST), which administers the program. Because U.S. companies have been faulted for being slow to bring new discoveries to market, it was hoped that this government stimulant would help. Commerce Secretary Robert Mosbacher praised the program as demonstrating "a new spirit of cooperation" between government, academia, and industry.[24]

During the late 1980s, it became clear that the manufacturing sector of the U.S. economy, particularly the medium to small-sized firms, was lagging behind competitors in other parts of the world. Thus the federal government's Manufacturing Technology Centers program was established, based on the model of the highly successful Agricultural Extension Centers that had been established around the country (early in the century) to help small farmers learn about modern farming technology. The Manufacturing Technology Centers program[25] (operated by the National Institute of Standards and Technology and authorized by the Omnibus Trade and Competitiveness Act of 1988) initially consisted of three centers: the Great Lakes Manufacturing Technology Center (Cleveland, Ohio), the Northeast Manufacturing Technology Center (Troy, N.Y.), and the Southeast Manufacturing Technology Center (Columbia, S.C.). Two of the three centers are located on university campuses, further strengthening partnerships between academia and manufacturing.

The last of the four major congressional initiatives recognized the fact that during the 1980s an adversarial relationship had developed between the government and industry. Although other nations help their industry, the U.S. government had been overly zealous in attempting to control its industry. For example, antitrust laws resulted in corporations not being able to work together on early research and technology investments. Firms argued that they should be allowed to work together in the "precompetitive" phase, to pool their resources rather than to inefficiently dilute them by, for example, meeting the requirement that each of the major domestic auto companies independently duplicate the same research. This basically represented a growing recognition of the fact that the real competition was not among domestic firms, but between domestic firms and foreign firms. In addition, there was an increasing separation, even isolation, among America's industry, universities, and government laboratories. With the congressional initiatives, three forms of consortia became legally acceptable: between government and industry; between universities/national laboratories and industry; and among corporations in the precompetitive phase of developments.

While these federal efforts were getting under way in the area of industrial stimulation, individual states were well ahead of the federal government in encouraging capital investments, R & D, training, technology transfer, and so on. By 1992, twenty-three state governments were spending over $50 million a year supporting twenty-seven Technology Extension Centers.[26] A small amount in comparison with the $500 million a year Japan was spending on 185 Technology Extension Centers, but significant in showing what could be done to improve America's manufacturing competitiveness.

Many state programs were aimed directly at the problems caused by the defense cutbacks and sought to improve productivity, upgrade workers' skills, and promote advanced manufacturing technologies. But they need more federal support to expand. The Office of Technology Assessment estimates that it would cost up to $480 million a year to run industrial extension services similar to the successful one in Georgia in all affected states.[27] For comparison, the current nationwide Agricultural Extension Program annually costs about $1.2 billion.

It was not until the early 1990s that America initiated national efforts to address the urgent need for a specific defense conversion program. The FY91 Defense Authorization Act contained the Defense Economic Adjustment, Diversification, Conversion and Stabilization Act of 1990, which transferred $200 million of DoD funds to the Departments of

Labor and Commerce for programs to assist defense-impacted workers
and communities. And DoD's Office of Economic Adjustment (OEA)—
established in 1961 to assist communities affected by defense base closures—received $3.4 million in additional funding for communities to
begin planning a local response.

In the last year of the Bush administration (1992), the democratic Congress initiated defense conversion programs totaling $1.7 billion. Most of
them were put off, but eventually they became the baseline for the initial
Clinton program in 1993. This program had four parts: (1) help for displaced government (military and civilian) and industry workers; (2) help
for the affected communities; (3) dual-use technology investments to help
the industrial transition; and (4) nondefense technology investments to
stimulate the economy and provide R & D opportunities for defense
firms.

The Clinton campaign promised to stimulate the U.S. economy and to
shift the focus from the defense to the civilian sector. The Clinton administration, however, soon realized that every defense program cancellation
meant additional unemployment. Thus, using the rationale that it was
"necessary to maintain the defense industrial base," President Clinton approved construction of another $1.8 billion Seawolf attack submarine
and another $3 billion aircraft carrier, which, analysts insist, the navy did
not truly need. Unemployment consideration was the overriding determi-
nant. President Clinton clearly recognized that a reevaluation of the defense program, as well as of his economic stimulation program, was
required. In the defense case, it was concluded that research and development should be maintained at approximately the historic levels (around
$35 billion per year) and that reductions, if any, would come from cuts
in DoD military and civilian manpower and from reduced production of
current-generation weapon systems. The worldwide proliferation of modern weapons and the necessity for the United States to stay ahead were the
primary reasons for the R & D expenditures. In addition, R & D would
provide government-sponsored maintenance of critical engineering and
even manufacturing through weapons' prototyping. As a result, each of
the critical sectors of the defense industrial base could be sustained in
a relatively strong position. Finally, it was decided to attempt to shift a
significant portion of the R & D investments toward those technologies

that were truly dual use in nature such as information technology, electronics, software, manufacturing technology, and new materials.

Although most of the other Clinton initial programs were largely a continuation of the congressional initiatives, the rhetoric was much stronger and more proactive. And funding continued to expand. In 1993, the president committed his administration to a $20.3 billion total "conversion program" for the 1994 through 1997 budgets (building up to $5.2 billion for 1997 alone). Many of these funds would flow through the Labor, Commerce, and Defense Departments. An interagency group, cochaired by DoD and the new National Economic Council, was established to coordinate the program, whose total allocation was $20 billion: $4 billion for retraining displaced defense and civilian workers; $1 billion to aid communities hit by defense cutbacks; $5 billion to promote dual-use technology; and $10 billion to spur new civilian technology that would help wean companies from reliance on defense funds. A significant portion of the assistance effort was to expand the regional Manufacturing Extension Centers.

Worker retraining funds were increased for enhancing skills, but there was also a need for achieving some control over the large number of existing programs. There were 125 federal programs in operation, costing over $18 billion each year, and hundreds more were offered by the states. Michigan alone offered seventy educational and training programs, overseen by nine separate departments. Overall, the Defense Conversion Commission found that there were a total of fifty-eight programs to assist the transition of individuals from the defense sector to other areas, and eighty-six programs to assist communities and firms.[28] Many of these provide similar services to the same target population,[29] some are more specific: six programs are designed for Native Americans; four for migrant workers; four for the homeless; and at least ten for veterans. These groups, however, are also eligible for other programs, and the General Accounting Office found that coordination among them is almost nonexistent. Most important, the programs are not focused on any long-term solution.

With the Republican congressional landslide in the 1994 elections, many of these initial "defense conversion" funding efforts began to come under serious attack. Nonetheless, the need for the industrial transformation still exists, and a strategy is clearly required.

5

Prior Lessons of Industrial Conversion

Thousands of firms have acquired experience with diversification through their attempts to add new products and/or new markets to their current business areas. And hundreds of defense plants have attempted to shift their production from military equipment and markets to the commercial world. In both cases there have been many more diversification/conversion failures than successes, perhaps suggesting that any effort is likely to be futile. Nonetheless, the effort must be made. For the overwhelming majority of firms in the defense industry, particularly at the lower tiers, the choice is either diversification/conversion or extinction.

Diversification

The choices here include: acquisition of, or merger with, a business in another product area or market; a shift in the nature of the business, for example, from being a direct supplier to the public to becoming a subcontractor to a manufacturing firm; the establishment of a separate organization within the company to pursue new business; and the attempt to introduce new products into current operations, utilizing existing labor and equipment.

An important study[1] of thirty-three large diversified U.S. companies (mostly commercial firms), between 1950 and 1986, found 2,644 attempted entries into new markets—70 percent through acquisitions, of which about half were in related businesses; 22 percent through startups; and 8 percent through joint ventures. By 1986, 74 percent of the unrelated acquisitions and 44 percent of the joint ventures had been divested. Even half of the diversifications into related businesses failed. And these were large diversified companies, accustomed to managing multiple commercial businesses.

Thus, even though all forms of diversification experience very high failure rates, there have also been many successes achieved via:[2] (1) internal growth through new investment; (2) creation of new startups; and (3) internal growth through redeployment of existing resources. Of the third category, approximately 20 percent survive for ten years after initial entry in the new field. For these successful efforts, the growth was a factor of 2.7.

Importantly, mergers and acquisitions have been a particularly unsuccessful route to diversification.[3] The difficulty of absorbing different corporate cultures and the lack of management knowledge of the new businesses have proven to be extreme barriers. Some researchers,[4] however, have found a significant short-term gain from mergers where the initial rationalization, that is, layoffs and plant closures, helped profits.

From these experiences, it appears that an important lesson is that the closer the new business is to the current business, the easier the transition will be. Equally important is that it is essential to assimilate the shift as rapidly as possible. A 1990 analysis[5] studied the characteristics of firms regarded as successful in marketing sophisticated technology-based products—exactly the kind of products expected of converting defense firms. This study examined firms in the United States, Japan, and Europe and concluded that four factors separated the leaders from the laggards: the successful companies introduce more products, faster, to more markets, and use more technologies; commercialize two to three times the number of new products and processes as their competitors; and compete in twice as many product and geographic markets.

Today, world-class firms achieve rapid new product realizations. The extremely long new product development cycles of defense firms—averaging over sixteen years for new weapon systems, from concept through first production—are totally incompatible with this diversification requirement.

Conversion

The term conversion has been applied to a variety of different initiatives.[6] In some cases it has meant a shift in an entire economic base, where the dominant employer in the area was either a defense firm or a Department of Defense facility. In other cases it has referred to the restructuring of a formerly defense-dominated corporation; and at the plant level, it has been used to refer to a reorientation of either the facility or the work force.

There is often confusion as to whether the term conversion applies when a facility only partially converts from defense to commercial production. Advocates of the "Lucas model" of conversion argue that the transition has to be total. In this model, worker teams establish the desired direction for the company to move (often into "socially desirable" products and markets) and the government then mandates total plant conversion. Although this may have some philosophical attractiveness, there is little empirical proof of success. Rather, the market pull from related but growing markets is undoubtedly a far more successful diversification/conversion model. When the selected markets make good business sense, the firm shifts to them voluntarily.

Even using the market-pull model, however, most conversions (three out of four) fail in their first three years.[7] Given the significant cultural differences between the defense world and the commercial world, the success rate for conversion of defense-oriented companies is not surprising: it used to be around 20 percent, increasing to 35 percent in recent years,[8] and in some cases into the 60 to 70 percent range, for closely related diversifications into commercial areas.[9]

There are a variety of reasons for the high failure rates: among them the companies often did not know the business they were entering; their products were sometimes over-engineered and too costly for the consumer marketplace; or the company lacked access to distribution channels and market savvy.[10] A National Science Foundation study of Western European experiences at conversion identified the following sixteen obstacles to diversification:[11]

1. Absence of an internal climate hospitable to change.
2. Priority commitment to military production.
3. Shortage of capital.
4. Competition from existing commercial firms.
5. Obstacles from other (commercial) divisions of the firm.
6. Problems of commercialization, for example, pricing and licensing.

7. Fragmented markets (versus a single government market).
8. Customer inability to specify needs.
9. Inadequate infrastructure, for example, product support.
10. Incomplete knowledge and patents (in commercial area).
11. Labor force inflexibility.
12. Low profitability of initial commercial investments.
13. Large scale of output, compared to defense.
14. Specialized resources required, for example, commercial contracting.
15. High cost of quality (particularly a problem at the lower tiers).
16. Inadequate marketing skills.

These obstacles were noted in Europe where the cultural differences between the civilian and military worlds are not as dramatic as they are in the United States. Therefore in the United States the barriers will be even higher.

Specific Industrial Cases and Lessons

There are no general rules or standard steps to conversion. Each case is different, and each requires a tailored approach designed by the firm involved. Nonetheless, some things have been found to be almost universally true. Perhaps the most important is that *most successful transfers from military to civilian production are at comparable high-technology levels,* not at a step down in technology. It is also almost universally true that *the overall key to success is a cultural reorientation, especially by the senior management,* to the activity involved. As summarized by Seymour Melman,[12] "Plainly, the top managers of military industry are, themselves, a major barrier to any potential conversion operation. Unless they are prepared to learn the skills of civilian-industry management, or are replaced by new men who are free of the burden of unlearning a set of skills that are inappropriate in civilian economy," the chances of success are very slim.

Below are a few additional general observations:

• All parties (labor, management, community leaders, and government officials) must participate.
• The longer the lead-time allowed for conversion, the better.
• Not all plants and facilities should be saved.

• Conversion efforts require both carrots and sticks to succeed.

• Engineering innovation, capital equipment, production labor forces, and skilled management are the assets to be maximized in any civil/military integration efforts.

Lucas Aerospace, a British firm, struggled for ten years to achieve conversion but failed in its efforts because it lacked management support. The attempt was driven by employees and by ideology, specifically, by workers who sought to produce socially useful products only. Corporate leadership and hard-nosed economics were both missing. By contrast, the United Kingdom's Atomic Energy Research Establishment (Harwell) succeeded because management took the lead, and through encouragement, incentives, and training cultivated their scientists' entrepreneurial skills, especially their marketing skills. Still, the diversification took ten years. An extreme conversion case was Kaman Corporation. This U.S. aerospace firm successfully converted to the manufacture of quality guitars, which was sparked by the president's personal interest in guitars.

The Japanese auto industry plants in the United States and Europe offer clear proof of the importance of leadership in any successful transformation. The new Japanese auto manufacturers utilized the same—previously uncompetitive—U.S. and European workers, until new management insisted on higher quality and greater efficiency in their operations.

Another vital aspect of defense conversion is *the importance of being market-driven*. According to a 1985 Report on Economic Adjustment/Conversion,[13] incomplete understanding of the new customer and the new market's competitive structure was a major contributor to the failure of Boeing-Vertol, a U.S. defense helicopter company, to successfully diversify into the civilian market for mass transit cars in the 1970s. The company also failed to address the need to change the design philosophy and practices of the defense engineers. More attention was given to retooling the factory than to retraining the design engineers. And too little time was allocated for prototype testing and conversion of engineering design skills. Many of the design problems appeared after the transit cars were in service; essentially, the cars failed to meet such crucial design criteria as simple maintainability and durability. They proved so unreliable, and required such costly repairs and modifications, that most were taken out of service after only a few years.[14] Lack of market understanding was also a major contributor to U.S. defense contractor Rohr's failure in its subway car venture.[15] After deciding to go into the mass transit area, Rohr went out to win all the metro systems contracts it could bid on. It won Bart (San Francisco, California), Metro (D.C.), and smaller "people mover" contracts for zoos and shopping centers. Unfortunately, the company had little engineering experience with the commercial practice of design-to-cost, and they tended to overspecify the systems. It went into production and large-volume sales far too soon and was not prepared to deal with the significant problems that developed in the field. To make matters worse, the market did not develop as Rohr expected.

By contrast, Raytheon, a U.S. missile firm, explicitly sought to gain marketing skills as part of its diversification effort. One Raytheon official admitted that the firm's earlier venture into the television industry was unsuccessful because "We knew almost nothing about commercial marketing." Raytheon's commercial acquisitions of Amana (refrigeration), Caloric (kitchen appliances), and Heath (textbook publisher) helped it develop marketing acumen and facilitated transfers of its military technology to commercial products. For example, prior to their purchase of Amana, Raytheon's Radarange had been on the market for several years, but sales had mainly been to institutions (hospitals and restaurants). Amana modified the product for the general public, and sales expanded rapidly.[16]

Raytheon increased its commercial sales from 15 percent in 1964 to 50 percent in 1970; during the same period it terminated 15 percent of the work force in its defense plants. This successful diversification illustrates yet another point, that *multiple product objectives should not be combined in a single product*. The dual-use approach cannot be accomplished by adding some additional civilian capability to a military product. Even when talking about a common product area, one needs to think in terms of a specific civilian product and a specific military product—if they can be designed and built in the same plant, all the better.[17] Another consideration for defense contractors is to *break the habit of depending on the buyer to completely define the characteristics of the product*. A survey of European defense producers[18] found that "most of the civil sectors are unable to describe their research needs" and, therefore, defense firms face a greater challenge in entering the market. This is especially critical since *"technology push" has been far less successful than "market pull" in achieving conversion.*

A successful way to ease this difficulty is to carefully pick a very few new markets to enter because widespread diversification makes market mastery almost impossible—and mastery of even one new market is usually quite expensive.[19]

Another major problem faced by defense firms in their conversion efforts is that their products are very frequently too expensive.[20] They also take too long to develop, the range of products is far too limited, and there is poor calculation of costs, insufficient marketing, and a lack of after-sales service.

Obviously conversion is easier to achieve if the commercial products selected can stand the added costs of utilizing an integrated plant, that is, continuing defense-based as well as commercial business. This has been the case, for example, with commercial communications satellites and aircraft jet engines where, in both instances, reliability is the big life-cycle cost driver.

One of the most difficult aspects of conversion is that *long time periods are required for any reasonable level of diversification.* MBB, a German aerospace firm, successfully diversified into the railroad car business, but it took thirty-five years. Matra, a French defense firm, was producing mostly tactical missiles when it decided to diversify. Its first effort into watchmaking, in 1970, was a failure. It subsequently moved into autos, subway cars, telecommunications, and space. By 1979, it was 50 percent civil and 50 percent defense; by 1989, it was 76 percent civil and 24 percent defense (autos and transportation 34 percent; missiles 24 percent, telecommunications and engineering/manufacturing software 24 percent, and space 18 percent). This transformation, however, took twenty years. The Swedes estimate that as many as eight to ten years may be necessary to create and introduce substitute products that would be successful in civilian markets.[21]

Studies have shown that after a product is selected for integration, it is reasonable to expect two years of planning time to blueprint the changeover. The absence of such careful planning can lead to failure.

Needless to say, unsuccessful commercial ventures can be extremely expensive. For example, from 1983 to 1985, Grumman lost $15 million in its nonaerospace commercial ventures. McDonnell-Douglas purchased Computer Sharing Services for $69 million in 1983. After losing $333 million in 1989, it phased out its commercial information systems division.[22]

Technology transfer is best achieved when commercial designers and users are involved right from the start. For example, in the late 1960s, British Rail successfully created a mixed research team of aerospace and traditional railway personnel to develop new suspension and braking systems. Similarly, West German workers in some plants move back and forth between ships and tank hulls, and between tanks and railroad cars. The Swedish firm Hagglunds successfully shifted workers from armored tracked vehicles (in the mid-1970s) to commercial ship cranes; and the SAAB auto was designed by aerospace engineers working with car designers. In general, the training period for shifting production workers has been found to be less than three months;[23] however, converting design engineers takes considerably longer.

The specific difficulties in converting scientific and technical personnel (based on U.S. studies)[24] were found to be: (1) the lack of cost consciousness in defense; (2) the view of business managers that defense engineers are not well suited to commercial work; and (3) the belief among engineers that the defense environment requires more specialists, and the commercial environment more generalists. Due to the large number of engineers in defense operations, these engineering conversion issues become important.

Overall, defense-related industries tend to employ a larger number of professional and technical staff (especially engineers), administrators, managers, and skilled (craft) workers than does the manufacturing sector generally; but they employ far fewer sales staff and semiskilled workers.[25] Thus, it must be recognized that to be successful in the civilian world, defense-oriented firms may have to significantly reduce their administrative and engineering staff. This move, many have argued, would be a desirable shift for defense businesses in any case.

Lack of familiarity with commercial marketing practices is one of the primary difficulties in converting administrators and managers. The higher salaries in the defense sector, especially in administrative areas, is another important barrier. These issues must be addressed head-on.

Retraining defense workers is, of course, possible. Programs can take from two weeks to four years and are most successful when being done for a specific new job, that is, on the way in, versus generic retraining, on the way out. Obviously, retraining is most successful when similar labor skills and capital equipment are involved. For example, ordnance and accessories (SIC 348) and construction machinery (SIC 353), or ammunition (SIC 3483) and turbines (SIC 3511) are two sets that meet this test.[26] Highly specialized skills or tools are usually not transferable very far afield. According to numerous diversification analyses, the contribution of a firm's specialized human, organizational, or physical assets to profitability are inversely related to the range of their application to other markets. In other words, the more these unique capabilities contribute to the firm's profitability, the less applicable they are likely to be to distant markets. Successful (profitable) diversifications, therefore, tend to occur close to home.

Closely related to the issue of common skills and capital equipment are "core competencies."[27] These can be technologies and/or production processes; they also could be management skills or marketing distribution. Again, successful diversification/conversion is most frequent when existing core competencies are used. For example, Kaman Corporation successfully applied its core competence in helicopter vibration-control techniques to the making of guitars.

At one end of the spectrum in core competence we find a U.S. defense cloth supplier making ammunition pouches, duffel bags, and the like, successfully moving into the student backpack business. Being the low bidder was no longer sufficient, however; it had to learn about quality, marketing, and distribution to make this transition. At the other end of the spectrum are the defense prime contractors, who are skilled in high technology and large systems integration. Their competence is in managing complex state-of-the-art mission systems. If they view that rather than defense systems as their core advantage, they have a better chance of succeeding in the nondefense world.

Thus it is very important that a corporation interested in conversion recognize that *it is often not similarities in end products, but similarities in core competence that can be critical to achieving success*—whether this is technology, production process, or cost sensitivity. Using this approach, military aircraft enterprises have considered entering such diverse fields as prefabricated building sections, railroad cars, monorail transportation systems, electric road vehicles, hydrofoils, surface-effects boats, and, of course, civil aircraft.[28]

An interesting example of a company that took advantage of its core competence and shifted into a widely different market area was the Swedish firm, Stansaab. They moved from air warning systems for the Swedish military to air traffic control and hospital monitoring systems. The latter required a total organizational shift, including the addition of new people with knowledge of hospitals. Yet it was a conscious selection of a market that took advantage of a core competence—monitoring distributed items. In the case of moving to civilian air traffic control systems, it was only a relatively short jump from air warning systems for the military. However, the link to hospital monitoring systems recognized the fact that air traffic control required centralized monitoring of distributed aircraft on a relatively continuous basis and with a wide variety of parameters. This is very similar to the requirement for monitoring a large number of parameters in a wide variety of patients from a central control room in a hospital.

This discussion of common technologies should be kept in perspective. Specifically, it is important to note that *institutional structure and corporate policy are even more important than compatible technologies.* Since many existing structures retard free market mechanisms from operating, a structural shake-up is usually needed to achieve the changes that will encourage conversion or civil/military integration. Either the recipient structure has to change to accept the new technology ("absorption") or the technology itself has to change to fit the recipient structure ("adaptation").

This structural barrier is difficult to remove. In fact, most managers would acknowledge that one of the greatest impediments to successful diversification is the inflexibility of the organization.[29] An extreme way of overcoming resistance is to create a new venture. One venture capitalist (Spectra Enterprise Associates) invested $25 million from 1986 to 1992 to launch seventeen electronics companies that had sprung from military research. Thirteen are now in the black. The other four failed because they "didn't think strategically, didn't think products. They think solutions [like engineers], but they're not trained to finish a task." For the successes, 70 percent of their combined revenues are in commercial work. Spectra still looks to the Pentagon for 10–20 percent of its sales, mainly from R & D contracts. Its objective is to subsidize commercial work with government R & D and progress payments,[30] a strategy that is good for the firm, for its employees, for the DoD, and for the nation's economic growth.

Defense research establishments and the big laboratories of the largest civilian firms rarely generate technological entrepreneurs. Only a few growth companies have been started by people who left the research labs of AT&T, General Electric, RCA, or the aerospace and defense firms. It is far more common for one technology startup company to generate others: Hewlett Packard played a major role in the genesis of Tandem, Apple, and other computer-related companies; Fairchild Semiconductor spawned Intel, AMD, and National Semiconductor.[31]

Bearing this in mind, however, one diversification technique that has sometimes worked is the setting up of a small, isolated group outside of the major defense activity, staffed only partially from the defense sector— essentially, an internal "venture." In general, diversifying through construction of new plants has been more successful (from the firm's perspective) than diversifying within a plant by varying the product mix.[32] Naturally, in companies where once-integrated factory operations were forced to separate their civil and military work because of government defense mandates, it would make economic and practical sense to recombine them if DoD practices were changed. For example, Boeing and McDonnell-Douglas both had to split their civil and military transport operations in the early 1990s.

Another particularly important area for conversion consideration is research and development. In a vertically integrated firm that has both suppliers and end-item producers, it matters very much whether R & D investment is made in the end item or in the supplier plants. It also makes a difference when the government is deciding how best to spend its R & D dollars. For a single defense application, it probably would be more effective to fund the end user of the R & D, that is, the defense prime contractor. If dual use is involved, however, it may make more sense to fund the suppliers, that is, the parts or material manufacturers. A classic example of this involved DoD funding of R & D for very high speed integrated circuits (VHSIC). Here the overriding concern was to help the United States get back into the commercial semiconductor business to ensure a domestic supply of components for the military's next-generation electronics equipment. Since the DoD was funding the program, traditional practices were followed and the Pentagon contracted directly with the large weapons manufacturers. It then directed them to select a semiconductor component supplier from the commercial world as a subcontractor. Because the defense contractors specified the requirements of defense equipment, they virtually ensured that the components developed would be unique to defense and would therefore not be of much interest in the commercial world. By contrast, had the DoD funded the commercial component suppliers and directed them to give subcontracts to defense firms, the lower-tier suppliers would almost certainly have developed products to satisfy both commercial and military needs.

The R & D strategy utilized clearly has a distinct influence on the evolution of technology. Therefore, specifying dual use (versus defense only) for an R & D program will very likely determine which technology is emphasized and how it evolves. For example, R & D on advanced military systems can stress either maximum performance or it can balance performance with cost, accepting the necessary trade-offs. If the R & D focuses on designing weapon systems to be lower cost, and only marginally decreases potential performance, it will have helped a firm to be internationally competitive in the civilian sector.

Moving from an end-item supplier to a subcontract supplier is another technique that industrial firms have used to successfully diversify/convert. The Vickers (U.K.) tank plant diversified by bidding, on a subcontract basis, for work on machinery, car parts, furnaces, and motor parts. Also, Northrop and LTV followed a subcontract route to conversion into similar aerospace businesses by making panels and parts for commercial aircraft.

Government Support Experiences

One conclusion gleaned from past defense conversions is that government initiatives on their own are less likely to be successful than strong industry initiatives with some government support. In mid-1964, the state of California, with federal support, initiated four efforts in conversion from military work to transportation, communications, waste management, and crime prevention and control. These efforts were not industry-led and were not successful.

Also, diversification/conversions are more likely to be successful when organizations use some of their own funds and look for areas of high return, instead of counting on the government for full subsidization. Thus when the U.S. government first began funding commercial ventures in the early 1990s, it insisted on a 50 percent cost sharing by industry.

In the same way, diversification is more likely to be successful in privately owned competitive firms, rather than in government-owned operations or in private firms supported as sole sources. Again, this is due to the use of market forces to drive entrepreneurial behavior. This is a strong argument for allowing a reduced long-term capital gains tax for entrepreneurs who start up their own company and hold the stock, or stock options, over an extended period of time. By allowing them to reap the benefits of their venture, there are far greater incentives to make it succeed and, in the process, create jobs and national economic growth.

There are a few other lessons that the government can learn by looking back over historic cases. For example, the maximum civilian sector benefits from defense funding are gained when the DoD funds are used to start up an "infant industry" that is doing dual-use work. This results in the creation of new physical and human resources that would not otherwise have occurred.

Another historic key role for the government has been that of the first buyer. Here DoD, by guaranteeing and then buying the first quantities of an item for the military, stimulates new fields of technology. The same item or a modified version is then sold in large quantities to the civilian sector. Successful examples of this first-buyer stimulation range from the parts level, such as semiconductors, through full systems, such as supercomputers. Such purchase guarantees are allowable under the Defense Production Act; they are not often used, however, as they force the government to adopt a long-term view in regard to the growth of an industry—something it has been reluctant to do in the past.

It should also be emphasized that startup firms, even after they have developed a prototype of a new product with or without government

R & D funding, often have difficulty attracting venture capital funding. Here, an initial contract from the government is a great benefit not only in launching the firm, but in helping it to obtain the funding needed to set up high-volume commercial production.

There are also negative lessons that come from prior government interventions. For example, there is no evidence at all that conversion can be legislated—as some still hope. Also, there is little proof that the government can save companies through bailouts, stretchouts, or additional procurements without some real commitment on the part of the firm to also take necessary difficult steps to transform itself. Finally, there is little evidence that protectionism alone is successful. It can be a useful tool when dealing with an infant industry or a firm during a transition period, but it must be time-limited, and the industry involved must ultimately help itself.

Actions taken in connection with military base closures are another set of cases from which conversion lessons might be learned. Here, through forced conversion and long-term government assistance in the planning and transition phases, the Pentagon's Office of Economic Adjustment claims that one and one-half new jobs have been created for every one lost due to base closings. From 1961 to 1990, they estimate that even though the actual conversion funding levels were relatively small, 158,104 new jobs were created to replace the loss of 93,424 civilian jobs at former military bases. They attribute this to long-term planning and direct involvement with the local communities. The catch to this long-term positive result is that, in the short term, there were a considerable number of layoffs and local hardships.

One base-closure case study highlights the above points. In 1967, the Strategic Air Command's largest base, in Roswell, New Mexico, was closed.[33] Almost overnight, the city of only 45,000 lost close to one-third of its population. Not only were the 6,000 people who worked on the base affected, but so were all of the surrounding businesses and support services dependent upon the base—the so-called multiplier effect. Real estate prices collapsed; unemployment rose to well over 20 percent; and the young people began moving away. However, there was quick reaction, strong leadership, a clear vision, and community support to prevent Roswell from becoming a ghost town. As a result, today the population is back to its pre-1967 level, and the old air base is now a successful industrial park.

A more recent finding is that of the eighty-six U.S. bases whose closures were announced in 1989, at least twenty-six were chemically contaminated (five severely). These old facilities were involved in defense processes that had severe environmental impacts. Future conversion efforts, for both industry and government, will be considerably complicated by environmental requirements—an area where government assistance can be of considerable value.

Summary

From these various examples it is possible to draw a few general conclusions. Specifically, there are eight considerations to be taken into account in defense conversion:

- the growth of the nation's economy;
- commitment of the company, especially management;
- commonality of technologies—products and, especially, processes;
- marketability of alternative products;
- availability of capital;
- flexibility of employees; again, especially management;
- defense dependence of firms; and
- support of the government.

In addition, it is clear that conversion takes time and is not an easy or quick solution to defense downsizing. Barriers to conversion created by the government make it that much harder. But even removing these, the major part of the effort is up to industry and its leadership. Full corporate management support and major changes in engineering, management, marketing, and factory operations are likely to be required to make the transition to new product lines economically viable and profitable, in national and international markets.[34]

Based on prior conversion experiences, suggested steps for industry are:

1. Identify core uniqueness.
2. Find growth markets to which these advantages are applicable; do not focus on selling existing or modified products.

3. Search for areas with generic, dual-use applicability and comparable technologies—especially comparable process technologies.

4. Transform, or reconstitute, the management.

5. Retrain, and/or hire, marketing and finance personnel.

6. Retrain technical workers in design and manufacturing, to have a focus on cost and quality.

7. Retrain production workers.

8. Transform plant and equipment.

9. Retrain administrative workers.

To achieve international competitiveness, the U.S. commercial industry has had to go through many cultural changes in the last few years. It is very clear that the firms that succeeded felt a crisis, created a new vision, had sustained leadership, and worked very hard.

To paraphrase Churchill's famous statement about democracy, "conversion may be the worst choice—except for all of the others."

6

The Best Structure for the Twenty-First Century

Even if there had been no dramatic geopolitical changes in the world, there would still have been a need for significant restructuring of the U.S. defense industry. The huge increases in individual weapons' costs, the long time required to develop new products, and the growing isolation of the defense industrial base from the state-of-the-art technological advances in the commercial sector (for example, in electronics) would have required it. But there were also dramatic changes in the world, leaving little question in anyone's mind about the need for major changes in how defense business is done.

The Choices

At the broadest level, there are three basic public policy options for the future U.S. defense industry:[1] (1) nationalization of the major defense contractors; (2) regulation of the contractors as a public utility; and (3) competition among the contractors according to market forces.

The economist John Stuart Mill first proposed nationalization for England in the nineteenth century, arguing that economies of scale would otherwise predominate in the defense sector and lead to monopoly.[2] More recently, John Kenneth Galbraith argued for nationalization in order to bring American defense firms under public control.[3] The question, however, is whether this would result in public control or just provide political shelter. Experience has shown that publicly owned facilities are even harder to close or control than those in the private sector, and are approximately 30 percent less efficient than their private counterparts, mainly because they operate without competition. When nationalization is proposed for the U.S. defense industry, it seems to be done more out of frustration than out of logic. Nonetheless, in a few sectors it may actually be the best solution.

The second alternative is to maintain the current isolation of the defense industry and essentially regulate the contractors as a kind of public utility—perhaps with a commission independent of the DoD.[4] Defense contractors are currently controlled by federal acquisition regulations, but the industry is never formally listed as "regulated" since there is no external regulatory commission and because the DoD conducts its regulation at the micro level (welding specifications, inspection details) rather than at the macro level (structure, profit, pricing) as is normal for regulated industries. Experience with airlines, trucking, and nuclear power has shown that regulated industries are quite prone to capture by their regulators, and that regulation tends to deter change. Today, rapid technological evolution requires a defense industry that can move quickly. Furthermore, regulated industries (especially utilities) are not known for cost consciousness since they simply pass on their cost increases to their customers; and profits tend to be significantly higher than those in the defense industry. Therefore, the only beneficiary of such a regulatory approach might be the defense industry itself. Yet this solution is pushed by Congress whenever the question of what to do about the defense industry comes up. In fact, during the 1980s, increased regulation was aggressively pursued as the best route to defense procurement reform. The regulations enacted then have yielded the adverse results described in chapter 2.

The third alternative is the preferred one: to create effective competition in the defense industry. The government, as the sole buyer of defense equipment, must exercise its monopsony power in a way that would promote, not supplant, natural market forces. Rather than issue detailed regulations, the government must allow defense firms to react to market changes and achieve an optimized equilibrium. Present constraints do not even permit natural market forces to register sufficiently for the industry to react. The government's aim should be to reduce overcapacity and obsolescence, but not through regulations, directives, and subsidies. Instead of maintaining the current adversarial, legalistic structure of defense market operations, the government must step back and assure (through administrative actions[5]) that significant, competitive market forces are present to achieve efficiency, effectiveness, innovation, and responsiveness from its suppliers. It must be emphasized that a national planning approach that enables bureaucrats to shift capital from firm to firm in order to nurture their favorite winners[6] is not what is being proposed. Rather, the suggestion is that, wherever applicable, policymakers should use free market forces and normal commercial laws to do the government's business instead of the unique laws associated with DoD procurement today. The DoD will still be required to perform independent price analyses (such as market surveys) to assure that the government is paying a reasonable price for the value of the goods and services received—so as to maintain the public's trust.

The question of how much government oversight is enough has long been one of the most challenging issues. Thomas More raised it in *Utopia*, as did George Orwell in *1984*, and as have many others in each generation. When we give certain people power in our society—as we must—and appoint others to watch them—as we had better—who is going to watch the watchers?

Civil/Military Integration

In the context of defense conversion, three forms of civil/military integration are relevant:

1. Dual-use R & D, to common requirements;
2. Dual-use plants, with common engineering, production, and support;
3. Dual-use equipment, especially parts, materials, software, and so on.

Dual use in these three areas will result in true interoperability between the military and civilian sectors of the industrial base. It means that the DoD will not just buy commercial parts, subsystems, or products when they fit, but that weapons will actually be designed with integration in mind, and will be planned to be built in fully integrated factories—using common tools, common labor, and, critically important, common information technology, the basis for the modern industrial world.

Perhaps the most important of the three integration areas is that of dual-use-by-design. This is critical in order for the DoD to take advantage of state-of-the-art technologies (both product and process) that exist in the commercial world, as well as to assure the high volume, low cost, and high quality that come from commercial production. It is essential that future weapon systems be explicitly designed to use commercial subsystems, components, software, and materials, and designed to be built on modern, flexible, commercial manufacturing equipment, in commercial (dual-use) plants.

This approach is considerably different from the historic R & D relationship between defense and the civilian world, where such close interaction was virtually unknown. For many years, defense had all the advantages—especially advanced technology and the best research facilities—to come up with new products to meet defense needs. These could then be "spun off" and, after appropriate modification for the commercial marketplace, be transitioned into the civilian world. Communication satellites, jet engines, and supercomputers are among many successful examples of spin-off. In many areas today, however, defense is no longer ahead in technology. Nor can the commercial world tolerate the long lead times associated with having the DoD develop new products.

The alternative model of "spin on," where commercial products are adjusted for defense needs, is also not satisfactory because defense systems are normally designed around their own unique requirements, which are not likely to be satisfied by an existing commercial item.

What is needed now is for new products to be broadly designed around the simultaneous set of conditions required for both military and civilian products. Obviously, the greatest commonality exists at the lower tiers, for example, semiconductor chips. But even when designing a weapon system, it should be possible to have a majority of the subsystems and components come from commercial operations, and even many unique defense items can be built on commercial factory equipment. Recognizing that the end-use requirements for military and commercial items are often dramatically different, the products themselves will be different. Nonetheless, they can be designed to be built in integrated facilities, with as much common production equipment as possible.

There will still be a few defense-unique plants required—particularly for final assembly and testing of some major weapon systems. Most of the major prime contractor operations, however, and almost all of the lower-tier and supplier level operations, can be dual use.

It must be emphasized that a key to integration is to look at what are now defense-unique production processes and/or defense-unique products and see if, for the next generation, the DoD is able to move to dual use—through either a different process or a different product technology.

Some areas of integration are relatively obvious, for example, commercial transports, jet engines, or communication satellites. In fact, many of these sectors in the past have been fully integrated, and to a certain extent, still are. Another important area for integration is software, since about 25 percent of a modern weapon's cost, and the major infrastructure areas (factory, office, and engineering), are affected by software.

To see how the dual-use-by-design activity can work, consider the case of the millimeter microwave integrated circuit (MIMIC) program, run by the Advanced Research Projects Agency of the Department of Defense. The DoD needed an advanced radar power supply for its weapon systems, and for a variety of technical reasons it chose to go to a gallium arsenide integrated circuit. What was interesting is that, instead of the traditional defense requirement for maximum performance as the sole design criterion, this project focused equally on low cost and high reliability. Therefore, before the device had even been deployed by the Department of Defense, it was picked up by the auto industry for collision avoidance and toll collection devices. In fact, one early application was for a radar transmit/receive module to observe areas around a school bus where the driver's view is obstructed. In its first use, it was claimed to have saved a child's life when she had gone under the bus to pick up something she had dropped. Because of the demand for high volume in the civilian world, the MIMIC supplier—a joint venture of Hughes and Delco—redesigned the production process and drove the costs down from $8,000 each to $200.

The MIMIC effort benefited the nation's economic growth. DoD picked up the R & D costs, thereby rapidly accelerating the new commercial product into the market. Because the United States is the first entrant, it can capture a large market share of not only the MIMIC devices but also the more expensive end items (such as the complete collision-avoidance system for cars) based on the devices—a clear example of the industrial "food chain" at work. In addition, the DoD will benefit from the lower cost and high quality that will come from the high-volume commercial production. To realize this synergism, it was necessary to waive normal DoD rules and to use commercial practices, specifications, and standards from the beginning. While the power and environmental requirements for the gallium arsenide defense device might be different, or the environmental requirements might be different from the school bus variants, both can be made in the same factory, using the same engineering, production, and support work force and the same factory capital equipment.[7]

Secretary of Defense William Perry estimated[8] that revising defense procurement laws to allow civil/military integration and encouraging more dual use of products, technologies, and industrial operations could save about $30 billion per year in defense expenditures (see chapter 9). He also noted that this might reduce the DoD acquisition staff significantly—his estimate was by well over 20 percent.

Despite such inevitable personnel dislocations, there are many reasons to encourage far greater dual use. The most obvious is the DoD's need to achieve lower-cost and higher-quality defense equipment. It also provides rapid access to state-of-the-art technology that defense would not otherwise be able to utilize; and it would provide a standby capability for military production surge requirements in times of crisis that would otherwise be totally unaffordable. The only alternative to this integrated base—in which you could rapidly shift from commercial production to military production—would be to pay for an enormous amount of excess military capability that would be sitting idle between crises and would likely become obsolete.

Another particularly important consideration in drawing on the broad overall U.S. industrial base for defense equipment is that it provides for much more competition in defense procurement. The alternative increasingly seems to be a single firm in each defense sector, specializing in defense-unique items. Needless to say, a single source, whether it be in the public or private sector, does not suggest either economic or time-related efficiency.[9]

Finally, civil and military integration will put more than $35 billion of annual defense research and development and more than $50 billion of annual defense procurements into the nation's commercial sector. This will go toward new product development, as well as for guarantees of initial purchases on the new outputs. This government/industry risk sharing could provide a very strong stimulant to the U.S. economy in the high-technology areas that form such an important part of economic growth and international industrial competitiveness in the world today.

Technological Facilitators

The recommendation for civil/military integration would have been far less practical in the past than it is now. During the 1980s, four major technological changes took place that make civil/military integration far more attractive and greatly facilitate its implementation. They are:

- the growing commonality of critical military and civilian technologies;
- the availability of highly reliable, rugged, and high-performance commercial parts;
- the development and application of flexible ("agile") manufacturing; and
- the widespread industrial application of electronic data interchange.

Historically there had been a distinct difference in the technologies of warfare (gunpowder, cannons, bombs) and those of the normal day-to-day, commercial economy. As defense has moved increasingly toward information-based warfare, however, and as the information age has moved the civilian economy into the high-tech environment, there has been a growing merger of the technologies for the two arenas. In fact, annual lists of critical technologies published by the Departments of Defense and Commerce overlap by more than 80 percent.[10]

Common technologies, however, are not enough to yield dual-use operations; other areas matter too. The commercial sector frequently offers lower-cost, higher-quality, faster new product realization times and the most state-of-the-art performance—and equipment that meets environmental requirements that are at least as rigid as those of the military. For example (as noted in chapter 2), there is a small computer chip that is mounted directly to the engine block of new cars. The environmental requirements on this part are similar to, or higher than, those of the military specifications. The temperature range for the commercial part is 10 degrees greater than that of the equivalent military part, and it meets all of the vibration, shock, humidity, and other requirements of the military. The equivalent military parts are significantly more expensive, less reliable, and two to three years later in state-of-the-art performance. Thus there would appear to be very little argument for continuing to utilize the specialized military parts, except that the DoD would have to allow commercial practices to dominate its buying activities.

Another important development was the dramatic change in both management and technology that transformed the manufacturing production process. Firms that have maintained their competitive status have had to introduce total cultural changes in their operations—incorporating such concepts as "concurrent engineering" (integrating R & D and production), just-in-time inventory control, and total quality management. In addition, there has been a dramatic shift from single (fixed) tools that were used on long production runs in the old mass production model to flexible (agile) manufacturing operations. Here robots are programmed to continuously change their tools and make small quantities of different items with the same efficiency that was previously possible only with large-volume production of the same item.

The last of the recent innovations that greatly facilitates civil/military integration has been the revolution in electronic data interchange. This has meant a dramatic change in the way factory and office processes operate, taking advantage of the quantity, speed, and accuracy of the additional information that is provided. Four major directions have been pursued simultaneously: within factories and offices; between companies; within the government; and between the government and industry. Together, these create a paperless, seamless data exchange, allowing rapid, high-accuracy, secure data links between and among buyers and suppliers. In fact, the DoD has focused its electronic data interchange systems (known as CALS), linking its computers and its industrial suppliers, on the use of commercial standards to greatly facilitate drawing more heavily on U.S. commercial industry.

The Vision

In the twenty-first century the DoD must not be forced to depend on a small, isolated, subsidized, largely obsolete industrial base—a set of firms forced to sell their goods on the international market to any willing buyer in order to survive. Rather, considering that in the future the commercial sector will establish the state-of-the-art in performance, quality, price, and response, the DoD must draw on this broad industrial base wherever it can. The current unique DoD way of doing business must be changed to allow this integration. Any new approach, however, must still assure that the public trust is well looked after.

In addition, it must be recognized that the dual-use concept will not be universally applicable for all defense products, and most important, that commonality largely lies in shared production processes. For example, a cannon is clearly a military item and has no commercial analog. But the large rotary forge on which a cannon is built is the identical machine used to produce railroad freight car axles. When the Department of Defense spent over $15 million in the mid-1970s for a new rotary forge to build its cannons, it should have put the forge into the private sector. It would then have had access to trained operators, available for three shifts if necessary, and would have had the benefit of overhead absorption that comes from the commercial use of the machine.[11] (Instead it went into an Army arsenal originally built in the Civil War era.)

Five steps are required for the Department of Defense to achieve the necessary procurement transformation:[12]

• Whenever feasible, buy products that are already available on the commercial market.
• Use commercial specifications in preference to government specifications.
• Adopt buying procedures similar to those used by commercial buyers.
• Adopt contract administration procedures, such as quality control procedures, similar to those used by commercial buyers.
• Use commercial terms and conditions in government contracts.

Even though these goals are intertwined, they are also separate in that each requires different action—statutory, regulatory, or administrative. Specific actions will be discussed in a later chapter, but one can already see the broad changes that are necessary. First, and perhaps foremost, the Department of Defense must make low-cost weapons an important military priority, equal to that of high-performance weapons. The recognition that lower cost and higher performance can be simultaneously achieved has been driving the commercial world in recent years.

Second, the government must recognize that its traditional cost-based contracting neither provides a low-cost solution nor the required assurances for public trust. The current approach of auditing defense costs simply assures that all of the allocated money was legitimately spent, which is very different from being cost effective.

Third, the DoD must recognize the importance of manufacturing as equal to that of design. Historically the DoD has stressed engineering design as the dominant factor in its resource allocations. Weapons technology advances thus have been achieved with very severe cost and time penalties. By emphasizing concurrent engineering in all of its new weapons developments, the DoD will be forced to simultaneously address both the new product and the new production process requirements, as is customary in commercial practices. This change will also satisfy the DoD need for rapid development of low-cost, high-quality, and high-performance new systems.

Fourth, the DoD must recognize the critical importance of widely applying advanced information technology: Costs and times can be greatly reduced, quality dramatically improved, and whole new industrial structures, along with new government/industry relations, can be developed. Again, this is the direction in which world-class commercial firms are moving, and the DoD must be part of that transformation.

Finally, the DoD must decide it wants an integrated industrial base. If not, it will find ample reasons to explain why "it doesn't make sense" and why "it can't be done," even though the barriers are all procedural, not technological.

Historically, many types of defense downsizing adjustments have been tried: company diversification, community economic redevelopment, worker readjustment, and facility conversion.[13] What has not been tried is a DoD shift to civilian buying practices and, therefore, a dramatic move toward civil/military integration of the industrial base. This change, of course, would require the removal of much of the current government-unique oversight provided by the specialized accounting, auditing, and procurement practices, replacing these with commercial laws, practices, and, particularly, market forces.

Arguments against Integration

In spite of the potential benefits, there is far from universal agreement that an integration strategy is the best alternative for the American defense industrial base. In fact, some defense industry leaders consider it a "cynical myth being perpetuated by unrealistic advocates,"[14] while others describe it as a "false promise."[15]

These objections are based on two concerns: first, the many unsuccessful conversion attempts of the past, and second, the reality that the magnitude of the defense cuts, particularly as they affect procurement dollars available for the defense industry, dwarf any possibilities of conversion in the near term. Obviously, both of these points are valid. To overcome the difficulty of past efforts, the government must take a very active role in helping bring about civil/military integration—something it has not done before. The government must remove barriers and facilitate the conversion process through a variety of legislative, funding, and training initiatives. In dealing with the second concern, it is true that downsizing will undoubtedly occur during the transition. The alternative, however, is to simply shrink down and wait until defense budgets perhaps increase again. This is an extremely undesirable long-term position for most firms and certainly for most employees. Even more important, it does not solve the Defense Department's future need for state-of-the-art, low-cost military equipment.

Another negative argument that is frequently raised is that increased purchases of commercial equipment could result in greater U.S. dependence on foreign suppliers. It is true that the DoD will be drawing on the international marketplace for commercial parts, and many of these do in fact come from offshore. But a counterargument is that the stimulation of American high-technology industries that will result from the availability of the large defense R & D and production dollars will help domestic firms become more competitive. The expectation is that there will be more, not fewer, high-quality domestic sources available.

It is equally true, however, that there will be a significant reduction in those domestic lower-tier suppliers, who today exist only because they are able to get away with supplying high-cost defense-unique products to the military. These firms could not compete in worldwide commercial markets and are likely to be replaced either by domestic commercial suppliers or by a variety of foreign suppliers. As noted, as long as there are many suppliers in different companies and in different countries, there is very little U.S. vulnerability to supplies being cut off. Most end-item defense goods will still be produced domestically; and, even at the parts level, the shift from domestic to offshore production is likely to be relatively small. In fact, some shift is likely to take place with or without the transition toward civil/military integration.

Another argument against civil/military integration is that it will make defense technologies and equipment less protected, and thus more vulnerable to widespread proliferation. As with the other arguments, this too has some valid basis; and if nothing else, it certainly is an argument for maintaining U.S. defense R & D. As in the commercial world, the best way to avoid competition is to stay ahead.

With regard to the proliferation issue, however, there are important counterarguments to be made. Rapid advances in commercial technologies and a growing overlap between the critical technologies of the two sectors have diminished the feasibility of protecting defense know-how. In fact, the overlap has served to improve defense capabilities rather than harm them. Commercial advances in computing speed and power, as well as miniaturization, are examples of benefits applied by the military. Yet even if desirable, it would be impossible to control the spread of commercial and/or dual-use technologies in the future. The only ones that could be controlled would be the obsolete technologies that continued to be utilized in the defense-unique sectors.

It will still be possible, however, to control final weapon systems. In fact, the output of the few remaining defense-unique (largely weapons final assembly) plants may be far easier to control than before. Their defense mission will be clearly identified, and they can be the focus of particularly intensive attention.

The concern about proliferation must also be balanced against the security benefits of a significant reduction in incentives for foreign military sales. Since most plants will become dependent on commercial sales for survival, they will not feel compelled to sell weapons. In general, however, much of the proliferation issue is "uncontainable" because many of the advanced commercial systems made by civilian firms could be used directly for military applications. For example, many of the earth-resource satellites are now gathering data with accuracies approaching—and soon exceeding—those of the intelligence satellites; commercial communication satellites are now being designed with great concern for security; and commercial navigation satellites (required for commercial air traffic control, for example) will be able to provide worldwide location accuracy comparable to that provided by military systems. Such analogies continue to expand, as civilian needs increasingly overlap with those of defense requirements in such diverse areas as supercomputing, advanced communications, new materials, advanced electronics, and even industrial security. Continuing to fight such trends, through isolating the defense industry, will prove to be both an expensive and fruitless exercise.

Finally, it should be emphasized that the U.S. advantage in many weapon systems is not at the component level, which is very difficult to control in terms of security, but rather at the much more controllable level of weapons systems. For example, although Japan has the full capability to build most of the elements of an advanced aircraft, they lack the systems integration capability to assure that the combination of the engine, the wings, the airframe design, and the avionics will work effectively together to achieve the desired performance. Secretary of Defense William Perry argued[16] that to maintain U.S. technological superiority, "it is neither necessary not sufficient to control the sale of technology," because such military hardware contains, for example, advanced electronics that are already on the international market. Rather, "the U.S. advantage in this new military technology is not in components, but in systems, training, and operational experience."

Since it is virtually impossible to stop the flow of knowledge, information, and human capital across international boundaries, the alternative is to track the source and regulate the use of the final product. The United Nations' register of arm sales (initiated in 1993)[17] and a more extensive international program of transparency (multinational disclosure agreements) will be first steps in achieving this visibility.

Two other concerns raised in objection to dual-use integration relate to the fact that some high-tech American firms may choose to move offshore for competitiveness reasons, and that, as a result, critical engineering and manufacturing for the defense sector of the U.S. economy would be lost.

One way to avoid this would be to require at least some defense R & D and production to be performed domestically, creating a considerable incentive for defense contractors to stay here. The other concern is that as the DoD moves toward greater emphasis on dual use, it would receive bids from domestically located but foreign-owned firms, which would then both gain the benefit of DoD resources and have some degree of control over defense products. Controls, however, exist for regulating technology transfer with foreign-owned firms on critical defense technologies.[18] In addition, the DoD could place constraints on its funding to make sure that engineering and manufacturing remain domestic. Finally, if there was concern about dependability of the source, a second source could be established or a credible licensee secured. Again, it must be emphasized that by opening up the defense market to commercial firms, there will be much greater competition in dual-use areas, and thus far less vulnerability to the action of a single firm, whether located domestically or offshore.

In general, autarky in most defense technologies and systems is no longer a possibility. Rather, one may be able to protect a few military technological breakthroughs, for a period of time, primarily through security classification; but the primary focus of future efforts first will be to stay ahead—through continued defense R & D—and then to achieve weapons proliferation control through multinational supplier and/or purchaser agreements. Here the benefits of an industrial base that is not dependent on military sales for its sole livelihood represents an enormous potential for the United States in taking the lead in achieving such multinational agreements.

Finally, one other concern that frequently has been raised in connection with civil/military integration is that although a defense-unique firm is dependent on the DoD for its livelihood, it may be difficult to keep a dual-use firm interested in doing defense business. As with all of the other arguments against integration, this too has some validity. If the DoD continues to be such an unattractive client—making it difficult for firms to do business with them, and difficult to make a competitive profit—then in fact the DoD will have trouble getting world-class companies to bid on their business. They will always find someone to bid, but there is a very real question as to whether the DoD really wants only the losers to show interest in their contracts. Many world-class U.S. companies—who have the option—are simply exiting from the defense arena, leaving the field open to those who cannot compete anywhere else. It is up to the DoD to make their business attractive enough to bring back these suppliers.

Dual Use by Other Nations

Japan has the second largest defense expenditure of any nation in the world, now that the Soviet Union has collapsed and the Russian economy is in shambles. After the Meiji Restoration and Japan's relatively late shift to industrialization, most of the country's effort was focused in the defense area; heavy industry was developed before light industry, and it was almost exclusively for military purposes.[19] These heavy industries still form the nucleus of Japan's defense sector, along with the later addition of the electronics firms. Today, however, these multibillion-dollar corporations (e.g., Mitsubishi Heavy Industries, Fuji Heavy Industries, and Kawasaki Heavy Industries) have only a very small percentage of their total business in the defense sector and are much more deeply involved in other industries, such as automobiles and ships.

The major Japanese firms therefore are fully integrated at the corporate level and have very little dependency on defense for their livelihood. In some individual plants of these heavy industries, however, there is an overwhelming dependence on defense, with an average of over 80 percent of their business coming from the Japanese Defense Agency. Their facilities are extremely impressive in terms of modern capital equipment, and identical equipment is used (for example) to build both commercial and military aircraft—the military FSX and major portions of the Boeing 777, advanced commercial transport. What is particularly important is that the Japanese Defense Agency is largely paying for this investment in dual use and offers incentives for companies to pursue it. The government often provides rapid tax write-offs for the equipment, for example, over a five-year period, and at replacement value. By contrast, the DoD has even longer write-off periods than those mandated by the U.S. tax laws, requiring that the write-off period be the life of the equipment, which is then written off at its purchase value.

Dual use has been going on for some time in Japan. In the early 1980s, Mitsubishi Heavy Industries produced the Diamond 2000 business jet and the F-15J fighter aircraft (manufactured through U.S. license) under the same roof.[20] Mitsubishi Electric Corporation's microwave millimeter integrated circuit production facilities develop, manufacture, and test semiconductor chips for both commercial and military applications using the same personnel and equipment.[21] (The military components are used for the phased-array radar systems for the FSX.)

In 1970, when future Prime Minister Nakasone was director general of Japan's Defense Agency, he published a defense industrial policy[22] entitled "Basic Policy for Development and Production of Defense Equipment." The five stated goals were: to maintain Japan's industrial base as a key factor in national security; to acquire equipment from Japan's domestic R & D and production efforts; to use civilian industries; to have long-term plans for R & D and production; and to introduce the principle of competition into defense production. The Japanese have built on this emphasis on civil/military integration ever since.

Japan's Ministry of International Trade and Industry (MITI) has an oversight and guidance role in both the civilian and military sectors; and, as a ministry, it outranks the Japanese Defense Agency. While most capital investment for integrated activities has so far come from the defense side, a leading role in technology is coming from the civilian side. As the head of research and development for Japan's Defense Agency stated, "We must depend on the civilian sector. In current technology there is no distinction between civilian and military technology."[23] Although approximately 80 percent of Japan's aircraft industry is the result of building American military aircraft under licenses, the stated long-range target of both MITI and the Japanese aircraft industry is the $50 billion annual business of building commercial aircraft for the world market.[24] Clearly, this is an integrated strategy.

In 1993, the Japanese government conducted a study that concluded that if a new transport aircraft were to be developed and produced domestically, it should serve both civil and military needs, and to achieve economies of scale, it should be jointly sponsored by MITI and the Japanese Defense Agency. Such an approach has not been typical in the United States: when the DoD developed the extremely expensive C-17 military transport, it did so in a facility separate from any commercial aircraft activity, even though it was done by a firm in the commercial aircraft business, McDonnell-Douglas.

The president of Fujitsu Systems Integration Laboratories stated recently that "Commercial and military technologies are converging so rapidly that the day when there was such a thing as military technology is fast disappearing."[25] An example of a nonmilitary export with obvious military applications is that of radar-proof ferrite paint, in which Japan is a world leader. The U.S. Department of Defense bought it from Japan for use on the stealth bomber.[26]

Perhaps one of the most remarkable aspects of the Japanese dual-use approach is that, when questioned about it, policymakers will strongly deny that they are employing such a strategy. One reason is that they have a hypersensitivity to any export of defense goods, so that any implication that products have dual use, or even that the production processes that built the products have dual use, raises a strong political issue within the country. Second, they argue strongly—although the evidence is even stronger in the other direction—that they have a totally free-market economy and that they do not provide subsidies to their civilian business from their defense work. The reason for this position is that such subsidies could be considered a threat to the General Agreement on Tariffs and Trade (GATT). Interestingly, they do accuse the United States of subsidizing its commercial industries through the defense R & D and production expenditures, for example, on aircraft. Yet the reality is that in the United States, these defense expenditures are increasingly unrelated to the commercial economy, often being made by different firms and/or in isolated plants. In fact, they have little or no benefit for commercial competitiveness.

The European Community in general and many of the nations within Europe individually appear to be emulating Japan in heading toward the development of an explicit civil/military integration strategy. In the United Kingdom, a 1989 cabinet-level Advisory Council on Science and Technology stated as its number-one recommendation that "the Ministry of Defense should utilize its research and contractual procedures, as well as developing its informed customer role, in ways that take greater account of the nation's future technological capability; principally by encouraging investment in a broader national technology base for defense from which both defense and civil sectors may benefit." [27]

Similarly, the French have stated that their policy would be one of an integrated strategy. [28] France has no legislative, regulatory, or accounting barriers between civil and military procurements, thus enabling firms to use commercial practices and facilities in the defense sector, and greatly facilitating civil/military integration. [29] Defense industrial planning is consciously integrated in the French government between the General Delegation for Armaments, the Ministry of Defense, and the Ministries of Economics and Finance, Industry and Foreign Trade, and Transportation. Therefore defense policy, as well as other industrial, economic, and social policies, are simultaneously considered—something the National Economic Council, established in the Clinton administration, has been moving toward in the United States. Also, the fact that the French Parliament only reviews the defense budget top line, and not each individual program, helps a great deal in achieving a broader national perspective and a more stable defense plan—both of which allow a more coherent long-range integration strategy.

Finally, Germany—which for many years followed the U.S. model— has also begun to shift toward a more integrated (civil/military) strategy. The largest of its defense firms, MBB, is now pursuing integration as a corporate policy.

From these examples, it appears that civil/military integration is the wave of the future. New technology not only allows, but greatly facilitates, this shift. Thus with the need and the possibilities both present, it is essential that the United States also expedites its move in this direction. Instead, this shift has been largely resisted—and, as a result, the industrial separation has actually increased. Only in the mid-1990s, under the leadership of Defense Secretary William Perry, were initial steps taken toward moving the DoD and its industrial suppliers in the direction of civil-military integration. Eventually the barriers will be removed and the large majority of activities will be totally integrated. There will, however, still be a few defense-unique plants left after the transformation; it is to these that we now turn.

7
A Few Defense-Unique Plants

The few remaining defense-unique plants will be mostly at the large weapon system final assembly level. They will remain unique because of differences in the final products and, particularly, because of specialized process requirements (such as nuclear weapons safety).

Obviously, many items purchased by the Department of Defense are different from anything made for the civilian world, but that does not make them unique, in the sense of requiring a separate plant for their design, fabrication, or support. As noted above, an army cannon, for example, has no commercial equivalent but is built on the same rotary forge on which railroad car axles are built. There are many examples of such defense-unique equipment that could easily be manufactured in integrated facilities.

Still, a few defense-unique plants will remain. Although it is difficult to estimate exactly how large this defense-unique sector will have to be, an upper limit might be seen from a 1990 analysis by Robert Kutscher, associate commissioner of the Labor Department in the Bush administration. Kutscher found that of the 3.2 million Americans working in private sector jobs financed by military spending, "fewer than 500,000 of these workers are making ammunition, missiles, warships, and other weaponry in factories that cannot be easily converted to civilian use."[1] Thus, the size of the defense-unique sector left after the full transformation of the U.S. defense industry should be less than 15 percent of the overall industry, probably significantly less, particularly as defense equipment becomes more electronics-intensive and as flexible manufacturing equipment becomes more widespread.

For these remaining plants, the government has a choice: it can either continue its current hands-off policy—making believe there is a free market operating, even though in the case of major weapon systems there is only one buyer, a very few suppliers, and a fully regulated market—or it can determine what it needs and what it can afford in order to structure an efficient and effective sector in these few defense-unique operations.

The current laissez-faire policy has resulted in each individual crisis being addressed in a vacuum. When a given sector gets down to one plant, there are extensive discussions as to whether it should be considered critical and saved. Or, when a foreign buyer wants to purchase one of the few remaining defense-unique plants, there is extensive public debate about whether this is a good idea. Or, if there is a question of preserving a private sector facility versus one in the public sector, there are strong political forces on both sides, and often no clear public policy decision is made, even though there is not enough money to support both. Or, when it is decided that an industry is critical and must be maintained, there is uncertainty over whether to subsidize engineering work on the next-generation system or to build one more of the last-generation systems in order to keep the factory open. These are difficult questions, but approaching them in an ad hoc fashion and having them debated in the press and/or on Capitol Hill is far less desirable than having some long-term sector-by-sector strategy. In the event a long-term industrial strategy is established, there is still the question of whether the government should continue to do business in the usual way or whether the weapons acquisition process can be dramatically changed to improve its efficiency. Empirically, there should be no debate—the evidence is overwhelmingly in favor of dramatic changes.

In the commercial world, performance of complex systems increases with each new generation while costs go down and development cycles for new products shrink. In the DoD process, while performance goes up costs rise at an equivalent rate, and acquisition times stretch out further. Thus there are many lessons that the DoD can learn from the commercial world.

Indicative of trends in the commercial arena is that Boeing aims to cut its production cycle from thirteen months to six months on its 737 aircraft, while lowering the cost by 25 to 30 percent. It is similarly committed to design and build a new United Parcel Service plane in twenty-eight months rather than its normal thirty-eight months. The average time for a new Department of Defense weapon (in 1991), from concept through first production, was 198 months—over sixteen years! Even worse, as budgets have been cut, the defense programs are being stretched out still further.

There are those in the DoD who feel that, since the United States currently has a technological lead in weapon systems, time no longer matters. The reality is exactly the opposite. Time is now far more critical for a number of reasons. First, time is money. The longer it takes to develop and produce a weapon system, the more expensive it will be. There are many people assigned to a program for its full duration (the program manager is an obvious example), and the longer it takes the more the costs will grow. In addition, as programs become stretched out and technology continues to evolve, the tendency is to keep trying to improve on the system under development, which increases costs even more. Weapon systems cannot be rushed into development or production before the basic technology has been proven. However, once it has been, and if it turns out to have a significant military advantage, then the only way the United States can maintain its technological superiority is to rapidly build and deploy the new systems. This is equivalent to the commercial need to speed up the time-to-market for new products to stay ahead of the competition.

Nations that are not encumbered by the unique U.S. laws and regulations that currently restrict the speed with which new U.S. weapon systems can be developed and produced will be taking advantage of these lessons from the commercial world. The United States must change its defense practices to take advantage of them as well.

Efficient and Effective Downsizing

One of the major incorrect assumptions about the U.S. defense industry over the last forty years has been to view it as a mass-production industry. During World War II, when the "arsenal of democracy" was turning out large volumes of military equipment to arm itself and its allies, mass-production efficiencies could certainly be achieved and sizing the industry for such an assumption was perfectly valid. Since that time, however, the mind-set has not changed, even as the annual quantities of weapons procured have plummeted. Looking to the future, with the extremely small annual quantities that are likely to be bought, it is absolutely essential to recognize that the defense-unique sectors of the industry must be scaled to be basically a craft industry, one that builds in small quantities and for which the capital equipment and labor are appropriately planned.

On the labor side, a craft industry requires a highly skilled and flexible work force, capable of performing multiple tasks on a few items, with those tasks and items changing over time. On the equipment side, it requires factories and machines that are scaled for small quantities and that can be used for multiple purposes. Today the typical defense plant builds only a single product, and as the volume drops the plant simply remains empty until the next program comes along.

Beyond a reconsideration of scale and flexibility, there is also consideration of ownership and capabilities. Defense-unique plants probably should remain under American ownership and should be domestically located. And because engineering, manufacturing, and support are becoming increasingly intertwined, each of the remaining facilities should have a capability for performing all of these functions. Although this may seem to require a very large subsidy, it must be kept in mind that these few defense-unique operations will almost all be at the major weapon system level.[2] The core groups that will have to be maintained (and subsidized) are primarily a few key teams of weapon system engineers (including some manufacturing engineers). Their expertise represents an essential national asset that will have to be maintained during the downsizing and supported thereafter to assure competition for new ideas and lower costs.

The need to maintain competition among suppliers is very important, particularly in the design arena. Yet this becomes increasingly difficult as the number of suppliers shrinks. For example, in an industry with two firms remaining, it will not be possible or desirable to have them both build similar items. Rather, one should be building the current generation

system and continuing to update it while the other is developing the next-generation system. This form of competition can be continued indefinitely, with the two firms alternating back and forth as to which one is the current producer. There might even be some distribution of the work in the current production and support activities ("competitive allocation") to assure that both plants are able to maintain manufacturing capability, not just engineering. Since in most sectors the DoD will have product improvements and maintenance activities going on at almost all times, this is a viable way to provide work for plants that do not have a current production program.

In many cases the government has to make a choice between attempting to run one plant at a relatively efficient level and subsidizing a second one in order to maintain long-term competition. Because of the inherent disadvantages associated with monopoly industries, it is clearly worth some subsidy to maintain the second firm. This may not even be an actual subsidy, since the reduced prices and improved innovation from competition could more than save the added cost of the second, small engineering group maintained for its competitive value.[3]

At this level of downsizing—to one or two firms—antitrust implications become increasingly significant. It is highly likely that in some sectors it may not be possible to maintain more than two firms, and very possibly not even two. It is at this point that the DoD needs to search out possible alternatives, such as firms in complementary industries that either represent potential competition—because they can do the same job in a different way—or could be co-opted for some small engineering jobs to have them act as a competitor. If that can be done, then the Justice Department must allow a far broader interpretation of the relevant market in evaluating the antitrust implications of defense industry downsizing. At some point it will be in the nation's interest to move from two firms to one, and even one may be difficult to maintain at some funding levels. Then the Justice Department simply will have to acknowledge the national security issue as overriding compared to the antitrust issue.

In this dramatic move to one firm, the government must consider the availability of alternatives on an international basis. Even though it is highly desirable for the United States to maintain domestic sources, the

existence of a foreign supplier who might offer similar or better equipment, particularly at lower cost, provides a sufficiently credible supplier to keep competitive pressures on the domestic firm.

Finally, the ultimate difficulty is presented when there are no dollars allocated in a given sector for weapons procurement because the services feel they have enough of that item. Here it still may be necessary to maintain at least one source in that industry for the long term. The DoD will likely need next-generation products in this area, and it may need to rapidly increase its production of current products should world conditions change. Because it takes many years to rebuild a competent engineering and manufacturing capability once it has been closed down, this is an important consideration. One way to maintain a viable minimum capability is to establish joint production with foreign partners, an approach that is increasingly being considered in Europe. Another option is to continue to support just a few critical design people, and a few highly skilled production engineers in that sector to work on the continuous development of next-generation systems, a few of which would be built and then tested in the field. If they prove to be of dramatically higher military capability, then some would be produced and deployed. However, if they only represented a marginal performance gain or were too expensive to build in adequate quantities, the firm would be funded to design—and build—the prototypes for the subsequent generation.

An important consideration at this minimum-sustaining level of only one plant is the concern that there will be inadequate efforts on breakthrough technologies for next-generation systems. For example, it is very likely that a plant that is fully equipped for, say, metal cutting, might not place heavy emphasis on a next-generation composite (plastics) system—which requires a totally different set of engineering and manufacturing skills and equipment. On the other hand, such a nontraditional technology approach may offer the DoD the option of a second source, working in a totally new field. This approach would keep weapon's evolution moving ahead and would provide an extremely valuable form of subsidization that increases competition and at the same time greatly broadens the industrial base.

These types of choices require a conscious sector-by-sector strategy, different for aircraft, shipbuilding, missiles, satellites, and so on. Where

civil/military integration does not come about, and where subsidies are needed, the government should not select the winners but rather allow market forces to make these choices. The ideal role of the government is to establish broad industry goals on a sector-by-sector basis; perform analyses for each of them to determine what is the minimum need; set specific objectives as to how many firms, at what size, and in what technology areas are required; and, finally, provide adequate guidance to the firms as well as to government decisionmakers on a program-by-program basis, so that market forces can be utilized to shape the industry.

This is an extremely delicate process. The government must avoid managing, while still assuring the ongoing efficiency and effectiveness of each industrial defense sector. And decisions must be removed (as much as possible) from the political process. Fortunately, in each of these defense-unique sectors, by the time they are down to one, two, or three firms it is clear that what the Japanese refer to as "administrative guidance" is ideally suited to their subsequent restructuring.[4] The Japanese experience suggests the outcome would be a very few relatively large plants that are heavily, if not totally, dependent on government contracting and are generally recognized as national assets for the nation's future security.

It is clear that the United States cannot afford to simultaneously maintain and subsidize greatly underutilized operations in both the private and public sectors. To date, great duplication has been allowed to exist in the areas of maintenance, production, R & D, and services. It need not continue.

Public versus Private

Ask any U.S. military man or woman or any member of Congress whether they favor capitalism or socialism as the basic economic system for America and most will immediately respond by saying "the cold war is over, Russia lost, and America won; capitalism is now the undisputed wave of the future." They might note that most socialist countries around the world are shifting from state-owned means of production to private ownership. Further, they might add that in many capitalist countries where there had previously been public ownership of large industrial sectors, these too are being "privatized." In fact, in the 1990–92 time period there were an average of 150 firms annually privatized around the world, and essentially no nationalizations. From 1986 to 1992 this privatization activity reached a cumulative value of $325 billion.[5]

Perhaps surprisingly, the only major portion of the world's economy that has been moving significantly toward socialism is the industrial base of the U.S. Department of Defense. To understand how and why this is happening, it is necessary to look briefly at the history of the publicly owned (and quasi-public) sectors of this base. Specifically, these include the *government depots* for maintaining, overhauling, upgrading, and repairing military equipment; the *arsenals* for building new equipment; the *defense laboratories* for R & D; and the *federally funded research and development centers* (FFRDCs), which range from the large, quasi-governmental nuclear weapons laboratories to large systems engineering, quasi-governmental think tanks. Each of these activities has a special history and rationale, and together they represent tens of billions of dollars a year of defense industrial base expenditures. Because of their long history[6] and very strong political support, these institutions have been shrinking much less rapidly than the private portion of the defense base. A brief history of each area follows.

Weapons Support   Each of the armed services maintains large depots for support of major weapons and, in some cases, for subsystems as well. The concept evolved to its current structure during World War II. Since private industry was consumed with producing as much new equipment as possible, the services set up in-house ("organic") depots to repair equipment that was damaged during the long war, as well as to maintain and upgrade equipment. In the period immediately after World War II, it was assumed that future wars would be of a similar type—that is, an all-out, extended-duration conflict against the Soviet Union in central Europe—so the depots were maintained as large installations in the event they would be required to perform similar functions as in the past.

In a sense the depots were an insurance policy since, during peacetime, the DoD did not need to have the extensive support capability that would be required during a long-duration conflict. In addition, the armed services have long worried that they could not depend on industry to maintain their equipment, arguing that "they won't be around when we need them" and "we certainly can't expect them to go overseas to maintain this equipment." Over the years industry of course has strongly disagreed with many of the inherent assumptions associated with this rationale. In the post–cold war era, however, it is becoming increasingly difficult to justify the government depots. For one thing, likely scenarios do not include high-intensity, extended-duration conflicts; more probable is a conflict similar to Desert Storm, that is, a brief engagement with no time to send equipment back for repair and maintenance. Had there been time, the underutilized private sector plants could have easily handled the workload. And during the Vietnam War as well as in Desert Storm, private industry did in fact have maintenance people overseas, some even in the war zone. Large international corporations today routinely maintain their equipment on a worldwide basis. Many in the defense industry argue that since very little new equipment will be purchased in the post–cold war era, their major defense business will actually be in maintaining and upgrading existing systems.

Thus if the DoD is to maintain a viable defense industry, it will have to give this work to the private sector instead of to its own depots. In 1991, 69 percent of DoD maintenance and repair was done "in-house," at over thirty major government facilities, employing 175,113 civilian and 3,031 military personnel. Annual costs were approximately $14 billion in repair and overhaul work and another $9 billion in major weapon system modifications and equipment upgrades.[7] Clearly this represents a major portion of the current U.S. defense industry.

Weapons Production   The second category of public sector facilities is U.S. government arsenals and their navy counterpart, government shipyards. These have a very long history, with some of those still in use dating back to the Civil War. They evolved because until the cold war the country had a tradition of arming for wars and then totally disarming afterward— the farmer-soldier model. The only way the army could maintain any capability for rapidly building rifles, bullets, cannons, and other munitions, or the navy for building ships, was to maintain the production facilities themselves, as publicly owned industrial operations. After World War II, when it was possible to get much of this equipment in the private sector, the services argued that they had to have control over the facilities and over the work force in the event they had to respond to crises. Critics of the government-owned production facilities argued that similar defense work could be done in the private sector, and with much greater flexibility. For example, when a defense-related program was over, private-sector workers could be laid off and the facility could be converted to other products, including commercial items. By contrast, the civil service employees who work in the arsenals are extremely difficult to lay off.

There have also been repeated arguments made as to the relative efficiency of public versus private production facilities. One study comparing ship construction in the public and private yards showed a 33 percent greater efficiency in the private sector.[8] Nonetheless, billions of dollars are spent annually largely to maintain the arsenals in a standby position, since there is very little production going on. Again, they are primarily an "insurance policy"—and a very important one *if* there is no alternative in the private sector—for the needed production in a period of crisis.

R & D   The third and fourth of the activities in the public and quasi-public sectors fall into the broad category of research and development. Here we have the federal laboratories, both in the Department of Defense and in the form of the large nuclear laboratories run by the Department of Energy. Overall, there are over 700 government laboratories in America, with an annual budget of over $20 billion—which is almost one-third of the government's total expenditure on R & D, and nearly one-sixth of the nation's total. The largest labs are the three nuclear facilities—Sandia and Los Alamos, in New Mexico, and Lawrence Livermore, in California. Each has close to 8,000 employees and budgets of over a billion dollars a year.[9] For comparison, even the laboratories of such giants as IBM and AT&T (the Bell Laboratories) have only 3,200 and 1,400 employees respectively and budgets of less than half of the weapons laboratories.

Many of the defense laboratories were established when there was a need for a particular type of technology that did not exist in the private sector, or because the armed services wanted control over the research that was being done. (The research ranged from work on new materials for uniforms, as done in the army's materials lab, to work on advanced radars and communication systems, as is done in the air force's Rome

Development Laboratory.) Today almost all of these facilities duplicate activities carried out by private industry, and in many cases, lag far behind their civil counterparts. The armed services, however, have continued to argue for the maintenance of these laboratories, stating that an advanced in-house engineering capability would make them smarter buyers. Their argument (which has considerable validity) is that unless they understand the state of the art, they will not know what to ask for or whether they are getting what they should. Those who reject the government arguments say that while the government does need to have a corps of technical competence, the overwhelming majority of the research should be done in the competitive private sector. They point to independent engineering and research firms that could help the government "buy smart" without the large expenses associated with maintaining duplicative in-house research facilities. Many of the government laboratories have begun to shift some work to funding the private sector, but still keep a very large share in-house.

Another part of the government R & D community is the subgroup of FFRDCs that do laboratory work—particularly in the nuclear weapons area. These are primarily a legacy of World War II. As the nation began research on first atomic and later, nuclear weapons, it was felt that this work required extreme secrecy and physical security. Thus research and production were done within these "national laboratories." As the complexity of the projects increased, the laboratories—by necessity—branched into related fields such as supercomputing and high-energy lasers. With the defense buildup in the 1980s they expanded even further, so that there currently is enormous excess capacity.

These special-purpose laboratories are valued national resources, and there is a consensus that the United States must maintain its engineering and manufacturing capability in nuclear weapons. It is also very clear, however, that significant downsizing is required. The alternatives are dramatic downsizing to a small, highly specialized corps or conversion into other areas: however, many believe they should not be allowed to compete with private sector research.

FFRDCs also perform systems engineering and studies and analyses for the DoD. The Aerospace Corporation supports the air force in the space business; the MITRE Corporation supports the air force in the electronics business. The first of this type of organization was the Rand Corporation, which was established after World War II to do research for the air force.[10] At the time, the Department of Defense was beginning to develop extremely sophisticated weapon systems and it needed help in defining and managing them. It was unable to pay civil servants a sufficient salary to attract the very best engineers, so they established FFRDCs as non-profit, tax-exempt systems engineering and analysis companies. Since that time, both their numbers and their size have grown significantly; both the Aerospace Corporation and the MITRE Corporation now have thousands of employees. Over the last few decades, however, a private sector professional services industry has built up that offers essentially identical services. In fact, many of these private sector firms refuse to take contracts from the large defense contractors and only work for the government to maintain total objectivity and avoid even the appearance of conflict of interest—as has been the case with the FFRDCs.

In many ways these various aspects of government weapons support, production, and R & D work represent redundancy with work that could be done in the private sector. Obviously this is not a black-and-white situation, and it can be argued that the right answer to the public/private mix is some combination of the two. There are clearly some unique capabilities (such as work on nuclear weapons) that can be satisfied only by work now done in the depots, arsenals, laboratories, and FFRDCs. But duplication to the extent it now exists is not something that the government can afford as it downsizes the defense industry.

In the first five years of the defense downturn (from its peak in 1987), private sector defense employment fell by 14 percent, while the public sector had an employment reduction of only 4 percent. When it became clear that employment had to drop in the public sector as well and when depots were added to the base closure list (in 1993), a comparison of the total drop from 1987 to 1994 still showed private sector defense employment falling by 38 percent and total civilian defense employment (depots, arsenals, labs, etc.) falling by only half that.[11] In some areas, the difference was even more glaring: from 1987 to 1992, while the total defense acquisition budget fell by over 25 percent, the DoD in-house laboratory expenditures were reduced by only 3 percent.[12] Between 1987 and 1994, the ratio of DoD in-house civilian employment to private sector defense industry employment *rose* by 20 percent.[13]

By the mid-1990s these trends had begun to cause considerable alarm—particularly within the defense industry. Surprisingly, the industry had been relatively quiet during the preceding ten years, as the defense budget shrunk and the percentage of work was shifting dramatically to the public sector. This government sector had been exerting strong political pressure on the Congress because of the military's desire to maintain its own facilities and the government unions' desire to support its civil service workers. In many cases the DoD facilities were the largest employer in a congressional district and in some cases even the largest in the state (e.g., the national laboratories in New Mexico). They were well represented by lobbyists; and one of the largest and strongest "lobbies" in the U.S. Congress was the 108-congressional-member military depot caucus.[14]

Thus, it should be no surprise that Congress has gone out of its way to support the public sector—in many cases at the expense of the private sector. For example, in the Defense Authorization Bill (FY93) there was an explicit requirement that 60 percent of all work that could be done in government depots must be done there, and the other 40 percent must be awarded competitively between the depots and industry.[15] The following year (FY94) the Senate reemphasized the 60 percent requirement, but the House went further by stating that no new weapons programs could be planned to be maintained in the private sector; no transfers of maintenance work could occur from the public to the private sector on current programs; no consolidation of air force and navy depots could take place; a plan to maintain the current work load in the government depots must be submitted to the Congress by each service secretary; and government shipyards and depots would henceforth be authorized to bid on all relevant defense-related production and services.[16]

The intent of the Congress was clear. As these laws continue to be on the books, as work on new production in the private sector is reduced, and as an increasing share of the defense budget goes for work done in government depots, there will be an even more dramatic shift toward the public sector for the overall defense industrial base.

Yet as noted earlier, if the choice of socialism versus capitalism were given to a member of Congress, the answer would undoubtedly be "capitalism." Similarly, most members give speeches about the importance of free enterprise and the governments' responsibility to steer but not implement the direction of the economy. When defense workers and local votes are involved, however, both the military and the Congress go against private industry. The rationale is that these actions are required to "maintain the defense industrial base."

Increasingly, the Congress and the military have been arguing that the way to resolve this public versus private issue is to let the two sectors compete. Many argue, however, that this competitive approach has three fundamental flaws: first, it departs sharply from the nation's democratic/capitalistic tradition of a government that discharges unique, inherently governmental, public sector functions, and a private sector that performs commercial functions in support of the federal government. Second, the public-private competition model inevitably erodes mutual trust and the needed sense of partnership because the private sector faces a government counterpart that is both a direct competitor and the possessor of the right to decide who wins and loses. (This may actually be the most dramatic conflict-of-interest situation in the federal acquisition system.) And third, the competitive cost comparison methodology is basically unsound: The government's accounting system and cost collection processes do not reflect substantial portions of their indirect costs, such as the allocation of the 20,000 managers in the Pentagon, which contractors by law and regulation must reflect in their cost proposals. And in government operations there is no penalty for an underbid—the taxpayers will simply pick up the tab in the next budget cycle.

These arguments have not had a great influence in the political arena. In fact, the government operations have recently been encouraged to compete directly against the private sector for work outside of their traditional products and customers. This began when the depots, which faced not only a declining defense budget but also reduced demands for maintenance due to the increased reliability of modern equipment, began taking maintenance, repair, and upgrade work from private defense industry. Congress passed laws to help the depots, and the services spent hundreds of millions of dollars to modernize them. By 1992, as the defense cutbacks built up, the depots even began to attempt to get some commercial overhaul and maintenance work, and Congress proposed legislation to allow them to subcontract for work from the private sector. Air Force material commander General Ronald Yates even proposed doing final assembly of a new military aircraft, the F-22 advanced fighter, in its own government facility. He stated "we are radically changing the way we do business in the United States Air Force. I don't intend to close any depots. I intend to take . . . work away from [the defense industry] to keep my depots open." [17] This same phenomenon then occurred in the government arsenals which were similarly threatened with dramatic cutbacks in work load. The army's Rock Island Arsenal began making half of the mounts for the 120-mm gun on the M1-A2 tank, which originally had all been made by General Dynamics Corporation.[18] This work could obviously be done in either public or private plants since it is not inherently governmental in nature, but it seems that the United States is headed toward the Russian defense industry model.

In this Russian prototype, not only is the means of production owned by the government, but there is a separation of research, production, and support in independent facilities (laboratories, arsenals, and depots). Unfortunately this is not a model that lends itself to rapid new product realizations, because of the separations, nor to low-cost designs, since concurrent engineering is discouraged by the separations. Further, there will be very little tendency toward true civil/military integration, since the government facilities do not even attempt to be competitive in the purely commercial arenas and should not expect to be, given their nature and their mission.

An obvious option to consider for the public sector industrial operations, perhaps beginning with the depots, would be privatization, including possible consolidation with private sector firms. The World Bank studied twelve cases of privatization in Britain, Chile, Malaysia, and Mexico. It found that in eleven of the twelve sales there was a net increase in wealth—due to managerial innovation, higher investment, better pricing of services, and the shedding of surplus workers—especially since the managers were freer to decide on which workers to hire and fire. Perhaps surprisingly, the remaining workers also often gained; there has been no serious labor trouble in any of the twelve privatized firms.[19]

To take advantage of the unique capabilities of some government operations such as the national labs and to assure rapid industrial application of output, another option is to let the operations submit proposals for funding as subcontractors to industrial firms. These firms, in turn, would submit a joint proposal for a research project to the government, or even to another private sector firm. This way, the government operations would have to meet the tests of the market for their funding. For this to work, however, the depots, arsenals, or labs would have to be capable of isolating this work into separate "profit centers," and would have to be capable of absorbing a loss, rather than passing it on to the taxpayers. Both of these conditions would be extremely difficult to implement. Privatization might therefore be a more attractive option. It would free them to operate totally in the private sector as either a prime contractor or subcontractor; and to operate in defense-unique areas, or in dual-use areas, or totally in the commercial market. In all cases, however, they would have to be competitive.

Finally, the desirability of maintaining a few small defense-unique public sector operations, because there is only a single firm in the private sector, has some merit if it is the only way to assure an alternative to that monopoly supplier. This has particular appeal when the government is unable to create a competitor in the private sector, either because the volume of work is so small or because it is unattractive from a business perspective to do so.[20]

This question of the private sector versus the public sector is one of the more critical issues associated with strategizing the desired defense industrial base structure for the twenty-first century. It obviously arises most frequently in those few defense-unique areas that must be maintained to assure a viable military posture in the future.

8

Current Barriers to Integration

During Operation Desert Storm, the U.S. Army found that it urgently needed a large number of modern radios. The model that Motorola was producing for city police forces was ideal to satisfy the army's communications requirements as well as its criteria for rough abuse and environmental extremes. However, since U.S. law makes it a crime for a company to sell an item to the government at anything but the lowest price offered to any other purchaser, and since Motorola could not guarantee that the army was getting the lowest price offered anywhere to anyone (because of discounts given to police by local sales distributors), it could not sign the necessary certificate. The army attempted to get someone at a high political level in the army to sign a waiver on this law, but was unsuccessful. No one was authorized to violate the law without congressional approval.

The solution to this dilemma was to have Japan purchase the radios from Motorola and then supply them to the U.S. Army as part of Japan's contribution to Operation Desert Storm. Obviously such an expeditious path is only possible under extremely extenuating circumstances—in this case, the urgencies of war. This law, however, is only one of a large number that create barriers to the DoD's purchase of commercial items or its use of commercial buying practices.

Built up over more than four decades of legislative and executive actions, there are now over 5,000 sections of U.S. code containing unique laws that relate to defense acquisition of goods and services.[1] Relevant regulations run to more than 125,000 pages; military product and process specifications and standards fill 32,000 documents. These rules become the detailed regulations governing the day-to-day activities of the hundreds of thousands of DoD personnel (military and civilian) who administer the DoD acquisition process.

To quote from a book describing the Ming dynasty in decline in the sixteenth century, "the bureaucratic rule had reached such an advanced stage that all the hidden needs and wants of thousands of individuals, along with their personal aspirations, were irreversibly linked to the gigantic status quo."[2] This was a primary cause of the failure to reform the dynasty. It is also the major problem in achieving the needed transformation of the U.S. defense industrial base at the end of the twentieth century.

Perhaps no point in this book should be more heavily emphasized than the extreme difficulty that will be faced in attempting to implement the changes required for civil/military integration. The problem is clearly seen in the response to a 1987 Defense Science Board (DSB) report recommending that commercial buying practices, including commercial (market-based) competition, be utilized for semiconductor procurements by the DoD. This recommendation by a very senior DoD advisory group was made to allow the government to have the advantage of purchasing the lower-cost, higher-reliability, higher-performance, commercially available semiconductors that met the military's rugged environmental needs. At the urging of Congress, the Government Accounting Office (GAO) found that the DSB panel "based its findings not on hard, factual evidence but on professional and legal opinion. It did not [unequivocally] show that CICA [the government's Competition in Contracting Act of 1984] had impeded commercial acquisition. Nor did the panel address the long-term consequences of their request to change the requirement for full and open competition"—which the DSB stated should be returned to its old wording of "effective competition"—a subtle difference that would reduce the bidders to primarily those who were qualified. Perhaps most significantly, the GAO stated that the DSB panel "did not address whether there are not fundamental differences between commercial and government operations and accountability which give rise to the need for different procedures."[3]

Chairman Brooks of the House Government Operations Committee was not so circumspect. In a statement accompanying the release of the

GAO review, he agreed that "increased procurement of commercial products . . . would no doubt save American taxpayers billions of dollars." However, he blasted the DSB panel's recommendation to adopt commercial-style competition, which he said "attempts to legitimize restrictive competition to a few, selected companies. It ignores the fundamental differences between commercial and government operations. . . . The Competition [in Contracting] Act was passed in 1984 over strong objections from the Defense Department. It is obvious the DoD and parts of the defense industry haven't given up and will go to any length, including the use of bogus studies, to get their way." [4]

It is not that Chairman Brooks is wrong on this issue, or that the DSB was wrong; rather, they are attempting to pursue two different objectives through the use of defense procurements. Chairman Brooks is clearly interested in the issue of "fairness," that is, allowing everyone to bid; and he is also pursuing the issue of public trust—believing that allowing defense buyers to make market judgments among differing products serving the same function would not be as objective a decision as writing a detailed specification for the item, allowing everyone to bid, and then awarding it to the lowest bidder. He is also basically influenced in his decision by a belief shared by many (inside and outside of government) that the underlying motivation of industry is greed, and that it is the government's role—and not the role of the free market—to control this greed. Chairman Brooks made it clear that even billions of dollars of annual savings does not override the issues of fairness and trust.

If the government is to shift its buying practices to the commercial way of doing business and allow its civil and military industrial bases to be integrated, it will require a very dramatic change in the balance of fairness and trust, versus efficiency and effectiveness. Currently, the weight is all on one side.

A critical point here is that the billions of extra dollars required for the unique defense buying practices are not provided for in any budget bill. The excess costs are simply absorbed into the costs of DoD weapon systems procurements. It is this separation of budgetary responsibility and legislative/regulatory actions that make the change to a civil/military industrial base so difficult. There are simply no fiscal constraints on adding more and more legislative and regulatory oversight to an already overburdened system. Yet with the shrinking defense budget and the continuing need to maintain the nation's security, some reconciliation is essential.

Background

In the overwhelming majority of industrial areas—such as electronics, communication systems, information systems, commercial aircraft, jet engines, wheeled vehicles, satellites, etc.—the cause of the military/civilian separation is not technological, but rather procedural. Concern about potential "waste, fraud, and abuse" results in the lack of trust in the adequacy of normal commercial codes and normal criminal penalties for illegal actions. The result is the enormous body of intrusive oversight requirements that exists in the defense world—from cost accounting regulations through extensive government inspection and auditing. Interestingly, we trust the normal commercial practices in areas as diverse and important as tax collection and aircraft safety—the latter an area in which we place our lives and those of our families. In aircraft, Boeing finds that the government only requires five oversight personnel in their facilities for all of the commercial aircraft business that they do, while the DoD has 680 people at Boeing to provide oversight on their far fewer military aircraft.

The second reason for the many laws that are unique to the defense world has to do with the fact that legislators use the tens of billions of dollars of defense procurements to achieve objectives other than simply the nation's security. Strong interest groups have seen these dollars as a way for the government to correct many of society's wrongs, through directing defense procurements toward high-unemployment districts, minority firms, unionized plants, small businesses, and so on. For each of these valid needs there is a set of laws to assure that special requirements—above and beyond those covered by normal U.S. commercial laws—are met by DoD purchases. The problem is not that these added requirements are not desirable, it is that they add huge costs to defense procurements. Further, since these additions are not identified as socioeconomic costs that are subsidized by the government, the DoD is accused of having paid too much for low-quality goods and services. The nation, meanwhile, receives far less security than is suggested by the dollars allocated to the defense budget.

Here we also get into the fairness arena. By allowing everyone to bid on government contracts, the government is forced to write a detailed specification for the characteristics of everything from fruitcakes to semiconductors. This would not be necessary if purchases were limited to those products and suppliers available in the commercial world. Instead, if a government buyer wanted to purchase spare semiconductors for his military base, he would be prohibited from doing so unless there was a small business listed as one of the suppliers in his district, since all government purchases under $100,000 must be made from a small business. Most of the world's competitive semiconductor makers are not small businesses, nor are the national discount stores that might retail them.

Although many defense procurement rules have a valid basis, they go well beyond the laws written for the rest of the economy. The overall impact is twofold: first, the differences cause significant cost increases; and second, they force a separation of the civilian and military industries, causing still further cost increases. Two simple cases illustrate the impact. A military specification for white gloves led one manufacturer to set up a separate assembly line with a unit cost of $32 per pair, versus an identical commercial product sold by the same manufacturer for $20 a pair.[5] Second, a military specification for buttons on mens' shirts causes the distance between buttons to be unequal and to vary from size to size. As a result, the standard industry practice of loading the shirt onto a pallet which is fed into a button-sewing machine cannot be used. A separate military pallet is needed.

These examples may seem trivial, but multiply them by the thousands of other examples caused by the unique defense practices and apply them to the tens of billions of dollars' worth of defense goods and services and one can appreciate the magnitude of the problem.

In general, military industrial plants appear to have four times the cost and number of people to administer government contracts than their comparable commercial equivalents. Defense plants are also far more engineering-intensive than their commercial equivalents, which requires a much higher ratio of management and administration (by three to one)[6] than in production-oriented plants. In fact, this same high administrative work force ratio seems to hold for almost all activities of defense plants. One survey of 206 firms found that overall administrative costs were three times higher (as a percentage of sales) in comparable defense plants than their commercial equivalents.[7]

Studies of the aggregated effect of these differences on the total cost of items vary: one study found that comparable defense goods were 30 to 50 percent higher priced;[8] another showed that for comparable high-technology systems, the variation might be as much as 200 to 500 percent more for defense goods.[9]

Many commercial suppliers who do defense business have set up separate plants (Motorola, IBM, Boeing); others (Hewlett Packard and Digital Equipment Corporation) simply refuse to accept defense contracts—unless the product can be provided on a purely commercial basis.

Today commercial equipment will often do the needed military job in the required military environments. But historically there has never been any government motivation to integrate the civil and military industrial bases. To the contrary, many laws were explicitly geared to discourage integration. For example, as far back as 1970 Senator Mike Mansfield passed an amendment to the Defense Authorization Bill that explicitly prohibited a company's independent research and development from being allocated to its defense contracts, unless it was exclusively for defense use. This attitude persisted for more than twenty years. When people in the early years of the Bush administration advocated that DoD consider dual use in its buying practices, they were either muzzled or fired. In 1992, Congress finally reversed the Mansfield amendment to explicitly encourage the use of a company's independent research and development expenditures on dual-use technology.

Barriers to integration are especially severe for the thousands of firms in the lower tiers of the defense industry. These firms either are in the commercial world and lack the resources to meet the added government requirements, or have a defense-based operation and are noncompetitive in the commercial arena. Yet this is the level where civil and military products and production processes are most often inherently the same.

In spite of the merging of civil and military basic technologies that occurred in the 1980s, the uniqueness of the government's acquisition laws and regulations increased dramatically in this time period. A study done in 1992 by the Government's Merit Systems Protection Board found[10] that federal procurement rules had become so complicated that they were overwhelming many of the government's 31,000 contracting officers. "The primary factor behind these problems appears to be the inability of contract specialists to deal with the increasingly complicated requirements under which they must work." They observed a work force "struggling to keep up with potentially counterproductive growth in federal procurement policy and procedures. . . . The bottom line was that they [procurement officers] cannot be creative and innovative because of the rules."

Yet the rules were in response to the public perception of the need for a change in the way the government does its business. In 1987, a public opinion survey[11] cited "fighting waste, fraud, and abuse in government" as the number-one resource issue for the president (86 percent); compared to foreign trade (70 percent), and improved early childhood health (70 percent). Importantly, neither the public nor the Congress made a distinction between waste, which is common and is measured in *billions* of dollars each year, and fraud, which is quite infrequent and measured in *millions* of dollars.[12]

In response to the need for change, the reforms could have moved in either of two directions: broad changes aimed at removing waste and achieving greater efficiency, or increased regulation and oversight aimed at greater visibility and control over fraud. The latter was easier and faster, so it was the solution chosen. Many believe the result was far less efficiency in government procurement.

The defense procurement reforms of the 1980s had two focal points. First, to increase the number of competitions held among defense firms. The logic was valid for commercial-style competitions, where individuals make choices about how much they are willing to pay for different levels of quality in goods and services. This is "value-based" buying. The defense procurement process, however, has historically been based on cost-based competition, where minimally acceptable goods and services (that meet minimal government specifications) is all that is believed required. Anyone who promises to meet this minimum requirement at the lowest bid is given the contract. Prior performance is not a consideration. In fact, the law permits anyone who has not been convicted of a felony to be allowed to bid.

During the 1980s there was a dramatic increase in the amount of cost-based (not value-based) competition done by the Department of Defense. It was even introduced, by Secretary of the Navy John Lehman and subsequently by the air force, into research and development contracts. High-technology, high-risk advanced weapon systems were simply awarded to the lowest (fixed-price) bidder. Firms anxious to get defense business would promise anything, bid low, and hope to get bailed out later—when they were the only supplier of a badly needed, next-generation weapon system. This practice was reversed by the Bush administration, but not before doing enormous damage to the health of the defense industry, including further separation from the broader commercial industrial base.

The second thrust of the defense procurement reform initiatives of the 1980s was aimed at criminalization of procurement abuses. Prior to this, there had been administrative ajudication over such things as signing a time card wrong. But in the 1980s, many administrative actions became subject to criminal law. Since the legal cost to the government of bringing cases does not have to be justified (in contrast to the commercial world, where firms pay for such prosecutions), and since federal prosecutors attract big headlines when pursuing "contractor abuse," litigation increased and the small defense businesses were very negatively affected. They could not afford the legal costs of defending themselves against the federal government, and in many cases they were forced to plead guilty. In addition, Congress passed legislation to encourage and protect so-called whistle blowers, and actually offered rewards to industry employees who would bring suits (known in legal terminology as "qui tam") against their defense employers.

These two broad sets of procurement reform initiatives were brought about by two sets of scandals. The first was the so-called spare parts scandal in which simple, commercially available items were purchased at exorbitant prices. The reason for it was primarily the way in which the government cost accounting process works. All overhead within a given facility was simply allocated on the basis of sales, to a wide variety of items. Some items would absorb more and others less; a hammer or a

bolt could come out costing a ridiculously large amount. The public believed that if a $12 hammer cost $500 when the DoD buys it, then the
same ratio must apply to the missiles, airplanes, and ships it purchases.
They felt that more auditors and more regulations were required to control these abuses. And Congress responded.

The second scandal (known as "ill wind") involved procurement
bribes. A few senior government officials (primarily in the navy) apparently accepted bribes from industry representatives, which was clearly illegal, and penalties were already on the books for it. Nonetheless,
Congress passed additional criminalizing legislation, whose effect was to
introduce greater fear, mistrust, and isolation into the government-
industry relationship.

One consequence of these two sets of "reforms" was that many firms
simply refused to do R & D business with the Defense Department. Others set up totally separate defense industrial operations, which previously
had been integrated. As each new bill was added by the Congress to correct a perceived problem, the burdens of the defense way of doing business grew greater, and the costs increased. Defense-only operations had
far higher costs and far greater (expensive) government oversight.[13] What
is particularly surprising is that during these reforms, there was very little
effort by the Department of Defense either to object to the increased legislation and regulation in the procurement arena or to address the issue. As
the GAO commented, there was a lot of speechmaking, but no sincere
efforts toward change. In fact, many people in the Department of Defense
felt that this increased oversight was necessary to satisfy the public and
to minimize personal risk. Obviously the more checkers, auditors, and
inspectors in the system, the more diffuse the responsibility.

By the beginning of the 1990s, it was clear that the costly defense-
unique procurement system was incompatible with the required defense
industry downsizing. One study[14] asked world-class firms that operate in
both the civil and military business arenas (IBM, Motorola, Boeing, etc.)
why they separated their operations and asked other commercial firms
(Hewlett Packard and Intel) why they refused to do R & D business with
the DoD. Four barriers to integration dominated all of the industry case
studies—and invariably in this order of priority: (1) the weapons requirements process, with its almost exclusive focus on performance; (2) the

government's cost-based (not value-based) contracting system; (3) the unique military specifications and standards; and (4) the specialized government procurement laws. The one additional area that frequently surfaced was the military's concern about the dependability of worldwide logistics support from commercial suppliers. Less important, but still mentioned by some of the respondents as barriers to integration, were: legal constraints; security considerations; trade considerations; unilateral change orders in which the government requires that it be allowed to make changes in equipment at its whim, but which would be very disruptive to commercial production; excess of government inspections; and regulation of the commercial use of government property. To confirm the findings of these case studies, a survey was conducted of over 200 other firms doing business in both the civil and military areas.[15] The new data echoed the old. In explaining the rationale for separating industrial operations, "companies that segregate [their civil and military business] overwhelmingly cite the requirements of federal contracting, rather than unique technology needs, as the primary reason." Significantly, companies did not assign priority to the traditionally cited rationales for segregation: lack of an equivalent commercial market for their military products, or lack of capability on the commercial side of their business to produce for government needs.

The survey results strongly supported the feasibility of a single defense/commercial operation. Eighty-nine percent of the companies said that the different products could be manufactured in a single operation. Only 4 respondents of the 200 sampled indicated that their products and processes were completely different, with no potential for co-production. The primary barriers to integration, then, are based almost entirely on the legislation, regulations, and practices that govern the defense way of doing business. Many of the rationales for these rules no longer exist.

The Military Requirements Process

When someone in the commercial world decides to buy a new television set, they consider such functional needs as screen size, cable capacity, and cost; and the cost factor places very real constraints on what they might otherwise ask for. But rarely do consumers ask about the details of the design, such as the number of decibels of amplification out of the third stage in the audio chain; nor do they tell the manufacturer how to solder the wires. They might, however, expect a warranty on the product, and they certainly would check on the potential suppliers' reputations.

Compare this with the military approach. In the first place, a military commander defines what is needed; and this need is unconstrained by any resource limitations. Thus, the process begins with the military defining what they call a "mission need," which is authenticated up the military chain-of-command, on through the Chairman of the Joint Chiefs of Staff. In this process of transitioning through the system, what began as a functional requirement—such as the need to destroy an enemy's command and control centers—evolves into the need for a specific type of equipment—a new bomber. To this, additional requirements/desires are added, so that the bomber is described in terms of its speed, altitude, bomb-carrying capacity, etc. Later, these aspects are described in considerable design detail, with all of the military specifications and standards, in a request-for-proposal (RFP) that goes out for industry bids.

In addition to the bomber specs, the RFP is burdened with all of the standard defense procurement requirements—the need for small business plans, domestic parts purchases, detailed drawings and data packages to defense specifications, and, most important, the specialized accounting, cost reporting systems, and auditing associated with cost-based contracting. Finally, bids are received from all qualified sources, that is, anyone who has not been convicted of a felony and is able to demonstrate financial capability to perform the job.

In fairness, it must be noted that throughout the process there is some attempt to consider cost—but only in terms of feasibility, that is, would it break the bank if we bought one; or in terms of the coming year's budget, that is, can we afford to fund the first year's development cost. The usual rationale is "we need this system, and we'll figure out how to pay for it when the time comes."

This extreme emphasis on performance is predicated on the belief that to get higher performance, you have to pay more for it. This has been true over the history of modern weapon systems, where costs have been rising at essentially the same rate as performance.[16] In the commercial world, however, while performance has similarly been rising, the costs have often been falling—thus proving that it is not a law of nature but rather that the weapon system curves are based on defense practices.

Finally, warranties are not a serious consideration in the military since it is a firm requirement to be able to "organically support" any new weapon system. As long as the delivered item meets the specifications, the service chooses to handle it after that.

From this (somewhat exaggerated) comparison of the two processes, it can be seen that costs, specifically production and support costs, are given equal weight to performance in commercial practices but are considered only secondarily in the military. The result is that in the commercial world manufacturing and logistics support become major design considerations (along with performance); whereas in the military, advanced product performance is almost the exclusive design factor. It is this difference, probably more than anything else, that tends to start the military system off on its own, much more costly path away from the commercial world.

This is not to suggest that the Defense Department does not care about cost. But by the time the basic concept of a new product or system has been agreed on, over 85 percent of the production and support costs have been designed in. For example, when a requirements decision is made as to whether a new fighter plane will have one jet engine or two, most cost decisions will have been made as well, since jet engine maintenance is the single largest logistics cost in the DoD. The debate over the number of engines, however, takes place almost totally on the military performance level rather than on economic considerations. This example, when multiplied by the thousands of decisions made as a product is being defined, virtually precludes the practice of concurrent engineering. The latter approach, which brings together design engineers with production and support engineers in the preliminary design stage, is increasingly used in the commercial world.

The absence of early consideration of resource constraints frequently results in the selection of a weapon system that might have been totally different if economic considerations had been brought to bear. For example, to destroy a command-and-control center, the choice could be a low-speed, cargo-like aircraft that stands off and launches cruise missiles, or a manned high-speed penetrating bomber. The cruise missile option has been available for many decades and is orders of magnitude less expensive. The military requirements process, however, essentially blocked this option from reaching high-level decisionmakers. What frequently forces the commercial world to go to a nontraditional solution to solve a functional need is the fact that it can be done for significantly less money. Without significant resource constraints, the traditional military way of doing things will always win out.

Yet the requirement for using design-to-cost in the weapon system acquisition process was actually stated as a Secretary of Defense policy in 1973. In 1975, a specific directive (DoD Directive 5000.28) was issued, imposing design-to-cost considerations on all major weapon system acquisitions and requiring that cost be weighted equally with performance. This was updated in April 1983 (DoD Directive 4245.3), defining design-to-cost as "an acquisition management technique . . . [that] embodies, early, the establishment of realistic but rigorous cost goals [production and support] and thresholds, and a determined effort to achieve them."

An independent study by the Institute for Defense Analysis (a Pentagon-controlled think tank) noted that design-to-cost has *not* been implemented as intended. For the eighty-nine systems that were analyzed, design-to-cost was applied in only thirty-two of them. The study also found that when it was applied, it was only as a cost-monitoring device, and then only in full-scale production, rather than during the concept formulation phase where design trade-offs based on cost are feasible.

Until the Department of Defense makes production and support costs major considerations in the preliminary stages of the design of its weapon systems, DoD will always be on a path that separates it from the commercial world. It will continue to be faced with rising cost-curve trends and be unable to reconcile weapons' costs with plunging defense budgets. This need to refocus the product definition phases of the military requirements process is essential for civil/military integration to occur, as well as for reversing the rising cost trends in defense-unique products.

Cost-Based Contracting

If there is a single government business practice that forces separation of civil and military industrial activities, it is cost-based (versus price- or value-based) contracting. This split reflects a basic philosophic difference—trust in the forces of market capitalism versus lack of trust. In the commercial world, market-based competition establishes the price for goods and services. Consumers compare different products for the same function and make a determination based on the best combination of performance and price, that is, value. The commercial buyer does not need detailed labor, material, and overhead cost breakdowns of the product; it is up to the commercial supplier to worry about providing the best product for the lowest cost. The incentives for the supplier to seek cost reduction, higher performance, and higher quality are built into the basic principle of competitive market capitalism.

The government, however, bases its defense contracting principles on the concept of cost-based pricing. It pays for all supplier costs (labor, material, overhead, etc.) that are associated with building a given item and allows a small profit on top of that. It wants full visibility into, control over, and auditing of each and every one of these costs. The government seems not to trust the forces of market capitalism, nor does it trust the civil laws that operate in the commercial world to control waste, fraud, and abuse. Therefore it has set up an elaborate system of cost-based accounting practices.

The government's Cost Accounting Standards Board operates according to a fair and reasonable set of cost accounting principles. The problem is that its objective is to make sure that all costs are valid (justifiable) charges on each item the government procures. This is very different from the commercial objective of reducing costs. This system of justifying costs, and therefore maximizing all allowable costs, rather than realizing reduced costs to the customer is unique to defense. For example, since firms receive progress payments against their costs, there is an incentive to build up inventories—cynically referred to as "just-in-case" inventory management—since these costs will be reimbursed and a fee paid on them. This is of course exactly the opposite of the increasingly common commercial practice of "just-in-time" inventory management, which minimizes the cost of carrying the inventory and thus minimizes total costs.

Another counter-commercial example occurs when a government contractor has the choice of putting on a lower-priced or an expensive worker. As long as the costs are justified, higher-priced workers will be utilized. Even the profit incentives operate in this perverse fashion, since a typical defense contract pays a percentage profit on the total costs incurred. If it is a development contract, then it is usually on current costs (termed a "cost-plus-fee" contract). If it is a fixed-price production contract, then the allowable negotiated profit is a percentage of last year's costs (each contract is renegotiated annually), and the price for the following year will be based on the costs for the prior year. Thus the contractor and the government tend to focus their attention on two issues: first, are all the costs justifiable?; and second, is the profit reasonable? Interestingly, a survey of government contracting officers indicated that they believed that their primary focus was supposed to be to reduce the profit on defense contracts.[17] Their response indicates that their attention was primarily devoted to the 10 percent, or less, of the costs that make up the profit on a typical defense contract. Then they would validate the justifiability of the other 90 percent of the costs—rather than working with the contractor on trying to minimize the 90 percent. Obviously, the government would be far better off if the 90 percent could be significantly reduced—even if it meant an increase in the profit being realized.

One of the greatest fallacies in the public's perception of defense contracting is that the high costs of defense goods are caused by companies making huge profits. The reality is that defense contractors make a significantly lower profit than even a formally regulated industry. Rather, weapon systems are expensive because the costs of designing, building, and supporting each weapon system are far higher than they would have to be were commercial practices utilized.

The result of the distinct difference between the commercial and defense cost accounting systems is that if a commercial firm wanted to do defense business, it would have to set up two sets of books. Intel, a world-class semiconductor supplier, tried to modify its accounting system to make it acceptable to the DoD. After spending over $2 million on this effort, the company gave up.[18]

The interesting anomaly in the defense cost accounting method is that it is a totally different system than the government uses for assuring that American industry pays its taxes to the IRS properly; or that it requires industry to use in accounting to the Securities and Exchange Commission. For both the IRS and the SEC the government does not even use government people to certify the cost data. Rather, they use independent outside auditors (certified public accountants). Only in the case of defense contracting has the government felt that additional reporting, auditing, and oversight were required. In fact, each time there is a defense costs scandal, oversight is increased. Clearly, the cost of doing this greatly exceeds the cost savings that result, but that is not the issue. The Congress is simply reacting to the public outcry for defense procurement reform.

As might be expected, there is an enormous amount of overlap and redundancy in defense-related oversight, with different people coming to check on such issues as small business contracting, equal-opportunity employment, contract compliance, accounting practices, etc. Some make periodic visits to defense plants, others are full-time residents within the plant. In addition, there are at least an equal number—and usually a ratio of two to one[19]—of company personnel who supply data to the government personnel. One case study of a company that performed both military and civilian contracts on similar products concluded that the military division of the company had higher product costs because the number of administrative personnel required in the military division was eight times higher, per dollar of sales, and twice as high, as a percentage of total personnel, than in the commercial division.[20]

It must be emphasized that this extensive oversight includes government officials who are not from the DoD. On the B-2 bomber program, in addition to the DoD's 183 full-time plant representatives at the prime contractor's (Northrop) facility, there were on-site GAO representatives in the plant from 1990 to 1993, performing a variety of investigations at congressional request; between 1981 and 1990, Northrop had close to 150 visits from senators and representatives. In addition, state and local agencies checked on everything at Northrop from air quality to equal employment and worker safety.[21]

All of this financial reporting, auditing, and oversight was to assure that Northrop's costs were fully justified and accounted for. None of it was to reduce the basic costs of the B-2 bomber program.

To address the desire for civil/military integration and the need to achieve far lower costs in weapon systems, the DoD will have to move eventually to a market- and value-based contracting and pricing system. And it will have to do so in a way that public trust is not forsaken (we will return to this issue in detail in the next chapter). At this point, however, it should be noted that one technique frequently recommended is to make greater use of independent accounting firms to perform the auditing functions. As world-class companies are moving more and more toward a practice known as activities-based costing, in which they have high visibility into each of the activities associated with their direct and indirect costs, this becomes a much more practical solution. As the DoD becomes more concerned with reducing costs, defense firms will also move toward activities-based cost systems. Thus all data would be available for independent auditing by accounting firms. Overall there are ways to address the public trust issue—once the government is committed philosophically to a change from its current cost-based contracting approach to a price-based contracting system.

Military Specifications and Standards

The phrase "military specifications and standards" describes the 32,000 documents in the DoD Index of Specifications and Standards that are uniquely military.[22] The specs describe the item that is needed and how it is to be incorporated into a larger system, that is, its form, fit, and function. They ensure, for example, that the department does not procure fifteen different variations of the same part that are not interchangeable or supportable. Uniquely military specifications and standards, however, create a barrier to commercial procurement when they:

• describe items which are essentially nonmilitary in nature: toothpicks, dog muzzles, money bags, mustard, etc.;
• require products or processes that are obsolete;
• detail process ("how to do it") rather than performance ("what is needed") requirements;
• are misapplied or inflexibly applied,
• are automatically imposed on subcontractors, even when they may be applicable only to the prime contractor; and
• differ unnecessarily from common commercial practices and standards.

Unfortunately, these abuses are increasingly prevalent, as independent reviews (including by the GAO) frequently point out.[23] Further, it has been found that defense procurements often reference other, subsidiary documents—many of which are out of print. This practice has been highlighted by the GAO as a particularly abusive practice, and attempts have been made to avoid it by requiring that only primary documents be utilized in defense contracts.

Most defense contractors simply accept military specifications and standards as part of the cost of doing business. These companies have experts who specialize in compliance, and their engineering designs and factories are set up to conform to them. Although these many "conditions" result in higher costs, they also have had a positive historic result associated with them. Many commercial industries, lacking any other standardized product norms, have come to rely heavily on military documents in the design and construction of their own products. One 1982 aerospace report indicated that about 5,000 military specifications and standards are regularly used in the construction of commercial airliners. This is representative of the technology transfer that has historically taken place in the aircraft industry from military to commercial products.

When the U.S. defense sector was the world leader in technology, it was quite common for the DoD to establish the standards that would then be transferred to the commercial world. However, this is frequently no longer the case. The military-specified mobile electric power unit that the DoD uses is basically a twenty-five-year old design. It is less efficient and more polluting and has lower reliability than current commercial units. There is no commercial supplier for such outdated equipment, so the DoD pays dearly to have a specially built, obsolete system. Literally thousands of other examples of such obsolete products and/or processes could be cited. In fact, the U.S. Air Force recently performed an analysis of the age distribution of the documents in the Index and found that some 45 percent were more than five years old and 29 percent were over seven. They concluded that the DoD has not been reviewing documents in a timely manner to determine if they reflect current technology.[24]

In the long run, a dual-use manufacturing base cannot be achieved if DoD continues to define design details and manufacturing procedures, rather than performance, in its specifications and standards. The basic assumption has to be that commercial specs and standards are the accepted norm. The DoD would still be able to ensure that performance targets are being met through a variety of means, including:

• acceptance of third-party (e.g., Underwriter's Laboratory) certifications;
• use of "qualified manufacturer's" certifications, that is, where the production process of a given plant has been approved;
• use of nongovernmental standards—either domestic commercial or, preferably, international standards;
• use of DoD's personnel to assess a contractor's in-house standard to ascertain whether it meets the system's requirements; and

• use of acceptance testing, for example, accept delivered goods only after performance tests have been made.

Each of these approaches offers a viable means for ensuring quality without requiring a defense-unique design, manufacturing, or management procedure.

An easy place to start would be by buying off-the-shelf commercial items—ketchup bottles, gloves, dog dishes, and other items for which the Defense Department receives annual ridicule from both Congress and the press. In fact, the DoD has developed a streamlined contracting format for commercial items procurement (known as DFARS 211) that prohibits the use of military-unique specifications on such procurements. The problem of course is that it is not often applied. For items that are not readily available commercially, the United States might emulate the approach of Germany and the United Kingdom. Both governments have entered into formal agreements with standards-setting bodies in the private sector to work together in preparing standards acceptable to all government agencies as well as to commercial business.[25]

As initial moves in the right direction, in 1994 the U.S. government took two significant actions to address the military specifications and standards barriers. First, the Secretary of Defense directed that all future DoD programs should shift to the use of commercial specifications and standards whenever possible. Second, the Congress passed a procurement reform bill aimed at easing the problems of the government in buying commercial items. The impacts of these actions remain to be seen; however, they must certainly be applauded.

Procurement Practices

Martin Marietta made two proposals for launching a communications satellite: one to a private sector firm to launch an Intelsat, and one to the U.S. government to launch a Geosat. The proposal to the private sector cost Martin Marietta $1,000 to prepare and was ten pages long. The proposal to the government cost $1,000,000 and was 10,000 pages long.[26] This is but one of the many horror stories that point out the difficulty of doing business with the Department of Defense. Similarly troubling is the time period required by the government to run one of its procurements.

A small government procurement averages nine to twelve months (commercial procurements average 2); complex larger contracts typically take eighteen to thirty-six months (commercial, five to six months).

Added to this long procurement cycle is the usual three- to six-month delay while one or more of the losers of the defense contract protests the award; and far more if, as often happens, it has to be recompeted. In the commercial world, if a firm loses a competition its only recourse is in the courts—and then only if an illegal action took place. In defense procurements, beside the courts, a contractor can protest to either the GAO or the General Services Board of Contract Appeals. In 1984, the Competition in Contracting Act explicitly encouraged losing bidders to protest, allegedly in the interest of greater fairness. The result was that between 1984 and 1991 there was a 63 percent increase in grievances filed (2071 to 3372). Similarly, in the area of large software-intensive systems (where the "Brooks Act" applies, and where protests are also encouraged), in recent years more than 90 percent of the contract awards have been protested, and about 40 percent of the procurements have had to be recompeted. In addition, under the "Equal Access to Justice Act" the government provides payments to cover the protesting firm's costs. These laws are apparently achieving their desired objective—however, at the expense of efficiency and effectiveness in defense procurements.

The complexity of the government contracting world (see table 8.1 for some examples) does not stop with the Department of Defense. It is compounded by differences within the DoD itself. For example, the GAO found that to sell the same commercial oscilloscopes to the army, navy, and air force required a supplier to deal with 205 different contract clauses in the three sets of contracts; and there was only 12 percent overlap among them. Needless to say, this makes good business for defense contract lawyers, but it is hard to imagine how it can do anything but significantly raise the cost of the items being delivered.

The only way to correct this problem is for the requirements that are covered in normal commercial business within the United States to be applied to defense business as well. The government must move toward using the Uniform Commercial Code for government business in the same way that it is used for commercial business. When this is done, the government becomes simply another buyer of high-quality goods and services from the best competitive sources available.

Table 8.1
Some special procurement requirements

- Truth In Negotiation Act [Requires Cost Data]; 10 USC 2306a
- Examination of Records by the Comptroller General; 10 USC 2313 (b)
- Cost Accounting Standards [Rule Compliance]; 41 USC 422
- Small Business and Small Disadvantaged Business Subcontracting Plan and DoD Clause Supplement; 15 USC 637(d) 4-(6)
- Liquidated Damages—Small Business Subcontracting Plan [Assessment of Damages]; 15 USC 637(d) (4) (f), (8)
- Utilization of Labor Surplus Area Concerns; 15 USC 644(d)-(f)
- Labor Surplus Area Subcontracting Program; 15 USC 644(d)-(f)
- Buy American Act Balance of Payments Program Certificates; Buy American Act and Balance of Payments Program; 42 USC 10a-d, 10b-1
- Limitations on Use of Appropriated Funds for DoD Procurement of Foreign-Made Items; 10 USC 2506
- Buy American Act—Trade Agreement Act—Balance of Payments Certificate and Trade Agreement Act; 19 USC 2501 eq seq
- Annual DoD Appropriation Act; Preference for Certain Domestic Commodities [e.g., food, clothing, wool, tents, specialty metals]; PL 101-511
- Annual DoD Appropriations Act; Preference for Domestic Hand or Measuring Tools; PL 97-377
- Restriction on Acquisition of Valves and Machine Tools; 10 USC 2507(d)
- Restrictions on Acquisition of Foreign Anchor and Mooring Chain; Annual DoD Appropriations Acts since FY 1988
- Restriction and Acquisition of Polyacrylonitrile (PAN) Based Carbon Fiber; PL 100-202 Sec. 8088
- Restriction of Acquisition of Carbonyl Iron Powders; 10 USC 2507(e)
- Restriction of Acquisition of Night Vision Image Intensifier Tubes and Devices; PL 101-165 and subsequent appropriations acts
- Required Sources for Jewel Bearings and Related Items; PL 90-496 and subsequent appropriation acts
- Representation of Extent of Transportation by Sea [Requires U.S. flag vessel]; 10 USC 2631
- Foreign Source Restrictions [many specific items]; DFARS 252.225-7025
- Walsh-Healey Public Contracts Act Representation; 41 USC 31-45
- Drug-Free Workplace; 41 USC 701 Note
- Utilization of Women-Owned Small Business; E.O. 12138
- Certification of Non-Segregated Facilities; E.O. 11246
- Pre-Award On-Site Equal Opportunity Compliance Review; E.O. 11246
- Affirmative Action Compliance; E.O. 11246
- Equal Opportunity Compliance; E.O. 11246
- Equal Opportunity Pre-award Clearance for Subcontracts; E.O. 11246
- Affirmative Action for Special Disabled and Vietnam Veterans and Employments Reports on Special Disabled and Vietnam Era Veterans; E.O. 11738
- Affirmative Action for Handicapped Workers; 29 USC 793

This shift requires a significant change in the government's view of the purpose of its procurement system. Today the objective is perfection— including absolute fairness and the prevention of any mistakes. It is an attempt to create rules that would prevent every possible instance of fraud or abuse. What is totally missing is any consideration of efficiency.

In 1993, Vice President Al Gore's task force on "reinventing government" to achieve greater effectiveness at lower costs had as its first procurement recommendation that government acquisition policy should "convert the 1,600 pages of the Federal Acquisition Regulations from a set of rigid rules to a set of guiding principles." [27] This would follow the practice of the Uniform Commercial Code, which begins each section with a simple statement of policy and contains a great deal of explanation, guidance, etc.

Business Practices

While the four major barriers to achieving integration of defense and civilian products and plants are clearly the absence of cost as a military requirement, cost-based contracting, military specifications and standards, and unique procurement practices, several other items have also been identified as significant deterrents. We will briefly consider them.

Budget Process   Multiyear procurement commitments enable manufacturers to plan production and manpower needs, and to purchase parts and material in advance, often benefitting from volume discounts. The U.S. government, however, has a one-year defense budget process. America is the only nation in the world that does its fiscal planning on a one-year basis; all other countries have a rolling multiyear budget process in which they annually debate the fifth or sixth year of their fiscal plan and then release the first year's dollars in that year's budget. Suppliers in their defense industries have a long-term forecast as to what the dollars will likely be and can plan accordingly. The only place this has been done in the U.S. Defense Department has been with the Polaris/Poseidon/Trident Ballistic Missile Program in the navy. Here, the program office makes a commitment to its suppliers for at least a three-year budget period. The program has continuously received praise from the Congress, the GAO, and others who observe the benefits of this budget stability. The long-term answer is for the entire U.S. government to move to a rolling multiyear budget process as well.[28] In the shorter term, however, the DoD should move in this direction.

Obviously there is some risk to the government in making a multiyear commitment, since a program could be terminated and some added costs may have been incurred—such as the extra parts bought for future systems that will now not be procured. Although this requires that the termination liability costs be covered, it is extremely unlikely that all programs would be cancelled at the same time in any given year. Thus it is not necessary for all program termination liabilities to be annually budgeted—as unfortunately has been the decision of the DoD controller in recent years—rather, it can be done on an actuarial basis (as with other insurance).

In the 1980s, the Congress passed a law (referred to as "Enterprise Programs") that allows the Department of Defense to budget its selected weapons programs from one major milestone to another (i.e., fully funding a weapon's multiyear development)—in effect, allowing multiyear budgeting on those designated programs. The DoD, however, has chosen not to do this because it takes away their budgeting flexibility. The choice is between efficiently managing a small number of programs (by keeping their funding stable) or inefficiently running a larger number of programs and maintaining the flexibility to change them annually—as has traditionally been the case. The Defense Department blames the Congress for making innumerable program changes during the annual budget process, and in fact it does change about 50 percent of the line items in any given budget. The DoD, however, tends to change almost all of them; so both sides are to blame. The corrective action is clearly to move toward multiyear contracting and a rolling multiyear budget to achieve the efficiency that comes from program stability.

Incremental Acquisition   A second defense-unique business practice that deters efficiency is the insistence on an incremental acquisition process. Although commercial operations have moved increasingly toward a development and production process that is fully integrated (engineering, manufacturing, and support functions), every point in the weapons development cycle is isolated and subject to intensive review and critique. The assumption in the defense world is that you have to constantly prove you should go on to the next stage; in the commercial world, it is assumed that once you have decided to do something, you will continue unless you get into trouble, and you will do it as rapidly as possible.

This philosophic difference does not imply that the commercial world does not have any visibility or control over its programs—to the contrary, it has even more. What it does mean, however, is that they are schedule-driven; they do not stop for six or nine months—as the Defense Department does—for major decisions during a program's development. World-class firms are being competitively driven to shorter and shorter cycles. The same change has to happen in defense.

Test and Evaluation   The testing and evaluation of weapon systems in the defense procurement process is done for entirely different reasons than in the commercial world. In the commercial world, the reason for testing and evaluating a new item is to determine where it will not work and to continuously improve it. One tests equipment outside of its boundaries, that is, to intentionally create failures, in order to learn from them. Again, the assumption is that product development will go ahead unless major problems are found. Thus testing and evaluation is primarily for the purpose of making the best possible product, and making it as robust as possible, that is, insensitive to variations in the manufacturing process or even to misuse and abuse by users. By contrast, testing and evaluation in the Department of Defense has tended to be a final exam, or an audit, to determine if a product works.[29] Tests are not seen as a critical element in enhancing the development process; tests therefore are designed not to fail. In this way very little is learned through the testing and evaluation process; the assumption is that the product will work and it usually does. Under these conditions, the less testing the better—preferably none at all. This rather perverse use of testing causes huge cost and time increases on the defense side, since tests are postponed until the final exam and flaws are found late rather than early. It is another major barrier to integration of commercial and military operations.

Data Rights The fourth business practice deterrent to integration relates to the DoD's desire to get rights to all proprietary data from its suppliers so that it can, if it chooses, use the drawings to create future competitors. Since the supplying of proprietary data is totally contrary to commercial business practices, many companies simply refuse to do defense business. Assuming that the DoD eventually is forced to use more and more commercial suppliers, it will automatically have more sources of comparable goods—not identical, but performing the same function. Thus this issue of government reprocurement rights should become much less critical. In addition, it seems that any firm doing business with the government would certainly be willing to give it the rights to any product that it stopped producing, so that the DoD could have the drawings and could have someone reproduce the item if necessary. Similarly, a firm would certainly be willing to sell the rights to the DoD, for any use, if they could receive a sufficiently high price—but this should not be necessary very often.

Logistics Support

The last of the major deterrents to civil/military integration, and the one most frequently raised by military personnel, is that of the DoD's valid need to assure logistic support of its equipment—at all times and in all places. The traditional DoD model of logistics support has been one of transferring responsibility for the products from industry to the government after delivery, then having organic support supplied at all levels of equipment maintenance, overhaul, repair, and upgrade. Although other countries send their products back to the industrial factory, the United States has its own depots. Although others call the manufacturer for spare parts, the DoD has a huge system of warehousing and supply of spare parts. And, although the DoD does use contractors for initial maintenance of its equipment until the government is fully up to speed, the basic model of the DoD is do-it-yourself.

This DoD approach is no longer justifiable since today's equipment is extremely reliable—for example, modern electronics. In fact, the commercial maintenance approach is often simply to throw it out because it is so unlikely to fail that when and if it does, labor costs make it much more expensive to repair than to replace it. In addition, defense logistics have changed since the time of high-intensity long wars, when defense industry factories were required to turn out high volumes of equipment. Then, they could not be distracted by maintenance or repair work on existing equipment, and thus the government depots were justified. Today very few people envision high-intensity long-duration conflicts, and there is ample excess industrial capacity to handle maintenance, repair, and overhaul in defense and/or commercial industry facilities.

Finally, historically most U.S. companies were domestically based, and their markets were here as well, so that the DoD's requirement for worldwide support could not easily be handled by the typical U.S. contractor. Today most successful firms operate on a worldwide basis. They have customers all over the world and can fly parts and repair personnel to them immediately in response to a phone call or a fax.

Boeing promises spare parts delivery of any commercial aircraft part, anywhere in the world, within twenty-four hours. Other suppliers provide similar support. The U.S. Army stocks numerous parts made by Caterpillar; average government supply system delivery time for those parts, when a base runs out, ranges from twenty-one to thirty-six days for bases within the continental United States to fifty to sixty-eight days for bases overseas. Caterpillar itself resupplies commercial dealers carrying those same parts in more than one hundred countries; its delivery times range from one to two days within the continental United States to two to four days for remote overseas destinations.[30] And if delivery time exceeds four days, they pay for the part.

When it comes to worldwide distribution needs, the military is now a bit player. For example, even during Operation Desert Shield, daily requisitions—measured with a three-day moving average—peaked at 35,000. By comparison, United Parcel Service averages 11.5 million orders per day.[31]

Nonetheless, when the argument for civil/military integration is made and the DoD is urged to use far more commercial equipment, you still hear arguments such as "you can't count on the contractors being there when you need them"; and "you can't direct them to go there." This is in spite of the fact that during both the Vietnam War and Desert Storm, contractors were there, maintaining the equipment and supplying a significant share of the support. In fact, 4,500 people from over thirty companies were present in the Persian Gulf during the Desert Storm conflict.[32] Interestingly, many of the industrial maintenance people involved in this support work were former military maintenance personnel who had gone to work for the defense companies and had been trained, by their firms, on the new equipment. They were required in the conflict countries because of their skills and knowledge on this advanced equipment. Clearly, if there is a concern on the DoD's part about support to any operation, it could be written into the supplier's contract, as is the case in many commercial contracts written today. In fact, because of the great uncertainty as to where and when such a need will occur, one can prearrange the contract terms and conditions on a "reimbursement for labor time and materials expended" basis, and not even have to pay the standby costs, if they are not required. Thus, as in most other cases, the government can be a self-insurer.

The other common logistics argument heard from the military is that "we keep our equipment for twenty years or more and commercial users don't; therefore, the company won't be around when we need them, and they certainly won't be producing the same spare parts that we need for our equipment." Again, this concern can easily be addressed. To begin with, DoD is not the only one to keep its equipment for a long time. Commercial airlines have kept their aircraft flying for more than twenty years, and they keep upgrading them over time, as required. Warranties are possible; and/or it can be a condition of the contract that a company will provide such long-term support. This is simply an argument for dealing with reliable high-quality companies, not necessarily the lowest bidder.

In addition, new products today are developed with computer-aided design and manufacturing, so that the data for any part is now safely stored away. If a part is needed for equipment no longer in production, it can be called up from the computer and produced in a relatively short time. Although this has certain constraints, for example, in terms of the availability of the manufacturing tools, it is clearly the trend for the future; and with flexible manufacturing it represents a very strong option for future logistics support. In fact, the navy is building a special facility in which it will be able to manufacture equipment that is out of production, simply by using the digital drawings—even if the original manufacturer is no longer in existence.

The important thing in all of these long-term maintenance requirements is that the DoD shift to the use of functional specifications—in terms of the form, fit, and function of an item, rather than its detailed design. When this is done, replacement becomes relatively easy.

In reviewing the various barriers to integration it seems clear that all have a valid historic basis. Together, they form a unique defense culture, but one that is no longer affordable—or needed—in today's world. Removing these barriers means changing from a system based on regulations to one based on market forces. The change not only makes sense; it is the American way. But to achieve it will be extremely difficult.

9

A Three-Part Transformation Strategy

Ultimately the transformation of the defense industrial base rests on the day-to-day decisions made by individual industrial—and, particularly, plant—managers. The closer they come to emulating the lessons learned from successful conversion efforts (and avoiding those of the unsuccessful efforts), the better their own chances. The overall industrial transformation, however, can be greatly facilitated—and accelerated—through governmental action. Specifically, the largely integrated civil/military industrial structure that is needed for the twenty-first century can be brought about through a three-part transformation strategy: (1) the government must remove many of the current barriers and provide guidelines and incentives for industry to achieve the desired objectives; (2) the government must assure industrial technological leadership in critical areas by encouraging the rapid application of state-of-the-art product and manufacturing technologies; and (3) there must be greater human resource development at all levels of the work force.

Legislative, regulatory, and government acquisition practice changes—as well as investments in advanced technology and skilled workers—form the foundation of this strategy; to be successful, however, the thrust for the needed reforms must be industry-led.

Numerous analyses have shown[1] that the government's highest rate of return for the benefit of its citizens comes from three main activities: first, from R & D on new products and processes (estimated at 15 to 25 percent); second, through investment in labor skills (estimated to be at least 15 percent); and third, from capital investments in public infrastructure (estimated at approximately 12 percent). Since many other interests cry out for government funds, it is up to the public—and specifically to industry, because it has the most to gain—to convince the nation's elected and appointed officials to utilize our tax dollars where they will have the greatest payoff in the long run.

National macroeconomic and microeconomic policies are not currently compatible with this strategy: the huge debt burden must be removed; tax credits must be provided for long-term R & D and productivity-enhancing capital investments; low-cost financing must be available for such investments; and there must be a consistent trade policy. Within the defense industry, the transformation requires a cultural change in the way in which business is done in both government and industry. The single element most needed to bring about this fundamental change is strong and sustained leadership. As has been repeatedly demonstrated,[2] without such leadership success is highly unlikely.

It has also been shown that such cultural changes take years to achieve. Perhaps three to five years will be required for the initial transformation, and up to ten for full implementation. It simply compounds the difficulty of making such a change to attempt it in a democratic society in which the political officials who must provide the leadership typically stay in their positions an average of only two and a half years. New leaders often come in with their own agenda, and the government swings back and forth, without a long-term, consistent, and sustained direction. Yet the evidence is very clear that a cultural change requires a great deal of time and attention by senior management and a coherent vision and strategy for its successful implementation. It is up to the leaders to align and motivate the millions of people in the overall military-industrial complex if successful change is to be achieved.

Finally, the desired change must be supported by the Congress. Here again, there must be sustained leadership and it must be consistent with that of the executive branch. This is not a political issue, but rather a recognition that the many special interests that have successfully lobbied for much of the recent legislation are not operating in the best interests of the United States. For example, a vibrant American economy—stimulated by allowing free market forces to operate effectively in an integrated (civil/military) industrial structure—is far better for small businesses than special interest restrictions on defense procurements that force these firms to operate exclusively in a very unique and shrinking defense marketplace.

Governmental leadership can utilize a wide variety of market adjustment tools and apply them in a coordinated fashion.[3] Examples include the use of industrial consortia, perhaps partially funded by the government; the sponsorship of multiple firms, each working on a critical area of advanced technology, on related component and subsystem research projects; partially subsidized capital investments; financing incentives (targeted tax policies, cash payments, differentiated profit policies, loan guarantees); direct government procurement (to get a new industry started, or to create a second source); protectionism (for an infant industry, and to create initial domestic competition); and other trade policies.

The best means of achieving the desired industrial structures, however, is through the major contract awards made on each weapon system. Each large award dramatically alters the structure of the defense industry. This does not mean arbitrarily picking firm A over firm B. Rather, it means saying, "The DoD needs to have three firms in this sector," and "We want the engineering and manufacturing in critical areas to be done domestically, and we want the firms to be operating in both the civil and military sectors in the same plants." It also means applying the same techniques to the lower tiers of the defense industry; the degree of attention the DoD pays to tanks, aircraft, and strategic missiles must also be given to unique machine tools, supermaterials, specialized software, and certain electronic components. The results of this strategy will assure such desired elements as increased R & D and capital investments, worker training and development, adequate competition, and dual-use operations—at both the prime contractor and lower-tier levels.

The DoD must designate an organization (within the office of the secretary of defense) to be responsible for the implementation of such a defense industrial strategy and then give that organization authority for direct inputs into the major resource and weapon system decisions.[4] The selected group will have to have adequate insight into the health, innovativeness, and responsiveness of the defense industry—on a sector-by-sector basis—in order to determine the actions needed to support or enhance market forces, especially during periods of change. Again, it must be emphasized that the approach suggested here is not a highly activist industrial strategy, nor is it one that recommends a U.S. MITI, a single organization that coordinates overall U.S. industrial strategy. Rather, the idea is to have a defense-oriented organization geared to those segments of the economy that serve defense—either exclusively or in a dual-use role—and on which the nation's security depends. The focus would not be on individual firms but on the structure of crucial segments of the industry and their characteristics.

In the next three chapters we will deal in considerable detail with each of the major elements of the proposed three-part strategy, that is, technological leadership (chapter 10), human resource development (chapter 11), and the removal of barriers and the creation of incentives for moving toward an integrated civil/military industrial base (chapter 12). Before doing so, however, it is essential that two key issues be addressed, since they are the dominant constraints to implementation. The first is the need to replace defense-unique laws and regulations with commercial market forces and still maintain public trust. The second is the need to develop adequate public confidence that the defense transformation will be worth the effort, that is, that the result will be dramatic gains for both the nation's security and its economic growth.

Public Trust

When the benefits of moving the defense weapons acquisition process toward a market-based approach were recently discussed with a senior congressional staff member, the individual acknowledged that the logic of the case was very clear, as was the potential for achieving billions of dollars of savings. However, he went on to say, "It wouldn't work." When asked why, he responded, "The excessive regulation is required because of contractor greed." [5] There is a widespread perception that the extensive regulation over the defense industry is required to assure that the public trust is protected when government funds are involved.

Given that free-market capitalism is the basis of America's political and economic system, this lack of confidence in market forces may seem surprising. There is, however, a long American history of defense industry abuses going back to revolutionary times. It does little good to argue that these were scattered and isolated incidents or that similar abuses occur in the commercial sector. The reality is that this public perception exists, and it must be directly addressed if the required defense industrial transformation is to take place.

Five elements seem to dominate the public's concern with the government procurement system:

- Are the items procured necessary?
- Did the government receive a fair price?
- Did the items delivered meet expectations?
- Is there fairness and equal access to the process?
- Is there fraud or abuse?

These concerns are all valid. The present system of increasing regulation and oversight has not resolved them; some would argue that it has made them worse. For example, the current weapons acquisition system encourages the defense contractors to "gold plate" systems with unnecessary additions to increase weapons' costs, since profits are essentially granted as a percentage of costs. The current system also discourages the supplier from investing in more efficient production processes, since that would lower his costs and thus his long-term profit.

Today government auditors, accountants, lawyers, and other overseers constantly do battle with an equally large (or larger) number of suppliers. The result is a constant flow of charges and countercharges about false claims, unallowable costs, pricing deficiencies, and a host of other controversies. The current system, then, does not seem to satisfy many people; that is why there is an annual cry—from both the legislative and executive branches—for "defense procurement reform."

There are basically only two broad choices for satisfying the public trust: the first is that of the unsatisfactory system of more and more regulation and oversight. The second is to allow the "invisible hand" of the free market to assure that the desired objectives of the procurement system are being met. Although the free-market approach is clearly the American way, the regulatory approach is easier to implement. It has been the option of choice for generations of executive and legislative branch leaders—in spite of their almost daily exhortations for "increased competition" and "use of the free market."

If one were to choose to move away from the cost-based regulatory approach toward an acquisition system based on competitive market forces, there would still be tools available to the government to protect the public trust. In fact, many believe that these would do a far better job of satisfying the public's concerns. The most obvious tool available is greater use of competition, in a wide variety of forms. The market of potential suppliers could be greatly widened to include commercial suppliers, and there could be expanded forms of competition to include not only firms bidding against each other to a common performance specification (instead of the current detailed design specification), but also greater use of common form, fit, and function specifications. This is the technique that commercial airlines utilize in order to have interchangeability of products and to upgrade their current subsystems as technology evolves.

Competition among firms that provide items to satisfy the same needs is the most common form of competition in the commercial world. These products are not identical, but they perform the same functions, and they can be evaluated on their total value, in competition with each other. Using the case of destroying an enemy command center, for example, a manned penetrating bomber, a stand-off aircraft launching missiles to the target, and a ground-based ballistic missile going against the designated target all could perform the same function. Since each of these has a cost and a known level of effectiveness, they can be compared against each other to establish an appropriate value for doing that job.

Second, the government can be assured of getting a fair price for the items that it buys by doing formal market surveys of similar products. Market research "by analogy" has been refined to quite a sophisticated level in the commercial world and could help the DoD avoid paying $500 for a $12 hammer.

Another important commercial practice is to base part of the selection of suppliers on the basis of their prior record in meeting cost, schedule, and performance expectations. This would require that the government change its buying practices to emphasize past performance rather than future promises. New entrants to a market in the commercial world (with no past performance to measure) obtain venture capital to develop a new product and then to test-market it. In the case of the government, the new supplier would have to supply "bid samples" for the government to evaluate as part of its source-selection process. For small and disadvantaged businesses, there is even the possibility of receiving special government loans. Thus there would still be access to the market for new entrants, while suppliers who provided poor products in the past would be penalized. In this way there would be incentives for government suppliers to achieve high performance; in the current system it is sufficient simply to do an adequate job, while placing most management attention and investment resources on bidding for the next procurement.

In defense procurement and increasingly in the commercial world, firms are linking their futures to a single preferred supplier. To assure they are getting a fair price, they use a variety of techniques. The most obvious is an independent market and cost analysis. In addition, since the supplier's original contract was won competitively, and future prices and performance were projected, the buyer can simply monitor the sole producer over time. As long as performance continuously improves and the price of each new procurement continuously falls, the buyer is happy. Finally, there are always other suppliers offering newer items to do the same job; and the buyer is continuously monitoring the domestic and foreign market to assure that he is getting the best value for his money. These techniques can be applied in the defense world.

Many have suggested that the government is not strict enough on poor performance by defense contractors, and that contractors that misled the government, fail to live up to appropriate ethical standards, demonstrate a lack of business integrity and honesty, or willfully fail to perform on a government contract should receive a suspension, and perhaps even a debarment, for a considerable period of time. This policy of exclusion from DoD business for companies found guilty of violating commercial-like procurement practices might be very helpful in assuring public trust. It would also give the defense industry added incentives to achieve improved performance at lower costs. Companies would then do far more self-policing and self-regulating, while much of the external regulation and oversight could be removed.[6]

Finally, and most important, there are a wide range of legal and regulatory controls, oversights, and prohibitions that govern the normal conduct of commercial business in the United States. These include provisions covering criminal actions (bribery, fraud); socioeconomic requirements (minority hiring, antidiscrimination); commercial accounting and auditing standards and practices; and of course the Uniform Commercial Code for buying practices.

Clearly, the use of free-market forces would not totally eliminate improper actions. It does not in the commercial world. As a panel of outside procurement experts[7] stated, however, it would be "... an acceptable risk." They went on to say that "Proper management of this risk will require better training of contracting and requirements personnel in market research and price analysis techniques, as well as meaningful, thoughtful, and innovative regulatory implementation."

The most difficult challenge for any oversight system is to assure the first measure of public trust, that is, that the items procured are necessary. Rarely can the public judge whether a new bomber or the extra radar for that bomber is needed, or whether the power out of that radar is excessively specified ("gold plated"). And yet in this area, the current oversight system does not work well—if it works at all. The only way that it can be changed is through internal DoD changes—in this case, with the military requirements process becoming far more concerned about future weapons' costs. The procurement approach proposed here, which explicitly forces the system to evaluate alternative ways to do the job by having functional competitions between different approaches, will greatly minimize the current abuses.

Within this category of "unnecessary procurement" also lies the common practice of congressional pork barreling. This is the situation, for example, when a member of Congress extends the life of a program—often at the cost of hundreds of millions or even billions of dollars—when the DoD does not request it. Or, when a member of Congress initiates a so-called R & D program for a library in his or her district; or ... the list goes on and on and could fill a book of its own. Such annual congressional initiatives have a long history: They have been growing in frequency and magnitude as a result of the lessening of tensions since the end of the cold war and the declining defense budget's impact on local employment. For obvious reasons, this subject gets little congressional attention; and most members of Congress are reluctant to point the finger at their colleagues when they are often doing the same thing themselves. What is surprising is that it gets very little press attention. Perhaps this is because the press and public in any given district or state do not see the award of a contract in their area as an abuse. Rather, they see it as a benefit, and therefore it is presented in the local press in a very positive light. The national press tends to have very little interest in it because most people just assume "that's the way Congress does business" and further that it doesn't affect them. In fact, they expect the same treatment from their congressional representatives. As a result, congressional pork barreling is done each year as a regular part of the budget cycle. Putting a spotlight on its costs, however, may help to control it.

Moving to the second of the public trust issues—the achievement of a "fair price to the government"—this is best gauged by market assessments. It becomes more difficult as one moves from hammers to bombers; and it requires that government improve its ability to use price-based contracting. Yet this is done every day by sophisticated industrial firms in their purchasing activities.

A related issue is to make sure that the delivered price is the same as had been expected. The government procurement system has a long history of cost overruns. As noted, these overruns are frequently much larger in nondefense government business than they are in the defense world—for example, the overruns on construction of the Hart Senate Office Building and the Rayburn House Office Building. Nonetheless, this is an important area of public trust because if the public does not have confidence that the supplier will deliver at the price it planned on, it will clamor for more oversight and regulation. By shifting to a market-based system, where prices are based on the market and the value of an item, there should be far less tendency toward the defense industry and DoD practice of "buying in." This undesirable practice is where a contractor bids an initial low estimate to get the contract, and/or a military service establishes an initial low budget to assure that the program fits into the overall DoD budget; and then one or both go back later and explain (rationalize) why there were sufficient changes to the program to cause the cost to rise. In an environment in which the initial prices are based on value to the buyer, and in which a supplier's next award will be based on performance in prior contracts, many of the perverse incentives that now exist in defense procurement will be eliminated.

In addition, there has always been a concern that industry does not make an excessive profit on government business. This is perhaps the most interesting contrast between the commercial and defense worlds. In the former, the buyer is not interested in how much profit the supplier made as long as the buyer received a fair price. In the defense world, the buyer (the government) insists that the company's profit be kept very low. The proposed focus on price versus the current focus on cost (and profit as a percentage of cost) will hopefully shift the emphasis so that the government becomes a world-class buyer of world-class products and still pays a fair price.

The third element of public trust is that items procured meet their expectations. This gets to the critical question of specifying a weapon system's performance. Again, this is extremely difficult for the public or the Congress to assess. Historically, if an item had a reasonably good quality record, that was good enough. However, we have learned (particularly from the Japanese) that "good enough" should not be acceptable. Focusing on quality is becoming an increasingly common practice in the commercial world and should be in defense as well. In fact, it should be as important as a product's cost. If weapons show the same high reliability that we expect from commercial items, that should greatly increase the public's confidence in the defense acquisition system.

A related issue concerns the test and evaluation of weapon systems, where the purpose of the test should be to increase performance—and, thus, to encourage testing until failure to improve reliability. The function of testing should not be viewed as a pass/fail final exam.

The fourth element of public trust is that of fairness and equal access to the process. Sometimes equity conflicts with efficiency and effectiveness. The commercial focus is on achieving an adequate level of competition; the government seeks free and open competition, which allows anyone to bid, regardless of prior experience or qualifications. Adequate competition is a basic premise of the proposed new acquisition process. Totally unproven sources, however, will have the opportunity to become qualified either through having their production processes accepted or submitting bid samples for evaluation. Either way, such options must be available to all potential suppliers, and the system should be perceived as both fair and accessible.

Last, but by no means least, is the concern about fraud and abuse. Fortunately, current commercial legislation is adequate to cover this. Bribery, for example, has always been illegal.

In summary, it is believed that the proposed approach to defense acquisitions has the potential for assuring far greater public and governmental trust in the defense acquisition process when it is fully implemented.

This maintenance of public trust is key to any military/civilian transition. It will require the keepers of the public trust—the inspector general of the Department of Defense, the director of the Defense Contract Audit Agency, others in the administration, and particularly the leaders of the House and Senate Government Operations Committees and their associates on other congressional watchdog committees—to genuinely believe in the use of free-market forces for defense procurements.

It is important to realize that the purpose of the proposed change is to make dramatic savings of billions of dollars in the defense acquisition process. President Eisenhower set up a system to look explicitly at the fiscal implications of government policy decisions. This system has long since been dropped. It should be reinstituted, however, and applied to new legislation as well as to administration policy. Many of the barriers to civil/military integration created by well-intended legislation and/or DoD practices surely could not stand this test.

Costs and Potential Benefits

Throughout this book it has been emphasized repeatedly that the proposed transformation of the U.S. defense industrial base will be extremely difficult and will take years to achieve. There will also be some one-time costs—mostly for education and training on the new system—that are associated with early implementation and will easily be paid back within a year or two. But there will be big costs associated with the use of executive management time, as key DoD senior personnel lead the change process.

As the implementation begins to take place, there will be significant cutbacks in the number of government employees as the leadership group expands and as more and more of the remaining people become participants in the change process. There will certainly be some termination costs, both in the government and in industry. Incentives for early retirements will be offered; and there will be rewards (such as promotions) for those who adjust rapidly to the new system and provide success models for others to emulate. Finally, there will be some increased unemployment costs, unless the overall economy is growing and can absorb these people.

One significant expense associated with integrating defense and civilian plants is the high cost expected for environmental cleanup of former defense plants. This is now running into billions of dollars, yet it clearly needs to be done—regardless of whether integration is achieved. In fact, it is worth considering some increase in initial expenditures in this cleanup effort in order to expedite it.

Similarly, added up-front charges may also be advantageous for the defense industry to expedite a write-off of the undepreciated costs of the large amount of now excess plant and equipment that was purchased during the defense buildup of the 1980s. Over time these costs will naturally disappear, but they currently represent a heavy burden hanging over the defense firms. They make it extremely difficult to diversify, since the costs have to be covered in the commercial prices the firms can charge (as well as against their defense goods), making the firms less competitive in the commercial world. A one-time added cost for write-off of this equipment therefore may be fully justified for those plants that in fact are integrating.

In addition to each of these direct costs, there could be some significant adverse economic impacts in other areas. For example, community employment and taxes lost in the closure of some defense-unique facilities will hurt some localities. In addition, new antitrust legislation may be needed to allow the required mergers associated with defense downsizing, eliminating the inefficient firms that cannot compete.

Such direct and indirect costs are trivial in comparison to the tens of billions of dollars of anticipated annual efficiency gains. The biggest payoff, for a small investment cost, is that associated with an extensive education and training program for both government and industry. This investment has been necessary whenever industrial firms have chosen to make a dramatic change—such as from the old mass-production culture to the modern lean-production culture. They found that a significant investment in training, throughout the whole organization, was the only way that alignment and motivation could be rapidly achieved and a consensus built up relatively early to avoid much of the otherwise inherent chaos and inefficiency.

Unfortunately there is no absolute proof available of the projected defense efficiency gains from integration, since the identical equipment has rarely been built in both the military and civilian sectors. In the few instances where this has been done, however, the results have been striking. And there have been many cases in which comparable equipment has been built for the commercial world and the military world from which rough comparisons can be made. Finally, there are numerous examples of the impacts of "commercial" changes to current defense practices. Thus one can look at these examples to arrive at a rough estimate of the order of magnitude of efficiency gains that might be realized from the three-part transformation strategy.[8]

Consider the following cases:

• One of the few examples of an identical product that was built both using the full military approach and the commercial approach was a secure telephone system (the STU-III). The National Security Agency decided to develop this with commercial parts and practices in commercial facilities in order to meet a rapid delivery schedule, which could not be met by doing it the normal defense way. Commercial development time was three years versus a typical seven- to eleven-year DoD cycle for comparable systems. A comparison of the commercial system with an identical military system that was built subsequently shows that the cost of development and production was less than 10 percent of the cost of the defense-unique equipment. This ten-to-one cost saving was significantly influenced by the fact that there was a large commercial market for these items—in which the DoD could participate—and it was realized because of the waiving of normal defense cost reporting, data rights, and military specifications and standards. In this case the system was designed for dual use, and the benefits were realized by both the defense and commercial worlds.

• Westinghouse developed a sophisticated pulse-doppler radar (the Modular Avionics Radar) for detecting airborne wind shear for the C-130 military transport and the Airbus A-300 commercial aircraft. The radar uses all commercial parts but was built in facilities primarily used for supporting DoD requirements and therefore required much of the DoD oversight and other unique aspects of defense operations. Nonetheless, a properly adjusted comparison with the APG-66 radar developed under normal DoD procedures for use in the F-16 military fighter, for similar capabilities, indicates a 50 percent reduction in development time and a 60 percent cost reduction for the Modular Avionics Radar. The cost and time savings have been attributed to the system being initially designed for both defense and commercial use and the granting of waivers from typical military specifications.

• The army needed a new helicopter engine and chose to use an Alliance 250-C30R engine, certified for commercial use by the FAA, instead of developing a military specification engine. They did have to make some modifications to the commercial version by adding an electronic fuel-flow component. The engine, however, was procured essentially as an off-the-shelf item, thus eliminating five to eight years of development time and large development costs—except for the modifications, which required approximately thirty months to develop and certify. Compared to a military-developed and -qualified engine, which the army estimates would have cost $200 million, seven certified commercial engines were modified and procured for less than $2 million. In addition, the commercial warranties have proved to be as good as, if not better than, military equivalents. In addition, the army has been able to take advantage of several commercial-use changes, which provided extended life in the desert environment of the Gulf War.

• Rockwell International Corporation said it reduced the cost of a global-positioning system (GPS) receiver for the U.S. Air Force by 30 percent, because it was built to commercial-like performance specifications rather than military specs.[9]

• Raytheon, in cooperation with Digital Equipment Corporation, offered the government a basic military version of the commercial VAX computer, using off-the-shelf components. A 20 to 30 percent cost savings was estimated for this system, and the Department of Defense gained the benefit of all of the improvements made to the commercial systems at no added cost. In order to do so, however, the DoD had to waive over 300 product specifications normally associated with computer acquisitions.

• For jet engine casings, General Electric has been building units to satisfy both commercial and military requirements in the same facility. This dual use has allowed for an over 70 percent manufacturing time improvement and 30 to 50 percent cost reductions, compared to engine cases designed and procured for strictly military use.

• In the semiconductor arena, the DoD has had a long-standing prohibition against plastic parts, although they have been used extensively in rugged commercial applications. Recent advances in plastic encapsulation have largely eliminated the problems that concerned the DoD, and switching to commercial semiconductors with these improved plastic packages would allow for a 60 to 70 percent savings over the ceramic or metal packages the DoD now requires. In view of the fact that the Department of Defense buys over $2 billion worth of semiconductors a year, this becomes a significant savings.

• Hewlett Packard developed a frequency agile signal simulation device capable of simulating a wide range of complex signals that would have potential use in radar electronic warfare. By using commercial off-the-shelf components, the system is estimated to cost only 20 percent of the less agile but comparable DoD military specification systems.

• Collins Avionics (a division of Rockwell) has developed numerous communications/guidance systems and data links that use strictly commercial specifications and standards for DoD and industry users. Collins estimates that a 20 to 35 percent cost penalty would be incurred for these systems if they were only acquired by the DoD. Thus, dual use in these cases has had a payoff for both the government and industry.

• General Electric's CFM 56 jet engine was originally designed for use in the commercial Boeing 707, as well as for the military KC-135 tanker during the 1970s. The dual-use concept worked to the benefit of both the DoD and the airline industry until the early 1980s. Subsequently, five modifications were made to the engine—alterations that were used only by commercial users. U.S. Air Force standards required that only the original engine could be maintained in air force depots. This restriction eventually led to separate production lines, that is, a commercial one for modernized engines and a basic line for air force engines—so the DoD received an inferior engine at much higher costs than if it had come from a common line.

• Two tactical missiles of similar development difficulty were designed and produced by LTV at about the same time under essentially fixed-priced contracts, including priced production options. One missile (the ATACMS) was a DoD contract with all the government requirements, oversight, and testing. The other (the VT-1) was a contract with a French company (Thompson) with more flexible requirements, minimal oversight, and much less—but adequate—testing. Both programs resulted in the development of very successful missiles and took roughly the same amount of production time. The predevelopment contract period, however, was much longer for the DoD program; and total contract development costs were more than twice as much for the DoD program than for the French firm. When the government costs and the estimated contractor costs were included, it would appear to be between two and one-half and three times more expensive for the DoD development approach than the French approach, which does not have any unique military requirements in its procurement process.

• Last, one of the greatest potentials for savings is in the software area. It is estimated that 25 percent or more of future defense weapon system costs will be software, where the ability to use commercial off-the-shelf items has already begun to show an enormous potential payoff. In one example, the Ballistic Missile Defense Organization found that by using open systems architecture and commercially available software, they were able to eliminate about 75 to 95 percent of the requirements for totally new software generation. This cut an enormous amount of time and cost out of software acquisition—to about $1 per line compared to hundreds or even thousands of dollars per line.

Testimony presented to the Acquisition Law Advisory Panel of the Department of Defense in June 1992 and statements made to the House Armed Services Committee in July 1992 show that defense-related specifications typically add 30 to 50 percent to the cost of doing business and impede the introduction of commercially developed technological innovations into defense systems. Even with conservative estimates and realistic impediments to implementation, savings could be in the tens of billions of dollars annually.

Estimated Savings

The basic inefficiencies in the current weapons acquisition system fall essentially into three categories:

1. program definition;
2. program execution; and
3. the defense industrial base.

Since there is obviously a good deal of overlap here, it would be inaccurate to simply add up the potential savings in each area to determine the total impact. Nor would projected savings be realized in the first year, so that the numbers to be calculated are those that might be realized after, say, a five–year time period when a significant portion of the transformation will have taken place. Finally, it should be noted that the calculations that follow are based on a fiscal year 1994 defense budget, which allocated $98 billion for acquisition. As the defense budget declines, the actual magnitude of the savings would also be reduced, but the percentage saving would remain approximately the same.

"Program definition" refers to the way the government goes about deciding what weapon systems it wants to buy. Often this process is not included within the framework of acquisition; yet it is in defining the initial product that some of the greatest savings can be realized. For example, it might be more cost-effective to specify a mission need or a required functional capability, rather than focusing on a specific weapon. This distinction is critical because from that initial point on, all one can accomplish are cost/performance trade-offs within, say, a given airplane, ship, or tank—as contrasted to considering other, totally different, lower-cost ways of satisfying that same mission need, for example, a low-cost missile.

A major cost driver in this category is the fact that most defense programs assume that "this will be the last new system for the next two decades," so they include all possible new, and often unproved, technology at the start of development (a more incremental approach is used in commercial practice). This defense approach is then exacerbated by the fact that, during the long development cycle, new requirements and technologies are constantly being inserted into the development process—causing disruptions, further inefficiencies, and costly program stretch-outs.

In addition, there is a common defense practice of overspecifying requirements, as well as making initial, optimistic estimates of the large quantities to be produced and the low level of support required. Since the military requirements are considered firm, there is very little opportunity to trade off their added future costs against their marginal value. For example, the unrealistically large quantities that are often planned for result in considerable excess production facilities and therefore excess costs.

Similarly, unrealistic initial budgeting ("buying in") results in significant program instabilities, because quantities almost always have to be adjusted downward in order to live with the (inadequate) funds granted.

One can estimate the dollar impact of these inefficiencies by using the FY94 numbers. There was approximately $45 billion budgeted for major weapon systems acquisition (out of an overall acquisition budget of $98 billion). Since this is the area most directly affected by the current military requirements process, we can start with these dollars, which, through the use of a more incremental approach, might be cut by more than 20 percent, or over $9 billion.

The use of commercial specifications and standards in defining the product to be developed should reduce equipment costs by 30 to 50 percent. If even half of the weapon system designs could take advantage of these efficiencies, then gains of perhaps 15 percent of the total, or at least $7 billion annually, should be feasible. It should be emphasized that subsystems alone make up around 50 percent of a typical weapon system's cost, so additional savings are certainly possible. In addition, the use of commercial specifications and standards have far wider application than just in weapon systems and should be extended to items from fruitcakes to dog collars.

Estimates from prior studies, such as those of the Packard Commission,[10] attribute significant cost savings of at least 15 percent to the gains that could be realized from reducing program and budget instabilities. Obviously, longer-term multiyear budgeting processes would have a significant impact here; but even multiyear contracts, such as those used in the commercial world, would create very real savings. If even half this gain can be achieved by smoothing weapon system funding levels, this represents an annual efficiency gain of $7 billion.

As noted, these numbers have considerable overlap. Given their conservative nature and the magnitude of their estimates, however, it would certainly seem realistic to assume that annual efficiency gains in the weapons acquisition process through changes in the program definition area could result in annual efficiency gains of perhaps $15 billion a year—out of the total $98 billion of acquisition dollars.

Moving to the second category of "program executions," we are considering the acquisition process for weapon systems as well as for all other

Table 9.1
Estimated potential annual efficiency improvements in the program execution area after a five-year period

	FY94 cost ($ billions)	Difference (%)	FY94 saving ($ billions)
Commercial items			
Food, clothing, fuel, etc.	3.7	3	.1
Construction	8.2	8	.6
Electronics and software	3.0	20	.6
Small purchases	8.0	10	.8
Subtotal	22.9		2.1
"Commercial-like" items			
Systems (e.g., transport A/ C, jet engines, vehicles, munitions, etc.)	7.8	20	1.6
Electronics and software	7.7	25	1.9
Subsystems and parts	21.5	25	5.4
Services	16.4	10	1.6
Maintenance and overhaul (excl. organic)	6.5	20	1.3
Subtotal	59.9		11.8
"Defense-unique" platforms and equipment			
Missiles and space	4.6	15	.7
Ships	1.9	15	.3
Military aircraft	7.3	15	1.1
Tanks and armor vehicles	.6	15	.1
Weapons and ammunition	8.0	10	.1
Subtotal	15.2		2.3
Government acq. employ. (approx. 150,000)	15.0	25	3.7
Total	113		19.9

areas of defense procurement. Here the proposed transformation would result in potential efficiency gains in four broad categories: commercial items; commercial-like items; defense-unique platforms and equipment; and government acquisitions employment (table 9.1).

Many of the items the government actually buys (electronic components, software, spare parts, and materials) could be purchased directly off the commercial shelves by the Defense Department—and the estimated savings would be at least $2 billion annually.

For "commercial-like" items, that is, where the specific equipment is unique to defense but sufficiently similar that it could be designed and built in an integrated plant (transport aircraft, jet engines, communication satellites, electronic systems, and software), integration would result in even greater savings. Almost all of the major subsystems and parts of even defense-unique weapon systems fit into this category, which represents approximately 50 percent of the total cost of defense weapon systems. Estimated annual savings are around $12 billion.

Defense-unique items include final weapon systems such as strategic missiles and nuclear submarines, which likely would end up being built in unique facilities. Even here, however, significant efficiency gains are possible. The adaptation of commercial practices to the defense-unique arena can have significant streamlining effects on the approximately $15 billion annual platforms and equipment budget. Annual savings of over $2 billion should be achievable.

Finally, there are the approximately 300,000 government employees involved in the acquisition process. Of these, perhaps 150,000 could be eliminated by the commercialization of the acquisition process. If even only 25 percent of the latter could be eliminated by the end of a five-year period, about $3.7 billion of annual savings would be realized.

Combining all of the above estimates, of a total $113 billion of acquisition-related costs (industry and government), there ought to be at least $20 billion of potential savings available annually.

The third major acquisition category is directly associated with the defense industrial base itself. Here the basic burden is maintaining separate defense and commercial industrial bases. Since the cost of defense facilities averages about 7 percent of equipment costs, and since at least half of the defense procurements are produced in single-use plants, if even some of these single-use activities can be shifted to dual-use facilities, there ought to be annual efficiency gains in the range of $2 billion.

In addition, the government also maintains a very large public sector industrial base. The depots, arsenals, laboratories, and the FFRDCs are almost entirely duplicative of capabilities in the commercial world. Maintaining these facilities costs approximately $21 billion each year. If a 25 percent efficiency gain would result from consolidation of these efforts with the private sector, then savings in the range of $5 billion a year would be possible.

The government also pays significantly for additional acquisition requirements that derive from its assumption that it will organically support its weapons systems. Added test equipment, spare parts, and maintenance manuals are just part of this support system. If the commercial industrial base were used to do this work, through greater use of contractors, a savings of just 4 percent (in weapons systems cost) could realize annual efficiency gains of over $2 billion.

There is also a significant cost for excess capacity in the defense industrial base, both in the public and private sectors, which is maintained solely for potential surges in production in times of crisis. If an integrated base existed, this additional capacity requirement could be satisfied largely by temporarily shifting work from the commercial to the military area, within the same facility.

An additional capacity demand comes from maintaining some sectors of the defense industry in business at all. The Congress annually adds significant dollars to the defense budget simply to "maintain the industrial base," by which it means the defense-unique facilities. In the FY92 budget Congress added $8 billion for programs that were not even requested by the DoD and for grossly inefficient stretch-out programs. If the need to preserve the defense industrial base could be satisfied by dual-use facilities, the potential savings could be in the range of $5–$10 billion a year.

Based on the above estimates, the potential savings from inefficiencies in the overall defense industrial base, private and public, should be at least $10 billion a year.

Combining the three broad areas of potential cost savings, we find:

* reduced inefficiencies in program definition ($15 billion per year).
* reduced inefficiencies in program execution ($20 billion per year).
* reduced inefficiencies in maintaining the defense industrial base ($10 billion per year).

Again, because these categories overlap and therefore cannot be added, it is not possible to estimate easily the total potential savings. From this, however, it should be possible to conclude that *the potential savings is certainly in the tens of billions of dollars annually,* or well over 20 percent of the total acquisition dollars spent by the Defense Department.

To add additional credibility to this estimate, in 1994 a very significant study investigated the regulatory cost impacts (of doing government business) within representative design and manufacturing plants. The objective was to determine the difference in doing a given task between defense practices and best commercial practices.[11] After months of analyzing a significant number of defense supplier facilities, the study concluded that the regulatory impacts alone represented approximately 18 percent of the value-added cost in an individual plant. The detailed analysis was done at both prime contractor and lower-tier facilities; therefore the numbers can be extrapolated across the overall defense acquisition budget. Thus, without considering many of the other inefficiencies noted above (the weapons' requirements process, added government employees, and the redundant industrial base), the study found that, solely due to regulatory impacts, the costs to the government were 18 percent greater than they would be if best commercial practices (by high-quality, world-class firms) were utilized. The study also found that the more engineering-intensive or high technology-based the activities were, the greater the regulatory cost impacts became (going well over 25 percent). The combination of these activities-based costing plant analyses and the numerous case studies of military and commercial equipment clearly indicates that the potential savings, as a result of moving from government practices to world-class commercial practices, can be extremely significant and fully justifies the efforts required to implement the actions recommended in this book.

10

Technological Leadership

Research and development fuel the engine that drives the U.S. economy. In the civilian arena, new products and new manufacturing processes yield competitive advantage, resulting in the creation of new jobs and national economic growth. In the military, R & D help sustain its strategy of technological superiority. Both civilian and military R & D are therefore critical; and wherever possible the nation should benefit from the coupling of the two.

The payoff from this coupling—and from increased civilian R & D investment—could be huge. Economic studies suggest that the rate of return on effective R & D spending runs as high as 50 percent a year, including indirect benefits to the economy.[1] R & D requires three sets of complementary investments: capital equipment, infrastructure, and skilled labor.

First, incentives must be created for capital investment, if the United States is to fully realize the gains from its R & D leadership. Increasingly, the nation that "wins" is not the one that carried out the original R & D but the one that gets the new products to the market most rapidly. This is true in both the economic and security spheres.

Second, there are huge benefits to be gained from national infrastructure investments. In the last generation, it was highway building (justified on the basis of national security) that stimulated the U.S. auto industry. Today, in the information age, these investments must be made in the national information infrastructure. Since this infrastructure is a public good, it is unlikely that private sector investments will be adequate. Government incentives and investments will be required.

Third, technological leadership requires a skilled labor force. Again, this is a public good in which it will be necessary to make significant public sector investments.

Thus there are four areas that require significant investment: R & D, capital equipment, infrastructure, and education and training. Since there are often inadequate long-term incentives for the U.S. private sector to make large enough investments in these areas, it is imperative that the government step in and help. American firms will often underinvest in R & D for one of the following reasons: they are not in a position to capitalize on the payoff (there may be richer, or faster, competition); the project is too risky; the benefits will accrue more to the public than to the firm; or, particularly, there may be a negative short-term profit impact. For these reasons, the United States may continue to lose its leadership position in many critical technology areas without government involvement in R & D—both in the creation of incentives through public policy and in selected direct investments.

When resources are constrained, as they certainly are for the federal government, programs must be justified on economic, quality of life, and/or security arguments. Federal projects such as the $120 billion space station become increasingly difficult to defend. As one European observer commented, "I can't understand your country putting billions into placing a man in orbit when your highways and railroads don't work."[2] Although this may be an exaggeration, it highlights the disparity between research levels on ground- and air-based transportation versus other projects.

The point is that it is not solely a question of how much money a nation devotes to R & D, but rather what it is spent on and how efficiently and effectively it is used. It also matters where it is spent; if manufacturing goes offshore, engineering will soon follow.[3] Therefore the nation must not just increase the amount spent on R & D but must assess the particulars of the funding. These become critical public policy questions.

Some general guidelines can be established. For example, a good deal of evidence shows that multiple smaller projects have a higher payoff than one or two "big science" projects. Similarly, it is possible to identify several industries/technologies where R & D investment by the government makes the most sense: (1) those essential to long-term economic growth and security; (2) those where investment will speed up their competitive advancement, that is, industries with high rates of change of technology and high barriers to entry or reentry; (3) those where industrial technologies are closely linked (in a "food chain"), so progress in one will rapidly carry over to others, for example, the semiconductor, computer, and telecommunications industries; (4) those areas in which reasonable levels of government investment can truly make a difference (where it would not be swamped by the current levels of alternative investments); and (5) those areas that are vulnerable to the loss of rapid access (the foreign dependency/vulnerability issue). These five key measures (critical, fast-changing, linked, leveraged, and vulnerable) describe areas for government targeting, either through private sector incentives and/or public R & D investments.

Critical R & D investment decisions can be made only by individuals who are technologically literate. Unfortunately, most U.S. industry, government, and labor leaders are technologically illiterate, often with a background in law, finance, or marketing. The decisions are made even more difficult because there are no good models to follow. It is easy to calculate the equations for return on investment once the likely market is defined. It is much harder to know the likely market created by a new-technology R & D investment; and judgments cannot easily be tested in the short term, since these investments are aimed at returns over many years.

Recent conflict-of-interest legislation greatly discourages people from high-technology industrial management positions to enter the government. Yet most senior government officials do not traditionally have a high-technology management background or experience in making high-risk investment decisions. As we will discuss in the next chapter, this lack of experienced government leaders may be a fatal flaw—unless corrected in the near term—in view of the very significant impact that the federal government has on R & D in the United States.

Government Role

The U.S. federal government funds approximately 50 percent of the nation's R & D. In fiscal year 1994, government R & D spending totaled

$75.5 billion, of which 56 percent ($42.5 billion) was for military R & D. There has been a significant rise in nonmilitary R & D in the last few years, and that trend is expected to continue. Overall, the intent of the government investments is threefold: to act as a catalyst in stimulating economic growth through investments in areas such as transportation, energy, and agriculture; to help improve the quality of life through investments in health, safety, and the environment; and to assure national security.

The government should act as a wise investor in areas that have a large public benefit either directly, for example, for national security, or through the stimulation of economic growth. In addition, the government has responsibility for assuring harmonization of both public and private interests and for creating incentives for private investment that are consistent with these.

This government role (in civilian R & D) is not new. In 1836 Congress appropriated $30,000 to Samuel Morse for the experimental telegraph line from Washington, D.C., to Baltimore, Maryland. But most U.S. government investments have been in basic science and defense, whereas many of the nation's economic competitors have emphasized nondefense R & D. As a percent of GNP in 1990, nondefense R & D was: Japan, 3.0 percent, Germany, 2.75 percent, United States, 1.9 percent.[4]

The U.S. government has often treated science and technology as if they were separable entities. In 1945, Vannevar Bush's report to President Truman, *Science: The Endless Frontier,* put in place this country's first federal science policy but assigned the government no role in technology development. At the time, America's industrial technology base was very strong, but its science base was relatively weak. Today, the opposite is true— America's science, basic research, and higher education systems are world leaders; its civilian technology base is faltering.

For nearly forty years after World War II, strategic technology in American was developed mainly in the context of military and space programs. This gave the United States world leadership in integrated circuits, advanced computers, aerospace, lasers, nuclear energy, polymers, and many other fields. Today the world is very different. The emergence of the civilian sector as the precursor of new technology developments (supplanting the military sector); the end of the cold war and the dramatic decline in defense expenditures; and the aggressive investment by foreign competitors in coordinated, public-private sector initiatives for technology development, are all typical of the new environment. As a result, the traditional U.S. approach to supporting strategic technology development and utilization through military and space programs has become less effective than it was in the past.[5]

The need for America to transfer some of its R & D focus from research to technology, and from defense to the civilian sector, is exacerbated by two significant shifts: first, the obvious decline in overall defense expenditures, which is bound to have an impact on defense R & D expenditures over the long term; and second, the increasingly short-term perspective of the private sector, resulting in cutbacks on high-risk, long-term industrial R & D investments in the interest of boosting quarterly financial reports.

Increased R & D investments in commercial and dual-use (civil and military) technologies must take two forms: greater government incentives for industry investments, and far larger direct government investments. The risk in the latter recommendation is that government investments frequently are not sufficiently market-driven. Also, there is a very real possibility—given industry and Wall Street's short-term perspectives—that government money would simply be a replacement for industry money—and thus not a net gain. For both reasons, it is critical that government support for civilian R & D be only in highly selected areas. Lewis Branscomb of Harvard has suggested the following three guidelines for the government's civilian sector investments:

• Support pathbreaking technologies that are long-range and high-risk, but promise to stimulate large new industries;
• Support infrastructural technologies that are public goods; and
• Support nationally vital technologies where they involve significant commitments on the part of the subsidized industry.

Civilian sector R & D investments by the government must be based on industry-led market analyses and indications of areas of long-term high payoff. Their expected value must be explicitly identified prior to making the investment. Where the payoff would be dual, with significant benefits to both U.S. economic growth and to national security, funding could come through either the DoD or the relevant civilian mission agency. In fact, the Departments of Transportation, Energy, Labor, Education, Environment, and Commerce all have significant mission-oriented, long-term, high-risk R & D that needs to be done, much of which would be relevant to defense. For example, there is a $200 billion environmental cleanup program required for the U.S. nuclear weapons plants over the next thirty years. R & D in this area that is focused on reducing costs and/or time could potentially have enormous payoffs.

In view of the potential for government/industry conflict in areas of dual use, it is essential that government-funded civilian R & D have very explicit guidelines. One set that appears credible includes:

• cost sharing between government and industry;
• industry involvement in project initiation and design;
• diversification of investments;
• project selection removed from the political process; and
• a rigorous project evaluation program.

Civilian sector technology investments will also require new institutional structures within government departments. The National Science Foundation historically has done an outstanding job of coordinating long-term science investments, and the Department of Defense has achieved a similar coordination function through its director of Defense Research and Engineering (in the Office of the Secretary of Defense). As the nation begins to emphasize technology investments in transportation, communications, environment, and so on, there will need to be similarly strong R & D organizations within the relevant agencies. Most important is that high-quality people with industrial technology experience be recruited to fill these jobs, and that they are able to receive expert outside opinion to guide them—as the Defense Department has historically done with its Defense Science Board.[6]

A first step toward addressing the institutional questions associated with civilian and dual-use technology investments was taken at the end of the Bush administration. A Federal Coordinating Council for Science, Engineering, and Technology (FCCSET, and pronounced "fix it") was established under the Office of Science and Technology Policy in the White House. Although this is an interagency committee, not an operational organization—and thus does not control either budgets or projects—it did initiate a series of steps that were carried into the Clinton administration. It was renamed the National Science and Technology Council; elevated to the level of the National Security Council and the National Economic Council; and is now headed by the president.[7] All of its initiatives are to be funded by the relevant agencies, but the council can have a very strong influence on integration and direction. By identifying specific areas and integrating the resources from the separate agencies, the council can provide guidance for private sector long-term investments and can make sure that the nation is getting the maximum benefit from the government's R & D investments.

The six specific areas initially selected (and the level of investment in FY93) were: advanced manufacturing ($1.4 billion); high-performance computing and communications ($1.0 billion); global change research ($1.5 billion); advanced materials and processing ($2.0 billion); biotechnology research ($4.3 billion); and science, math, engineering, and technology education ($2.3 billion). On an annual basis, these are clearly significant funding levels; and the interagency coordination should help to enhance their effectiveness.

Other civilian R & D initiatives that began in the early 1990s included the Advanced Technology Program started by Congress to provide grants for the development of "precompetitive, generic technologies." The National Institute for Standards and Technology (NIST) in the Department of Commerce was designated as the lead agency. Although initial funding was modest, it has been growing rapidly and requires cost sharing by industry. In 1993, Congress created the Technology Reinvestment Program, also a cost sharing effort, but this one was aimed at dual-use R & D and was to be administered through the Advanced Research Projects Agency (ARPA) in the Department of Defense. Its initial funding was $500 million, and it immediately generated enormous interest around the country (almost 3,000 proposals were submitted). It planned a wide range of dual-use areas for stimulation, including technology development for: information, electronics, machine tools and robotics, materials and structures, health care, training, the environment, aeronautics, vehicles, shipbuilding, and advanced batteries.

Another major initiative that got started in the early 1990s was a significant R & D program funded by the Department of Transportation. It included R & D on intelligent vehicle/highway systems, high-speed rail systems, magnetic levitation, and environmentally clean vehicles.

At the beginning of the Clinton administration, the president announced a new U.S. technology policy aimed specifically at economic growth. It had four key elements:

• directly supporting the development, commercialization, and deployment of new technology;
• fiscal and regulatory policies that indirectly promote these activities—from R & D tax credits to dramatic changes in government procurement policy;
• investments in scientific and technical education and training; and,
• support for critical transportation and communication infrastructures.

As shown in table 10.1, there are a wide range of methods available to the government to implement this policy. At one end are incentives that encourage industry, allowing them full responsibility for project selection (tax incentives, university support, and permitting corporate independent research and development (IR & D) as an overhead expense on government contracts). At the other end are government-sponsored R & D projects, funded by project-specific authorizations and appropriations. The most appealing options are those that create incentives for industry to invest in areas with the greatest market return.

The independent research and development (IR & D) program in 1990, along with bid and proposal dollars, had a level of $3.6 billion. This is a fully reimbursed expense under defense contracts and in recent years was changed to encourage its application for dual-use R & D. The contractor selects the areas for investment; and these have often been extremely successful, in many cases leading to products that significantly advanced the state of the art. The debate is over whether government-funded R & D support (direct or indirect) should be based on government decisions or industry decisions. In areas such as defense, the government will claim to know its mission needs better; industry will claim greater technical expertise and will assert that the government should let market forces pick the best technologies. In general, the data appear to favor the industry arguments, especially in the civilian mission areas. Nonetheless, there is a definite catalytic role for the government that must be present to stimulate investment in new high-risk areas.

Table 10.1
Some potential government policy instruments

- Protection of domestic market until producers mature
- Advanced degree support for engineers/scientists
- Exemption from antitrust laws
- Investment funds provided through special mechanisms
- Procurement assistance (and/or guarantees) from government agencies
- Preferential interest rates on loans
- Special incentives to attract foreign firms
- Rebates of indirect taxes
- Raw materials subsidies
- Loans to exporters
- Export targeting
- Export financing programs
- Providing R & D funds
- Technical assistance for smaller firms (from national technology institutes)
- Support for skill upgrading for scientists and engineers
- Selection of technologies of "critical importance"
- Support primarily for precompetitive R & D
- Tax incentives/special privileges for private research institutes
- Setting standards well in advance of current levels
- Incentives for R & D cooperatives for smaller firms
- Joint efforts between government and private R & D labs
- Government labs take on high-risk, large-externality, long-time-horizon R & D
- Tax credits for R & D investment and commercialization of locally developed technology
- Corporate set-asides of profits for R & D in coming years

Consistent with this is the belief that the overwhelming majority of even government-funded R & D should be done in the private sector rather than in government laboratories. The arguments here relate directly to the competitive nature of the private sector marketplace, as well as to the far closer coupling that exists within firms between R & D and the manufacturing and marketing areas. The example here is the difference between the way ARPA does its government-sponsored research within the Department of Defense versus the way it is done in the large government laboratories (either in the defense or energy laboratories). In ARPA, a few government project directors are responsible for the selection and review of areas to be funded and for monitoring how well the contractors are doing in their research. The critical element is the selection of project directors and the freedom they are given in selecting and working with contractors. The execution is 100 percent outside of the government (either in industry or universities). It is usually awarded through "best ideas" competitions, not on proposed costs, and contracts are given to more than one researcher so competition continues to drive the programs and costs are controlled.

This ARPA approach has received universal recognition for its success in funding nontraditional areas and in starting up whole new industries. By contrast, the alternative of setting up a government laboratory (or utilizing an existing one) to research a given area—essentially in competition with industry—has had a far less positive effect and should be discouraged, particularly in any future civilian R & D work to be done by nondefense government agencies. Unfortunately, recent congressional legislation has significantly favored the use of the government laboratories.

Government R & D tax credits to industry would also encourage long-term technology investments. Current tax laws actually penalize an American firm that sells internationally but does its research in the United States.[8] The portion of R & D that is tax deductible is only equal to the U.S. share of a company's worldwide sales. Thus, if a company does all of its research in the United States but registers only half its sales in the domestic market, it can deduct only half of its R & D expenditures. The Treasury Department insists that the balance must be deducted from income earned abroad. Foreign governments, however, refuse to recognize these expenditures for their tax purposes, unless the firm actually conducts the research within their borders. Therefore the American companies must either forgo the U.S. tax deduction or move part of their R & D investments from American universities and labs to other nations. Indeed, many have. The firms most directly affected are the large companies that finance most of America's privately sponsored research. Since they already have international operations, it is relatively easy for them to shift research from the United States to overseas facilities. The consequences of this policy have repeatedly been brought to the attention of Treasury officials, who respond that they need the tax collections to relieve the deficit. Yet this inflexible shortsightedness will inevitably harm the national interest. It gives other nations access to some of America's most advanced technology. It takes funds away from American universities that are training the next generation of scientists and engineers. And it develops state-of-the-art engineers in other countries, instead of in the United States. Certainly, this appears to be a policy worthy of review.

Another policy worth reviewing is the government's role in technology data gathering, such as advanced technology forecasting and international benchmarking. Traditionally, the U.S. intelligence community closely monitored both classified and unclassified trends in military technology around the world, particularly in the former Soviet Union. The data was not applied in the area of economic competition, and in fact was rarely available to those outside of the defense community. By contrast, many other nations (especially France and Japan) believe the government's role should be in civilian technology as much as in military technology. Japan provides technology forecasting data for its industry and university researchers. For example, in September 1988 the Japanese Science and Technology Agency published an impressive report entitled "Future Technology in Japan: Forecast to the Year 2015." Japanese government-furnished data also covers foreign technology and intelligence data. The Japan External Trade Organization (JETRO) is considered "the intelligence arm" of MITI. It was set up in 1957 as a trade promotion group and serves the dual function of lobbying (in the United States and elsewhere) as well as data gathering. JETRO has over 300 government officials working in Japan's embassy and consulates in America and is assisted by 200 Japanese journalists. The data collected is widely shared among Japan's various industrial sectors, with MITI acting as distributor.[9]

Any national industrial or technology policy needs long-term investment financing. The government can back private capital for critical technology areas, or it can supply that capital. Small Business Administration loans, targeted to high technology rather than to the restaurant business—as they now primarily are—would make a great deal of sense. The Small Business Independent Research (SBIR) program, in which a percentage of each government agency's R & D is set aside for small business ventures, is another form of direct financing that would be more effective if targeted to critical technology areas. As noted, when direct government financing is involved in civilian R & D, there should be some industrial cost sharing, assuming the commercial potential warrants it, to prevent the taking of government money from becoming a business unto itself. Still, indirect financial incentives that are market-driven are the preferred route.

A national technology policy is often associated with a trade policy. Clearly, these must be integrated, but an R & D-oriented policy that stimulates competitiveness would be far more effective than a protectionist trade policy. In fact, protectionism is probably one of the least effective stimulation policies. Mike Scherer of Harvard found that when U.S. firms are given protection against high-tech imports, they actually cut back on their R & D investments in the area being protected.[10]

Protectionism is inherently a "beggar thy neighbor" policy. It is a negative-net-sum game, which is very bad public policy. To make it worse, as Raymond Vernon (also of Harvard) has observed, "One key reason for the striking protectionist sentiment in Congress and in the public press is that a coalition of protectionist interests in the United States has succeeded in a strategy that they have pursued persistently over the past thirty-five years. Fundamentally, the strategy has been to ensure that the problems associated with increased international trade are always addressed on a case-by-case basis rather than systematically. That result has been achieved by a succession of statutory measures that have given aggrieved domestic industries increasing power to initiate individual proposals for trade restrictions. As long as such issues arise case by case, the atmosphere surrounding discussions of trade policy is bound to be protectionist, and the costs of imposing import restrictions on the economy at large—costs such as the impact on consumers and the risk of retaliation—are likely to play a secondary role in the decisionmaking process."[11]

In a few selected cases it might make sense to have an infant-industry trade protection policy for a short time. Most of the legislation in this area, however, has been for protecting dying industries and is more political than constructive and has not been based on economic growth initiatives.

What is missing from U.S. government economic policy is the recognition that the primary markets have now shifted from internal domestic competition (where the government was reluctant to get involved lest it favor one firm over another) to an international competition in which U.S. firms are competing with foreign firms (and where the foreign firms have government support). As electronics expert Michael Borrus of the Berkeley Roundtable for the International Economy put it, "There is a growing conviction that competition in high tech, once between companies, is now between countries and their governments."

In recognition of this change, the Congress loosened the antitrust laws and began (with the National Cooperative Research Act of 1984) to allow "consortia to be established by U.S. firms to assist in the critical phase between pure research and production competition between firms"—known as the precompetitive research phase. More than one hundred consortia were formed in the first five years after 1984. By 1989 the legislation was further expanded, and such partnerships were extending their efforts into production, often with the government serving as banker.[12]

Companies participate in consortia when the benefits of the inventions that result could probably not be retained by a single company or when the investment required cannot be justified on a single-firm basis.

A number of initial consortia involved major defense contractors (eleven of them established a Software Productivity Consortium).[13] Politically, consortia appeal to the conservative right by overcoming the complaint that antitrust rules prevent American companies from cooperating on any project. They appeal to calls from the left for better planning— and because they suggest less government control and more coordination of industrial policy.

When should consortia be sponsored by the government? As a general guideline, the National Academy of Engineering recommended[14] that U.S. consortia be established only: (1) in areas where the United States lags behind foreign competitors; (2) for a specific narrow purpose; (3) for a lifetime determined at their formation; and (4) to promote competitive horizontal and cooperative vertical relationships among a company and its suppliers and its customers (there are no internal competitors).

Closely related to the industrial consortia are consortia between government research labs and industry. This initiative was pushed by Congress to help diffuse government research to industry and to help in the conversion of the defense and nuclear weapons labs to civilian R & D. The Stevenson-Wydler Technology Innovation Act of 1980 (Public Law

96-480) for the first time made technology transfer a formal part of the mission of all federal agencies carrying out research and development.[15] Specifically, it states that "it is the continuing responsibility of the federal government to ensure the full use of the results of the nation's federal investment in research and development. To this end the federal government shall strive where appropriate to transfer federally owned or originated technology to state and local governments and to the private sector."[16]

The Federal Technology Transfer Act of 1986 (Public Law 99-502) expanded this policy across agencies by authorizing government-operated laboratories to enter into cooperative research and development agreements (CRDAs) with other agencies, nonprofit organizations, state and local governments, and private industry (extended in 1989 to government-owned, contractor-operated labs as well).[17] Since then, CRDAs have grown like wildflowers.

One final significant role that the government can play in accelerating new products into the marketplace is through the development of standards. Traditionally, private sector groups, usually made up of representatives from the firms in a given industry, develop either national or international standards via a very slow and poorly funded process, and the standards do not apply to defense-unique products. The government can supply the needed resources to accelerate the process, and it can support and encourage the development of dual-use standards. The Commerce Department's National Institute of Standards and Technology has traditionally played a significant coordination role in the standards area; but there is no reason why the DoD could not also fund some private sector efforts. Without the existence of such standards, there is a tendency for a great deal of duplicative effort on nonconforming products. The governments of many of America's international economic competitors have helped their industries accelerate their standards developments. The United States needs to get involved on an equal level.

Lewis Branscomb of Harvard has suggested five requirements for an emerging (international) U.S. technology strategy:

• its benefits should accrue largely to the United States;
• it should avoid conflicts of interest, and the appearance thereof;

• it should expect, and be able to shut off, projects that fail or are no longer useful;

• it should be informed by (even led by) competent advice, particularly from the private sector; and

• it should take into account the global marketplace and answer the question "who is us?"

In addition, it should provide the one thing that has clearly been missing from U.S. technology strategy, namely, any form of rigorous, independent evaluation of past policies. Not knowing when to stop government-sponsored R & D poses a real danger. Once a project gets started, there is a strong tendency to continue it, even though any good research analysis will show that the right thing to do is to start multiple approaches and continue only those that make sense. Politics and institutional biases must not stand in the way of terminating unsuccessful research projects. And there must be no penalty for failure.

Defense Needs

The Department of Defense today has a crying need nor just for technological superiority but for high performance at an affordable price. The addition of this cost requirement dramatically changes the R & D agenda for the department. The DoD still must push the edge of the performance envelope outward, but instead of paying more and more for each new system, it now has to use advanced technology—in new products as well as in manufacturing and support—to dramatically reverse the historic cost-growth curves.

There are two ways that the DoD can achieve this. The first, and by far the more difficult, is by focusing on breakthrough technologies and "nontraditional" approaches. The second is to pursue the traditional weapon systems acquisition route but focus on achieving much lower-cost weapons in the next generation.

An increased emphasis on the search for breakthroughs entails a much greater willingness to accept occasional technical failures than America has evidenced in recent years.[18] The idea is to pursue totally nontraditional approaches that can result in orders-of-magnitude improvement in performance but can still do this at significantly lower cost. For example, replacing the bomber with a cruise missile is a different way of doing the same job; by applying new technologies, the result is dramatically lower costs to do the same mission.

The problem of course is that the army, navy, and air force have built-in institutional resistance to such nontraditional approaches. The solution may be to set up totally new organizations. After the Soviet Union launched *Sputnik*—clearly, a nontraditional item up to that point—DoD reacted by establishing ARPA.[19] At the time, Secretary of Defense Neil McElroy stated, "I want an agency that makes sure no important thing remains undone because it doesn't fit somebody's mission." Since that time, ARPA has in fact created many new technologies and many new capabilities that were not likely to have come, and certainly not come as rapidly, out of traditional ways of addressing military problems. The challenge for the DoD is to establish new institutional structures to pursue nontraditional approaches.

In the more traditional R & D arena an "upgraded" approach to weapons design involves the use of "concurrent engineering," where manufacturing and support people are brought into the design process at the preliminary design stage. Four typical examples of the benefits of concurrent engineering (for military and commercial applications) include:[20]

• Boeing's Ballistic Systems Division, which realized 30 percent cost savings and 67 percent inspection ratio reduction;
• McDonnell-Douglas's TAV-8B, which found 68 percent fewer drawing changes and 58 percent scrap reduction;
• Hewlett Packard's Instruments, which had 35 percent less development time and 60 percent lower field failure rates;
• John Deere & Company, which realized 30 percent development cost savings and 60 percent development time reduction.

Since the largest portion of the life-cycle costs of a weapon system are often in the support area, improved quality has a double cost benefit: it reduces support costs dramatically, and it requires the procurement of significantly fewer systems, because more equipment will be working when needed.

As to time savings, although it is generally recognized how important it is to rapidly get a new product into the field in the commercial world, there has been some question of whether this is still an important requirement in the defense arena. It is. For example, during Desert Storm it became clear that the United States badly needed a technique for identifying vehicles on the ground as being either friend or foe. ARPA designed and delivered a brand new identification system in sixteen days (by totally bypassing all of the required DoD procedures). In contrast, the average time for new product realization cycles in defense is over sixteen years—and even under acceleration (crisis) conditions is still measured in years, not days or months.

The DoD not only has to focus on developing rapid new product realization cycles, but also has to plan for ongoing upgrades as newer technology becomes available. This requires initial planning for relatively small quantities of production and for the use of the most advanced manufacturing equipment and management techniques to achieve efficient production in small quantities. It also requires a dramatic shift in the investment resource balance between new product technologies and new process technologies.

Today, the DoD devotes almost all of its $38 billion of annual R & D to generate maximum performance from new product developments, leaving a trivial amount to investigating advanced manufacturing (process) developments—aimed at lowering costs and improving quality. Yet in many products, such as next-generation semiconductors, the product and process changes must go together to achieve state-of-the art performance—and certainly to achieve it at lower costs.

One of the biggest benefits in the manufacturing technology area comes (again) from taking a relatively nontraditional approach. Until recently, the focus in the process area has been on robotics and other forms of machine automation. Although this clearly will remain the focus in the next generation, two additional technologies are becoming very significant. First is that of information technology; second is simulation and modeling. Data systems and electronic networks throughout the factory linked directly into the engineering operation will allow simultaneous computer-assisted design and manufacturing. Essentially, the engineer designs the product on a computer and simultaneously programs the robots that control the production process. The data system then monitors the production results (statistically) and highlights areas that need process or product improvements. In simulation and modeling, the production process itself is modeled in detail and simulated on digital computers. Major changes can easily be tried on the computer and implemented at low risk to yield great benefits in both cost and time. The purpose is not simply to simulate the current production processes, but rather to develop totally new processes as a result of the availability of advanced information technology ("reengineering").

Finally, new accounting systems are being developed for factory operations to measure the cost and time of each activity, including the engineering and management functions. These systems, known as "activities-based costing," or when used as a management tool, "activities-based management," can be used to empirically validate the process simulations, as well as to measure the effectiveness of process improvements as they are introduced. To achieve the dramatic savings that are projected for these various techniques, however, far more research and development—including prototyping—on advanced manufacturing processes are also required. Today funding for such activities is minimal.

When these techniques are applied across a wide variety of products, the United States will become far more competitive in many dual-use areas. For example, the United States is basically out of the commercial shipbuilding industry. Yet because shipbuilding is so important to the U.S. Navy, if some of the new techniques can result in dramatic savings, it is conceivable that the United States could profitably get back into shipbuilding. (Germany currently designs and builds ships in an average of sixteen months; while the United States takes an average of thirty months.)

Apart from reentering an old commercial industry, there are other major advantages to dual-use R & D. The DoD would gain the benefit of the higher quality and lower cost that comes from the greater commercial volume. In addition, it would speed up the development cycle and reduce the cost for defense R & D to design future weapon systems, based on the use of existing commercial components and even subsystems. As noted, when this was done for a secure phone (by the National Security Agency) it cut the development time by a factor of five to one, and the production cost by ten to one.

The traditional front-end emphasis on new product technologies and prototyping has relegated manufacturing considerations to secondary importance, usually put off until production or—at the very earliest—full-scale weapons development. In the future, process technology should be considered just as critical as product technology.

There will always be a few very expensive investments required for new weapons production on systems that are essential for military needs. For example, the multibillion-dollar development and production of an advanced antiballistic missile system was found to be needed in the Persian Gulf conflict. The problem with these next-generation systems is the incredible cost for both the products themselves as well as the manufacturing equipment on which they are built. The R & D alone for a new aircraft is in the range of $2–$4 billion and for a new jet engine or even a new semiconductor facility, over $1 billion each. On projects of this magnitude, it is essential that the DoD fully utilize every technique for reducing cost and time. Needless to say, many of these new concepts represent a cultural change in the way DoD does business. For example, the apparently simple concept of activities-based costing was tried in the early 1990s by a number of defense firms. The voluntary participation between 1991 and 1993 dropped from eleven active participants to only two,[21] clearly not evidence of strong support. Thus it will take active and continuous leadership for the DoD to implement any new systems for continuous performance improvements with continuous reductions of cost.

To maintain technological leadership in the twenty-first century, it is clear that continuing high levels of defense R & D investments will be required; that these investments should focus on dual-use applicability; and that they should be driven as much by cost considerations as by performance. Finally, one other action that would greatly enhance defense R & D is simply speeding up the procurement process. By using electronic information systems between the government and industry, the award cycle can be cut down from two years to a few weeks or, at worst, a few months. The approach has been demonstrated but not widely applied. In this area as in others, the DoD can capitalize on the true benefits of rapidly changing advanced information technology.

Manufacturing

The manufacturing problems of the U.S. weapons acquisition process deal with figuring out the best way to achieve mass production efficiencies in small quantities. The solution has been referred to as "lean," "agile," or "flexible" manufacturing. It incorporates many of the ideas that have been developing over the last decade, such as "just-in-time inventory," "integrated product and process development," "total quality management," "enterprise integration," and particularly "worker empowerment."

The concept—largely developed by the Japanese—is to strive for a process that allows the customer to tailor each product to his unique desires and yet have the total volume in the factory be high enough so that, through the multiple use of flexible manufacturing equipment and information systems that control the factory, each item can be produced rapidly with high quality and at low cost. The key to success in this process is to drastically reduce setup times on machines (transferring from one product to another), thus allowing efficient operation on much smaller batches of goods. At the same time, the work force in the factory is constantly striving to improve both process and product, an approach that can be tolerated by a flexible manufacturing system that accepts continuous changes and continuous improvements.

Under ideal conditions (always the objective) the system has no failures and virtually no maintenance costs. It is continuously restructured to remove all non-value-added elements, and there is little or no inventory kept around. The parts and material arrive "just in time" to be used in the production process; each item produced has been ordered, for immediate delivery, by a particular customer. The large costs of carrying inventory (including the plant space and warehouses) are largely eliminated. In fact, inventory turnover, which may have been three of four times a year, now is twenty-five to thirty times a year.

In this process, "good enough" is not acceptable. There is a constant quest for "better." You continuously have to try harder just to maintain your share of the market because someone else is trying harder still. Since all workers feel part of the process and are empowered to improve it, there is much higher employee motivation. In addition, workers are rewarded when the whole team does a better job. Obviously, it takes a highly skilled and intelligent work force to operate within a flexible system, so training and education become key elements of this process.

To take advantage of the potential benefits from manufacturing technologies, Japanese world-class firms devote about 64 percent of their total

R & D dollars to these processes; top U.S. firms allocate about 32 percent;[22] the DoD allocates between 1 and 2 percent! Of a defense R & D budget of approximately $38 billion, the only clearly identified process-technology funding is approximately $350 million, for the so-called Man-Tech program (for a variety of small, manufacturing technology efforts) and the Sematech program (for semiconductor manufacturing technology). Because the Department of Defense historically has had such an extreme focus on the design of new missiles, aircraft, and tanks, it will be extremely difficult to reallocate resources to manufacturing. Nonetheless, this is an essential step.

This resource shift must be complemented by a change in the type of people who are involved in the early design process, specifically bringing in people familiar with manufacturing. The post–cold war DoD shift toward more emphasis on weapons' prototypes and advanced technology demonstrations (rather than large quantities of production or even full-scale development of major weapon systems) in no way changes the need for a manufacturing perspective. It does, however, change the nature of what the prototypes are intended to demonstrate. Now, it is equally important to determine whether a low-cost weapon could be developed, as it was before to focus on a high-performance weapon. This makes prototypes more expensive because engineers will have to consider future production costs while designing them, but it makes the prototypes far more useful. If one wanted to subsequently produce them, they could be manufactured relatively quickly and at much lower cost.

One DoD success story in manufacturing technology was Sematech. Here, the DoD shared R & D investments fifty-fifty with an industry consortia. The objective was to reverse Japan's lead in semiconductor manufacturing equipment. Because the Defense Department believed microelectronics were so critical to future defense needs, and because the DoD was becoming increasingly dependent on Japanese chips for their weapon systems, it decided to make a significant investment in the area. It focused on the manufacturing tools that make the chips, since that was the key limiting factor in advancing the state of the art. It was recognized that defense needs were a trivial portion of the overall semiconductor industry, so for the DoD to be able to buy its chips domestically meant revitalizing the entire domestic commercial semiconductor industry. The only constraint placed on the DoD investment was that firms that took part had to agree to initially use the equipment only in their domestic plants.

The arrangement eventually worked out by the industry itself was that a consortia of twelve semiconductor firms—that became known as Sematech—would put in $100 million per year for five years, and this would be matched by the DoD. Although the Bush administration tried to back out at one point—claiming they did not want to support "industrial policy"—the program was successful in reversing Japan's leadership in the semiconductor equipment field. At the end of the five years, not only did the Clinton administration continue the funding, but it added a commitment by the Department of Energy of around $20 million per year for five years to have the Sandia National Laboratory (DoE) match funds (again fifty-fifty) with Sematech to conduct further research.

The Sematech model has subsequently been used to set up other public/private manufacturing efforts, and it has been suggested for electro-optics, superconductivity, high-definition television, and advanced transport aircraft. But this approach may not be suitable for every sector of the industrial base. Alternatives could include: having industry do the work on its own in an individual plant; having a consortia of industry members or a consortia between industry and government; or having a totally funded effort by the government, either to an individual firm or a consortia; or any one of the above, but including university linkages. What is clear is that there are significant benefits to having the DoD focus on manufacturing technology leadership.

Dual-Use Critical Technologies

Since the beginning of the cold war, the U.S. government, and particularly the DoD, have been deciding which technologies are critical for national security and which are not, as evidenced by their funding choices. The issue now is whether there should be a greater role for the government in helping to stimulate those areas it deems critical to the economy as well. The argument for greater involvement emphasizes the importance of technology leadership to future economic growth and international competitiveness. This means using the R & D dollars that are provided by the DoD and focusing them as much as possible in dual-use areas. It also means increasing the government's R & D activities in other essential civilian areas such as transportation, education, the environment, and energy.

These resources should come from a redirection of current expenditures. For example, the United States now spends billions of dollars to benefit the real estate and construction industries through tax subsidization; yet neither of these industries has a big export market, nor do they utilize rapidly changing technologies that require such government subsidization. In the same way, the Small Business Administration makes the largest share of its loans to small restaurants, which have an extremely limited export market and certainly are not considered high-technology growth industries. In addition, the United States provides an annual farm subsidy of $91 billion,[23] primarily to large agribusinesses that could do very well without it.

The government must also begin to think of using cost-effective new technologies in solving some of its more traditional problems. For example, in the massive highway construction arena, switching to intelligent vehicle/highway systems (using advanced information technology to make better use of existing highways) instead of traditional "more asphalt" solutions that cost between $1 million and $100 million per mile, depending on whether one is in a rural area or in downtown Los Angeles.

Experts who are asked to list "critical technologies" tend to identify a relatively common set of areas. The lists of the Department of Defense, the Commerce Department, and the Office of Science and Technology Policy have an amazingly high level of overlap. Even comparing these lists with those put out by the Japanese or the Europeans reveals an extremely high overlap. Typical of the items almost universally agreed to are:

- electronics technologies;
- biotechnologies;
- information technologies;
- manufacturing and process technologies;
- advanced materials technologies; and
- software.

These critical areas have a wide spectrum of future markets and are often referred to as "generic." They are critical for both defense needs and commercial competitiveness; many represent areas in which the United States has been losing its leadership position.

As American industry has become more and more short-term (profit) oriented, DoD funds for basic research have become more and more critical for developing the nation's future competitive and security positions. Unfortunately, in the second half of the 1980s, even though its budget remained high, the DoD reduced its basic research allocations by 43 percent.[24] This is something that the nation cannot afford. Fortunately, basic research and applied technology are incredibly inexpensive, compared to the full-scale development, production, and support of weapon systems that DoD has been funding. With savings of tens of billions of dollars anticipated in weapons systems, there are large numbers of prototypes and advanced technology demonstrations, as well as basic research, that can be undertaken while still dramatically reducing the total funding requirements. Equally important, this front-end R & D lends itself to a dual-use focus.

Yet as the budget is cut back, the military services have been tending to focus more and more of their resources on some of the truly defense-unique areas—for example, the air force focusing on stealthy, high-acceleration fighter aircraft or the army on enhanced armored vehicles. Although essential to the long-term missions of the services, these foci cause most of the resources to be expended in a more traditional fashion and do not place the appropriate emphasis on the quantum leaps that are possible when one focuses on the more basic, and generic, technologies listed above. Thus much of the funding for some of this basic and applied technology has been coming from ARPA. These areas should be receiving increased funding from the services as well.

If performed using the ARPA model, defense R & D can be extremely effective. With a $1.5 billion budget, ARPA accounts for only 4 percent of Pentagon research but has produced a rich harvest for U.S. industry (commercial and military). Technologies nurtured by ARPA are now used in robotics, advanced aircraft, artificial intelligence, and supercomputing. ARPA currently funds research in ceramics, advanced memory chips, and parallel-processing computer software[25]—all dual use and critical. ARPA has shown that by operating with a small, highly qualified team and by funding out all of its R & D budget, a great deal can be done with limited funds. World-class computer labs at MIT, Stanford, and Carnegie Mellon were developed with funds from ARPA. As John Gage (of Sun Microsystems) stated, "Everything America has [in advanced computers] came out of a small group of dreamers supported by ARPA."[26]

With the shift in private sector industrial research toward more short-term objectives, ARPA is one of the few places still left that significantly funds long-term research. What is particularly important about the ARPA effort is that it is explicitly geared toward breakthrough technologies. Not aimed at just making a percentage improvement in conventional areas, ARPA goes for nontraditional areas and quantum changes that would totally affect the way things are done, creating completely new industries and new ways of overcoming society's problems—including increased security—if the research is successful.

Essentially, ARPA's strategy is completely consistent with the Schumpeterian notion[27] of "gales of creative destruction"—wherein a new technology or product can make a qualitative difference. This has been the case with stealth, numerically controlled machine tools, and virtual reality. It is these technological breakthroughs that really spur a nation's growth. Without such major qualitative advances, even doubling net investment in plant and equipment only raises the growth rate of real income by less than half a percentage point a year.[28] If this new plant and equipment, however, is devoted to the development of a rapidly expanding, totally new industry—such as portable computers; handheld position locating devices (using navigation satellites); or secure portable communications equipment—devices that create their own new markets and that frequently have application for both commercial and military users—then the impacts of the added plant and equipment investments can be far more dramatic.

The problem in these breakthrough areas is in creating the initial market. In fact, this can be a bigger problem that creating the technology itself. Consumers often do not know quite what to do with the new device or how to use it to take advantage of it, since it never existed before. Often it actually changes the way people do things, so they cannot see its advantage until there has been considerable experience with it. Thus one of the greatest roles that government can play is as an initial purchaser of dual-use products. This is exactly the role that ARPA played in the supercomputer field. By buying the early units and demonstrating their capabilities in a wide variety of fields—from nuclear weapons design through meteorology and oceanography—the world began to buy them, and other firms entered the market as suppliers, thus driving the costs down and improving the performance. Interestingly, although the government is not normally allowed to make guaranteed purchases of items that take more than a year to develop—because that extends beyond its one-year budget constraints—there is an exception made through Title III of the Defense Production Act that allows guaranteed purchases for "defense industrial base reasons." In recent revisions of this act, the Congress has become increasingly lenient in its definition of the industrial base, expanding the interpretation into areas involving dual-use technologies and the general area of "economic security."

Other branches of the federal government could also use the initial-buyer stimulation of new technologies to help move along a critical industry. For example, were the U.S. Post Office to guarantee the purchase of large quantities of electric-powered vehicles for their next-generation mail delivery cars, this could provide a very significant stimulus to the industry. In the same way, a U.S. Army initial purchase of hybrid (conventionally fueled/electric-powered) vehicles could be a stimulant for that technology.

A Technology Strategy

The only way for America to achieve technological leadership in either the military or commercial arenas is to continue to strive to stay ahead. Although perhaps self-evident, this is by no means an easy task. In the first place, it is impossible to do it in every area, so the nation must be selective in which areas it is going to focus. Then in each of the selected critical technologies, it must have some overall integrated effort and make best use of its total resources—both public and private. The clear objective must be to achieve the desired leadership position against extremely competent worldwide competitors, who have every intention of establishing a leadership position themselves.

From the above discussion, certain key points stand out. The U.S. technology strategy—and associated actions and funding—must have year-to-year consistency. On the other hand, the policy must allow for flexibility and a good deal of diversity; and, in the most critical areas, multiple options should be pursued. In fact, if the strategy does not build in various forms of competition, it is unlikely to be successful. Competition is not duplicative; it represents a way to both manage risk and achieve rapid results for the lowest possible cost.[29]

Most important, the technology policies must be market-driven—whether this market be in the defense or the commercial arena, or preferably both.

To achieve the military's needed cost and cycle time objectives, the technology strategy must achieve a far greater balance between product and process technologies than has been true in the past, with perhaps even an overemphasis on process to counter over forty yeas of exclusive focus on performance. Part of this increased emphasis on process would include the acquisition and dissemination of benchmarking data from abroad. It would also include the creation of incentives for capital investments. Finally, it would shift the overwhelming balance of the government's R & D expenditures to the private sector because of the links between engineering, manufacturing, and markets—links that do not exist in government laboratories.

As with ARPA, the government's investment strategy must focus on high-risk breakthrough technologies. (Industry is more likely to use its own R & D funds to pursue low-risk incremental improvements in the current technologies.) Breakthroughs can come in either performance or in cost; the latter are becoming increasingly important for both the DoD and the commercial world. Thus a new product that has an order-of-magnitude lower cost is as much a breakthrough as one that has an order-of-magnitude higher performance.

The vast majority of the government-funded efforts should be dual use. Since new products will be designed using concurrent engineering, early consideration of the production and even the support phases of these systems is a critical portion of the technology strategy and must be explicitly stated.

Another key element of the technology strategy must be the continuous tracking (benchmarking) of best practices throughout the world. One way of gaining access to new developments is through joint programs with other countries. Another way is through a significant U.S. presence in these countries. Today, Sweden has 17 technology attachés in Detroit and 147 worldwide. The United States has almost none. A sole exception, and yet a very important example case, is the recent establishment of an office by the American Electronics Association in Japan. It receives support from the Commerce Department and gathers technology data for the U.S. electronics industry. Its representative also sits on a number of advisory boards within the Japanese Ministry of International Trade and Industry.

A 1992 Carnegie Commission report noted that "very few talented career foreign service officers have had experience with science or technology, and there are very few science officers abroad." France, Germany, and the United Kingdom have a total of thirty-four experts in science and technology staffing their diplomatic missions in Washington, D.C. By contrast, the State Department has only two foreign service science and technology positions in France, one in Germany, and one in the United Kingdom, for a total of four.[30] Some people argue that it would be hard to disseminate this data to only U.S. firms. In fact, it would be hard to even define what is a U.S. firm. That should be a secondary consideration, however. The data must be broadly disseminated once it has been obtained. The United States should have a diffusion-oriented R & D policy, extending all the way to small and mid-sized manufacturers. This is especially significant, since larger firms usually operate on a worldwide basis and have their own capability to gather benchmark data. It is the smaller and mid-sized firms that need help in gathering that data and understanding it.

Benchmark data may come not from an identical industry but from other industries in other fields that are using new techniques in a different way. Although each sector has unique characteristics, there is an important lesson in the fusion of multiple disciplines and technologies that may represent the greatest opportunities for rapid advancement in new directions.

Prior to becoming Secretary of Labor in the Clinton administration, Robert Reich proposed six steps to return to technological preeminence:[31]

• scan the globe for new insights (technology absorption);
• integrate government-funded research and development with commercial production (dual use);

- integrate corporate research and development with commercial production (concurrent engineering);
- establish technological standards (benchmarks);
- invest in technological learning; and
- provide a good basic education to all citizens.

Although the above discussion covered the first four of these points in detail, the last two stress the obvious fact that technology policy is critically dependent on a high-skill work force. Thus we now turn to a consideration of America's greatest asset—its work force.

11

The Critical Work Force

In the old mass-production model of manufacturing, workers were viewed as a cost that management tried to limit by minimizing their number, their hourly wages, and their benefits. Under the theory of Taylorism—which truly established America's world leadership in manufacturing until the 1980s—the objective was to break down the steps required by each worker to the minimum. Thus few skills were required either in the factory or in the office, and as automation was introduced, the machine would simply replace the laborer. In today's "lean" production model, labor is viewed as a company's most valuable asset. The machines are there to make the people more efficient; the worker is an asset to be developed through life-long learning, rather than a cost to be controlled.

Labor inputs account for roughly 70 percent of the U.S. gross domestic product.[1] To achieve national economic growth, labor is the area where there is both the greatest potential and the greatest payoff from investment. If America is to have a strong (defense and civilian) industrial base, with state-of-the-art technology and products, the most critical element for this is its work force. Yet in recent years the U.S. approach to international industrial competition has been to drive down the labor cost of an American worker, as shown by figure 11.1.[2] Real wages had been growing throughout the 1960s and 1970s. After 1978, however, wages went down, so that by 1990 they were actually lower than they were in 1964. The dream of the American worker—to have his children earn more and live a better life—will be increasingly difficult to realize if America continues to be a low-wage producer.

Two things must happen in order to reverse this trend. First, workers must be far better educated when they enter the job market. And second, they must be encouraged to continue to learn throughout their lives. Although education in America is probably the best in the world for the top 25 percent of the population, for the rest it is poor. In developing countries, it has been found that the lack of human capital (education) has prevented countries from ever catching up to their industrial neighbors. For these countries, education is a much more significant investment than an investment in physical capital. Although the United States is certainly not underdeveloped, the lessons are relevant.

There needs to be a new orientation to education in America. Rather than being viewed as something that is completed at the age of seventeen (high school) or twenty-one (college), education must be seen as something that does not end with graduation. Knowledge development and skill training for careers must be a life-long venture, whether it be for work on the factory floor or in the executive suite. It must be done for both the employee's benefit (higher skills, higher pay) and for the corporation's benefit (increased productivity and profits). The rapid technological, economic, and labor market changes constantly taking place demand new, and often more intellectually demanding, job skills for those finished with traditional education and already in the labor force. In fact, over 80 percent of the projected work force for the year 2000 is currently employed.[3]

The second prerequisite for educational progress is for American industrial leaders to recognize the inherent potential of their work force and to encourage the realization of that potential. American workers are not encouraged to excel. A Public Agenda research study[4] found that only one out of four jobholders (23 percent) say that they are currently working at their full potential. Nearly half (44 percent) say that they do not put much effort into their jobs over and above what is required to hold on to a job. The overwhelming majority (75 percent) say that they could be significantly more effective than they are now. Nearly three-quarters of the work force (73 percent) say that the quality and amount of effort that they put into their job has very little to do with how much they are paid. As perceived by the employee, they will be paid the same amount for certain tasks, whether done well or done poorly. Nearly three-quarters (73 per-

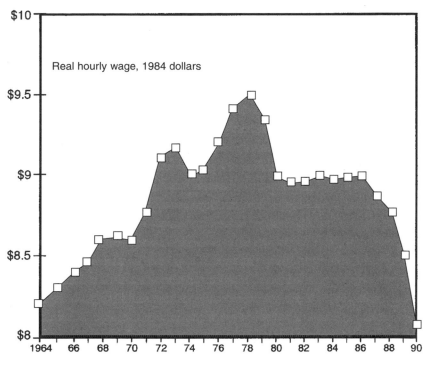

Figure 11.1
Real hourly wages, manufacturing
Source: U.S. Department of Labor Statistics, "Employment and Earnings," various issues.

cent) also believe that the absence of a close relation between pay and job performance is one of the main reasons why the work effort has deteriorated in America.

Clearly, improvement must be a two-way street. While management must encourage all employees to realize their potential, the workers must make every effort to continuously upgrade their knowledge and skills. Unfortunately, the data[5] show that most Americans—particularly those in the lower 75 percent—greatly overrate their personal literacy and skills and make little effort to upgrade them after leaving school.

In addition, many jobholders feel little connection between the productivity of their firms and their own welfare. A study conducted for the U.S. Chamber of Commerce found that only 9 percent of American workers believe that they themselves will be the primary beneficiaries of improvements in productivity. On the contrary, workers in the United States generally perceive that if they increase productivity and innovate, they will lose their jobs. In other nations, workers expect that, as the firm becomes more competitive and grows, the employees will benefit through higher wages, promotions, and greater job stability.

Japan's Ministry of Labor reports that of the country's firms with automated production, fully one-half have had to add workers to keep up with increased orders. Toyota states that it utilizes "automation with a human touch." The idea is not to remove the skill requirements of the workers but to build on their skills.[6] The recent experience of many American firms also indicates that effective use of automation can lead to expanded employment.[7]

Current Problems and Potentials

The United States has the highest overall levels of functional illiteracy of any major industrial power.[8] Thirteen percent of American students leave school without minimal reading skills; the percentage is 10 percent in the United Kingdom, 4 percent in France, Germany, and the Netherlands, and 1 percent in Japan. One of every five American adults is functionally illiterate, unable to read a job notice or make change correctly. In addition, one of every ten is impaired by drug or alcohol addiction. A majority of a generation of minority youths have never had a regular job. The problems are particularly acute among the young people entering the work force. For those between 21 and 25 years old:[9]

• Only 60 percent of whites, 40 percent of Hispanics, and 25 percent of blacks can locate information in a news article
• Only 25 percent of whites, 7 percent of Hispanics, and 3 percent of blacks can decipher a bus schedule
• Only 44 percent of whites, 20 percent of Hispanics, and 8 percent of blacks could correctly determine the change they were due from the purchase of a two-item restaurant menu.

Even when you look inside the factories and offices, the results are not very encouraging for the currently employed work force. There are 30 to

40 million functionally illiterate people working for American companies today.[10] Essentially, 20 percent of America's current workers are considered functionally illiterate, as compared to only 2 percent in Japan.[11] One-third of America's front-line workers are high school dropouts—often illiterate and innumerate. And 50 million people in the current work force need additional training just to perform their present jobs effectively.[12]

In spite of these crying needs, only 11 percent of American employees receive formal training from their companies.[13] This can partially be explained by the high worker turnover—"Why train them if they are only going to leave?" Some 40 percent of all U.S. workers have been in their jobs for less than two years. One-half of those in their first year will leave or be fired during the next year.[14] Of course with regard to turnover versus lack of training, one might argue about which is the cause and which is the effect.

Employers annually spend 11 percent of their equipment costs to maintain their equipment and less than 2 percent of their salary costs to maintain their employees' skills.[15] American firms invest primarily in plant, equipment, and college-educated employees. The 75 percent of the work force that does not have a college degree is largely neglected. As Ray Marshall and Marc Tucker have observed, "Our front-line workers . . . may be the least skilled among those of all the major industrial countries."[16]

When industry does invest in education and training, it is primarily for their college graduates. Correspondingly, there is a growing separation wages between the college-educated and others: in 1979 there was a percent differential, by 1989 the difference was 80 percent. In contr job distinctions and skill requirements between management and la are narrowing in world-class companies. Information technology eliminated the need for many middle managers, and empowerment c worker along with the flexibility required for lean production opera mean that there is a greater need for knowledge and skill across a br cross section of the work force.

Increasingly, there is evidence of the positive benefits of educatic training to the worker—but it must be geared to the skill levels re Productivity gains from on-the-job-training are twice those gaine the more general higher levels of education.[17] In addition, wor!

more motivated by education that is related to the skills that they will need, as evidenced by the fact that drop-out rates from vocational programs are significantly lower than those for comparable students exposed to general (high school) education programs.[18]

Because of both the need and the value of training to America's work force, one of the major thrusts of the defense conversion legislation that was pushed by Congress was geared to increased training for workers to help them gain new jobs. Unfortunately, most of this training was geared to workers on the way out from jobs. The evidence is overwhelming that there are far greater benefits of training for specific new employment—especially on-the-job training. The difficulty with attempting to retrain a worker to achieve a higher general skill capability—with no specific job in mind—is that there is very little motivation on the part of the worker and very little assurance that the right skills are being learned, since the new job is undefined. What modern companies have been learning is that the very best form of training is just-in-time training. In other words, if you need workers to do a specific job, train them right before asking them to do it, and then let them immediately apply those new skills. In this way there is no need for long-term retention. This integrated learning-and-doing process has an enormous synergistic payoff.

Certain basic skills are required today for almost all workers. These include computer operation; mathematics, to understand statistical quality control; and literacy to read instructions. Broad-based education—upgrading of higher-order thinking skills—is essential for the specific skills training needed for the work place. And because the technology of both the information age and the industrial world will continue to evolve rapidly over the coming years, life-long learning is an essential part of this worker education and training process. No world-class corporation can afford to let its greatest asset become obsolete. Nor can a worker who wants to maintain a high wage afford to.

This need for America's workers to be self-motivated (in continuously maintaining and increasing their skills and education) is compounded by the trend toward the "distributed workplace" (via telecommuting), as well as the trend toward a "contingent work force." The latter—frequently involuntary—includes part-time, contract, and self-employed workers and now composes 25 percent of America's work force.[19] (And

it is expected to grow to one in three workers by the year 2000.) Both the telecommuting and contingent workers require even greater self-motivation; yet it is not at all clear that the vast majority of American workers are sufficiently self-disciplined or motivated. In fact, the evidence is to the contrary.

In addition, a traditional motivation for self-improvement (through continuous education and training) has been the belief that the employee can gain significant rewards through promotion. With the leveling-out of modern organizational structures (the so-called delayering), many levels of management are being eliminated. Although this streamlining has obvious productivity benefits, twenty years ago an employee's chance of getting a promotion was one in five. Today, it is one in thirty. To properly motivate employees for continuous self-improvement, other reward systems will be necessary.

Engineers versus Lawyers

As the economy becomes more dependent on science and technology, American students are learning less science; fewer Americans are becoming engineers and physicists; and an increasingly smaller percent of the gross national product is being devoted to research and development of new technologies. To compensate, the nation is hiring more and more foreign-national scientists and engineers—to teach, to do research, and to manage industrial research.

The cause of America's science and engineering education problems begins in elementary school. "Children are being turned off to science, beginning the first day of first grade," Cornell University's Corson said. "The problem is so deep that I think it will take generations to solve."[20] Many elementary school science and math teachers are simply uncomfortable with the new technology. The National Science Teacher's Association has admitted on the record that a full 50 percent of its members were never qualified to teach the science courses that they are now trying to teach. In the elementary grades, estimates go as high as 95 percent.[21]

Since technology is evolving so rapidly, the half-life of an engineer's knowledge is now about five years. The majority of those teaching and practicing engineering have been out of school far longer than that, so their knowledge is basically obsolete. The only answer is continued education.

There is a death spiral at work here: math and science are poorly taught; students do not develop the required skills or interests for going on to engineering educations; companies cannot get the engineers they need; American firms move offshore, creating even fewer jobs and fewer incentives for students to study engineering; and the spiral continues downward. Even though engineering is critical for the future, industry and government are cutting back on long-term R & D funding as well as on support for capital equipment for research in universities. So the crisis deepens.

There is a particularly acute shortage of students in manufacturing engineering. In 1987 there were only two U.S. schools even offering degrees in manufacturing engineering (with 42 manufacturing degree graduates out of 75,735 total graduates that year). Only a few programs have been added since then. The result is that most people practicing manufacturing engineering in the United States today are not only without engineering degrees—only 4 percent have them[22]—but their knowledge is largely obsolete, relative to the rapid advances that have taken place. Clearly, massive retraining is called for in addition to the need for more university programs and students.

One study estimates that if an additional 10 percent of university students went into engineering, the growth rate of the economy would rise by 0.5 percent a year. By contrast, if law school enrollment doubled, the growth rate would fall by 0.3 percent annually.[23] Yet, the United States trains 1,000 lawyers for every 100 engineers—while in Japan the ratio is exactly the opposite: 1,000 engineers for every 100 lawyers.[24]

In 1987, Japan had only 18,000 lawyers, while the United States had over 500,000. Japan had one lawyer for every 6,693 citizens, the United States had one lawyer for every 360 citizens. By 1990, the U.S. lawyer population had swelled to 756,000. American universities graduate far more lawyers each year than exist in all of Japan.[25]

The shifting emphasis on litigation is visible even in the federal government. For example, from FY82 to FY88 the U.S. Department of Justice increased its personnel by 30.4 percent, while the Department of Education *decreased* its personnel by 31.6 percent.[26]

The lawyers in Washington are either in Congress, on their staffs, in the executive branch, or lobbyists (in 1993, there were 80,000 lobbyists in Washington, D.C.).[27] The fact that there are so many lawyers in Washington creates a continuing deluge of regulation and litigation—the antithesis of an environment that would focus on efficiency and effectiveness in the way the government does its business.

This general neglect of science and engineering at the expense of law, finance, and other fields has led some to compare the decline of America to that of England in the late nineteenth and early twentieth centuries—specifically, the British neglect of scientific and technical education for the masses.[28]

One clearly sees the American focus in the placement of financial incentives. Senior managers in industry frequently come from the financial or legal communities, while in Japan and Germany they come largely from the technical communities. Similarly, the phenomenal salaries of employees on Wall Street—mainly with legal and financial backgrounds—and in the large law firms dwarf the industry executive salaries.[29] Thus, even if American students are not discouraged from pursuing science and technology in the elementary and high schools, the market incentives discourage them when they get to college. Increasingly, American engineering schools are forced to recruit advanced engineering degree candidates, and even faculty, offshore. The result is that over one-half of the U.S. engineering graduate students are foreign students. While some of them, particularly from the underdeveloped world, stay on and contribute to America's economic growth, many go home. In fact, when one visits high-technology businesses in Europe and Japan today, one often deals with businessmen, entrepreneurs, engineers, and scientists who received their graduate education in some of America's finest universities.[30]

Interestingly, many of these foreign engineering students are subsidized by either an American state or the U.S. government. A National Science Foundation report noted that about 75 percent of the graduate students receiving financial support from university engineering departments are foreign nationals. Since a significant share of these are in state universities, the foreign students are being partially funded through state-subsidized tuition. And since much of the scholarship money comes from U.S. government (DoD) research grants, they are also being partially subsidized in that fashion. For the graduates who leave the United States, these engineering programs serve as an American-subsidized technology-transfer program.[31] Thus the DoD is actually making a significant contribution to the subsidization of America's foreign competitors—competitors both in the sense of economics and possibly future security.

The School System

In many ways, the problems in America's schools mirror those in the government, industry, and the military—namely, an overburdened overhead structure. In spite of the fact that manufacturing drives the economy, the data in figure 11.2 show that government employment (federal, state, and local) now exceeds that of manufacturing. Many of these jobs are bureaucratic overhead. Similarly, between 1980 and 1991 the number of officers in the U.S. Army grew by 7 percent, while the total number of soldiers shrank by 3.5 percent. Between 1965 and 1985 the number of non–teaching staff in school administration in the United States grew by 102 percent, while the number of students shrank by 8 percent.[32] This process has reached administrative nirvana in New York City, where 7,000 bureaucrats misrun the school system at an annual cost per pupil of nearly $7,000.[33]

The problem is basically not money. Spending per public school student (in real dollars, adjusted for inflation) rose from approximately $2,700 in 1970 to over $5,000 in 1992; yet the average SAT score for college-bound students fell (for example, on the verbal, from 460 to 420)—and those not bound for college fared even worse. The problems go beyond education. According to a 1985 survey of high school teachers in California, the most persistent school problems were: alcohol and drug use, depression, suicide, pregnancy, rape, and assault. In 1945 the same survey reported the most persistent problems as: talking in class, chewing gum, noise, running in the hall, cutting in line, and waste paper not making it to the wastebaskets.[34]

The federal government spends only 6 percent, or $26 billion, of the total spent on education in the United States. The Department of Education proudly points out that $330 billion of public money goes to education each year—40 percent more in real terms than ten years ago and more than the nation spends on defense. But, unlike defense, education

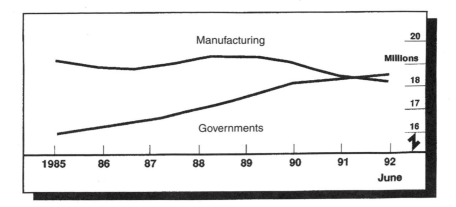

Figure 11.2
American employment
Source: *The Economist,* August 8, 1992, p. 16.

is almost entirely a state and local responsibility. Federal dollars have become even less significant (the 6 percent of total spending is down from 9 percent in 1980). The curriculum, teachers' pay, and most other school policies are fixed locally. This is actually highly desirable, since studies have shown[35] that the biggest contributor to good performance in America's schools is independence for school principals and teachers. This jars those anxious to impose tough management practices from above. It means that they would do better to delegate almost all authority and decisionmaking to individual schools—and let parents and pupils choose freely from among the results. But the results must be published.

With the growing problems, education is certainly an area in which the federal government needs to become more active—not in managing local schools, but in setting national standards for testing, in publishing the results for each school, and in doing research on the potential of modern information technology for education and training. One significant area for greater federal involvement is in developing the software that will greatly enhance the teaching ability of the teachers. There is growing evidence that new interactive, multimedia, computer-based teaching aides can be of considerable value in making teachers more effective.

The costs of developing the information technology are quite high and need to be funded. And the teachers must be trained in the use of the tools. Thus the federal government can have a significant role in education-oriented R & D, which is another area of dual use. The DoD has been extremely active in developing advanced teaching and education aides for its own work force (both military and civilian). In fact, it is leading the world in many areas of advanced simulation and modeling ("virtual reality") that offer a great deal of future promise, both for general education and particularly for skill development.

During the 1980s, education R & D was grossly underfunded by the Reagan and Bush administrations. In fact, President Reagan tried to abolish the Department of Education. The rationale for these actions, that is, the idea of less federal control over education, was undoubtedly valid. The need for research and development in applying modern information technology to America's education system, however, must be greatly stepped up—both for the school systems' use and for the lifelong development of the industrial work force.

Given the seriousness of the education problem in America, it is shocking that the total R & D budget for the Department of Education is only $350 million—less than 1 percent of the department's total budget and a truly trivial share of the $330 billion the nation annually spends on education.[36]

Industry

It is estimated that U.S. industry now spends between $30 and $80 billion a year on training—the spread indicates how little is known about it. It seems that most of this money (66 percent) goes to professional and management training,[37] while much of the rest goes to correcting the poor formal education of the workers, for example, teaching them to read instructions.

Top-flight companies that focus on worker training (such as Xerox, Motorola, and Hewlett Packard) spend about 3 percent of their total payroll on training. They are also world leaders in their fields; other companies are beginning to see the connection and want to emulate their programs.[38]

A significant number of leading firms are going to advanced interactive, computer-based individual training. For example, Federal Express has introduced a training program on quality for its 75,000 U.S. workers. They estimate this one-on-one method will save 80 percent, compared to comparable classroom training—and be equally, or more, effective.

Investments in worker education are easier for a firm in a growth marketplace than for a firm in a shrinking defense market. As defense plants become more dual use, however, they must also move in this direction. The defense work force is already a high-tech-oriented group, receiving a correspondingly higher salary as a result. In fact, Laura D'Andrea Tyson (head of President Clinton's Council of Economic Advisors) has found that the average high-tech worker receives about 22 percent higher wages than the average in all manufacturing.[39] The defense industry employs the highest proportion (30 percent) of minorities;[40] and it is the most highly union-organized sector of American industry.[41] Thus, as the defense cutbacks begin to displace workers and as the defense plants begin to diversify and convert to new businesses, this work force of highly skilled, highly paid workers should be completely amenable to advanced computer-based learning. Using the Bureau of Labor statistics, the following occupations have been identified[42] as "critical defense occupations" (in order of numbers of employees): aeronautical/astronautical engineers; aircraft assemblers; electrical and electronic engineers; engineering technicians; aircraft engine specialists; industrial engineers; shipfitters; system analysts and computer scientists; engineering, mathematical, and natural science managers; mechanical engineers; electrical and electronic equipment mechanics, installers, and repairers. Obviously, these high-technology areas lend themselves to a process of continuous learning; and, if pursued, to aiding firms achieve defense conversion. The absence of upgrade training, however, is a very big detriment to many former defense workers—especially engineers and managers—in aiding the transformation or in getting jobs in commercially oriented world-class companies. On the other hand, if both their management training and technical skills are up-to-date, then they are extremely desirable employees, especially to mid-sized U.S. companies attempting to capture some of the growing commercial markets.

Although many America firms have been increasing their focus on the importance of training, they must now shift from an emphasis on management to include total work force training. In fact, the more that one can train at the lower levels, the more it is possible to achieve worker empowerment and thus eliminate many of the layers of management and administration. The major hurdle is in overcoming the cultural barriers of many senior people—in both government and industry—to a clear recognition that labor must be viewed as an asset and must be invested in.

Government Education and Training

Apart from research and evaluation, there are two other major roles that the government has traditionally played in the training area: running programs for American workers, and running them for federal employees. The federal government spends $18 billion a year on 125 different training programs; the states have almost as many. Michigan, for example, runs seventy different programs, administered by nine separate departments. Unfortunately, as the British magazine *The Economist* observed, "Plenty of experts agree that a ragged army of state and federal programs [throughout the United States] delivers training in a pitifully scattershot fashion."[43] The incredible proliferation of "conversion" training programs at the state and federal levels (described in chapter 4) suggest the extent of this uncoordinated and overlapping effort. Nonetheless, the programs are probably better than none at all.

On the other hand, some of the very best and most widespread training is done by the federal government for its own employees. One of the largest training programs in the world is that which the Department of Defense provides to its military recruits. Here, about 250,000 people are trained each year in everything from basic reading and math to becoming electronic technicians and pilots. After serving just a few years, many return to the civilian economy far better educated and trained than when they entered. Defense cutbacks will result in significantly reduced training. Not only will the military suffer from this, but America's economy will also be dramatically affected. It will be hard to replace such basic education and skill training elsewhere. For one thing, the military environment and peer group influences are unique and conducive to positive results. Although industry may be forced to provide some of this training, it will add to their costs and thus make them less competitive (in the short term).

Both military and civilian personnel in the Department of Defense will have to have far higher skill levels themselves to deal with the information technology utilized by their weapons and their management systems. The need for increased technical and management skills by officers involved in the weapons acquisition and support area began to be recognized in the mid-1980s. Prior to that, military promotion had been primarily given to those on operational ("warfighting") career paths. Even the senior acquisition positions, such as program manager and materiel commander, were often filled by officers with little or no acquisition education or experience. In recent years, however, with a push from the Congress, there have been conscious efforts to develop career paths with promotion potential for the "providers"—to match those of the "warfighters." This includes specific training and education. This increased professionalism of the military members of the DoD acquisition corps has been matched by a similar effort on the civilian side. Although they represent very positive steps, there is still a long way to go.

According to a report by the Office of Personnel Management, the quality of the U.S. federal government work force at best "has remained fairly constant over time."[44] Given the need for greater decentralization of decisionmaking and the increased knowledge and skill levels required, this is simply not good enough.

Clearly, the problems of upgrading the education and skills of the government work force (military and civilian) directly mirror those of the industrial population, as well as the needs of American elementary and secondary education. For this reason, the work that the government does in developing its training tools and techniques can be of dual use. This could be funded by the Department of Education, the Department of Defense, the Department of Labor, or elsewhere. The Defense Department, however, has already developed a strong cadre of people working in this field, making it likely they will continue to take the lead in training and education. If advanced information-based tools and techniques can be made applicable to government, industry, and the school system, a small defense R & D investment can be of enormous benefit to the nation.

The political appointees who are put in charge of the acquisition work forces in the various government agencies are desperately in need of greater prior relevant education, training, and experience. Key agencies such as Defense, NASA, Transportation, and Energy have had greater and greater restrictions placed on potential candidates for their top acquisition jobs (including limits on their post–government employment) with the result that fewer and fewer of the appointees come to the job with any relevant experience. As one observer noted,[45] "imagine that every four or eight years, the Board of Directors of a company fired the chairman, president, vice-presidents, and all other executives, replacing them, in six months, with people who had little or no work experience at that company or even in that industry. This is precisely how the federal government selects most of its executives when a new administration takes office."

The solution to this problem is twofold. The first is to actually hire people with relevant experience. Clearly, this has the potential for possible conflict—for example, a senior executive coming from a defense firm. However, that can be (and is) handled simply by the executives excusing themselves from any decisions having to do with their former employer, and this can be monitored quite closely. A second (complementary) action that has been suggested relates to just-in-time training for those who are coming into the government. There usually is some extensive period between their selection and their approval—in recent years it has dragged into many months—during which they could receive extensive training. For those coming from industry who have the relevant technical and management experience, they can be trained in how the government works. Those coming from Washington law firms and Capitol Hill staffs, who understand how the government works but have no relevant industry experience, can at least be minimally educated in defense acquisitions, since they will be responsible for spending billions of dollars of the nation's resources. Again, the development of the software for such training programs would have to be sponsored by the government, which currently is not being done. The work itself could be accomplished in universities or elsewhere.

Education and training of government workers in other countries has always been a higher priority than it has in the United States. In many of those countries (ranging from Japan to France), government workers are looked upon as an elite corps. They come from the best schools, are paid well, receive extensive career development training, are given wide respect by industry and their peers, and can often look forward to high-level employment after leaving the government. By contrast, in the United States the government is often looked at as an employer of last resort. The fact that most politicians run against Washington and are constantly ridiculing the "bureaucrats in Washington" does not help at all. As much as many people would like the government to simply go away, that is obviously not going to happen. In fact, most people can easily list the things they expect government to do for them—ranging from local and international security through roads, schools, transportation, and communications. Government employees, like school teachers, are critical to American society; both need to be elevated in stature, if the nation is to realize its full potential.

Training in Other Countries

Both Germany and Japan spend two to three times as much on training as the United States does. Germany, with one quarter the population of the United States, has 1.7 million worker apprenticeships, while America has 300,000.[46] These positions are geared to the critical transition faced by the youth out of high school. Because German corporations recognize the value of the skill training provided to their future workers, they provide extensive funding (about 70 percent) of the vocational apprenticeships.[47]

More than 50 percent of the seventeen-year olds in Germany are enrolled in apprenticeship programs. Participation is encouraged in a couple of ways: by a substantial differential between trainee wages and those of a skilled craftsman, and by a well-organized and extensive multiyear system, with extensive industry involvement. Such programs are not available in the United States. The German system is financed and controlled by employers acting through industry associations and by local education authorities. Trade unions also provide important inputs. The formal written examinations and certifications assure that the skills acquired are highly transferable and are based on current technology.

Sweden also places great emphasis on education. A sample of Swedish workers was recently asked whether they had taken part in any form of education during the previous year. No fewer than 58 percent of professional workers, 54 percent of other white-collar workers, and 43 percent of unskilled workers said yes. But by far the most embracing form of adult study in Sweden are the informal study-circles, which are organized by voluntary organizations. In 1986–87 study-circles attracted 2.6 million adults, in a country of 8.4 million people. As a result, Sweden's well-educated workers are considered among the most productive in Europe.

European countries often use training and unemployment programs to help workers make the transition from shrinking occupations, such as bookkeeping, to growing ones, such as providing health care.

In addition, other countries place a great deal of emphasis on worker involvement. In one 1992 comparison,[48] for each 100 employees, U.S. firms receive only 12 suggestions for improvement, compared to 3,664 in Japan; while only 9 U.S. employees make suggestions, compared to 75 Japanese. In both countries, those suggestions made and adopted have been found to have a big payoff. So the need in America is to encourage more of them— to show employees that their suggestions will be welcomed.

The results of such employee involvement were borne out by the work of Daniel Roos[49] of MIT. He compared the Japanese emphasis on involvement and training in their plants in Japan as well as in their transplants in the United States with the activities of American-owned plants in North America and with European-owned plants in Europe. As shown in table 11.1, the Japanese provide the same teamwork environment in all their facilities but receive far fewer suggestions from their (mainly American) employees in the United States than they do from their workers in Japan. This is a cultural issue that the Japanese hope to overcome through additional training of their employees in the United States. New production workers in American-owned plants receive dramatically less training than those working for the Japanese—either in Japan or in the U.S. transplant operations. But as the data in table 11.1 show, training by itself is inadequate to enable U.S. workers to compete effectively with the Japanese. It must be built on a solid foundation of education, and it must go along with empowerment, teamwork, and other modern manufacturing management principles.

Two things that the Japanese have really focused on is the value of American higher education and the benefits of learning from your com-

Table 11.1
Average assembly plant characteristics (1989)

	Japanese in Japan	Japanese in North America	Americans in North America	All Europeans
Percentage of work force in teams	69.3	71.3	17.3	0.6
Suggestions per employee	61.6	1.4	0.4	0.4
Training of new production workers (hrs.)	380.3	370.0	46.4	173.3

petitors. In 1989 there were 18,000 Japanese studying in U.S. universities—many sent by their companies—while only 900 Americans were studying in Japan.[50] Similarly, there were about 5,000 Japanese scientists working in U.S. laboratories, while fewer than 150 U.S. scientists worked in Japan.[51]

Clearly, one requirement for advanced education in a foreign country, whether it be in universities or in industry, is to have the necessary language skills. Until very recently, studying Japanese generated little faculty or student interest and was certainly not stressed in engineering programs in America. By 1993, however, Japanese had become the number one foreign language taken by students at MIT[52] and number two at Harvard.

Nonetheless, for the overwhelming majority of future workers, the greatest payoff still comes from a solid education at the elementary school level and even earlier. Britain now establishes a national elementary school curriculum and a testing program for England and Wales, but allows each school to direct its budget to the specific needs of its students. In France, public preschools serve 85 percent of three-year-olds and 100 percent of five-year-olds, and there are state-funded supplemental classes for schools in impoverished districts, where the extra help is clearly required.

Finally, it must be emphasized that a key area of focus for many foreign countries has been the quality of their teachers—something that, unfortunately, America has not stressed. For example, Japan's well-paid teachers spend 40 percent of their school day in preparing lessons that encompass a variety of teaching methods in order to keep their students involved. The quality of education begins with the teacher.

Future Challenges

By the year 2000, 65 percent of all jobs in America will require some education beyond high school. However, even in professional and technical jobs—the largest single occupational category[53]—70 percent of the jobs will not require a college degree. This explains the growing interest in the German apprenticeship program for post–high school education.

About half of all service workers will be involved in collecting, analyzing, synthesizing, structuring, storing, or retrieving information as a basis of knowledge.[54] This will require far greater skills than the vast majority of today's service workers possess.

For both factory and service workers, computer skills will clearly be a basic requirement. The fastest growing employment sector in the economy will undoubtedly be in the software area—the engine that basically drives the information era.

Demographics in the twenty-first century will also change significantly, and both women and minorities will play an increasing role throughout the various levels of the work place. In fact, over the remainder of the decade, 85 percent of those entering the work force will be non-whites, women, and immigrants (with the native white male representing only 15 percent of the new entrants).[55]

The role of union leaders will also change. Rather than fighting technology, they must be involved in technology policy in a positive way. Indeed, labor and education policies must be integrated. Critical to this is the creation of a learning economy, which requires the support of industry, labor, government, and the educational establishment. Life-long learning means that the education market extends from preschoolers up to, and often beyond, retirement. In addition, as the world becomes more global, a significant part of life-long learning is foreign study. If we are to compete in the global marketplace, we must be able to speak other languages and understand other cultures.

America must become a high-skills/high-wage economy in the twenty-first century. A low-skills/high-wage economy will not be competitive; and a low-skills/low-wage economy will not achieve our objectives of a strong national security posture, economic growth, and a better life for the work force.

12
Achieving Civil/Military Integration

Survey data show that close to 85 percent of Americans simply are against change—on almost any issue. The changes required to achieve civil/military integration are in some cases major; the resistance, accordingly, can be expected to be severe. One must recall Machiavelli's warning on the difficulty of introducing change in government: ". . . it ought to be remembered that there is nothing more difficult to take in hand, more perilous to conduct, or more uncertain in its success, than to take the lead in the introduction of a new order of things. Because the innovator has for enemies all those who have done well under the old conditions, and lukewarm defenders in those who may do well under the new. This coolness arises partly from fear of the opponents, who have the laws on their side, and partly from the incredulity of men, who do not readily believe in new things until they have had a long experience of them. . . . Thus it happens that whenever those who are hostile have the opportunity to attack they do it like partisans, whilst the others defend lukewarmly. . . ."[1]

Yet the restructuring of the U.S. defense industrial base has to happen, for three basic reasons. *First,* the restructured military forces of the post–cold war era have to be equipped with the weapons to fight twenty-first century conflicts, but with far fewer dollars than in the past. *Second,* the U.S. needs to create an innovative, responsive, efficient, and effective domestic defense industrial base with lower costs, smaller quantity weapons production, and greatly reduced dependence on foreign military sales. *Third,* the tens of billions of dollars of annual defense R & D and production expenditures have to go beyond uniquely military applications to help overall U.S. economic growth and international industrial competitiveness (for DoD and the nation's mutual benefit).

In the same way that American industry has the primary responsibility for America's industrial competitiveness, it also has the dominant responsibility for coming up with an overall integration/conversion plan—and for taking initial actions—if it expects to get any government short-term help in making the transition. It is essential for American industry to apply the most advanced management techniques and the best technology toward improving U.S. competitiveness. In addition, it must help assure that America's greatest asset, its work force, is not only well educated and trained, but also fully challenged and utilized to its potential capacity.

Today individual firms and industry associations ask the federal government for help with foreign military sales, with weapons' production, loan payments, depreciation for capital investments, research and development funding, worker training, and so on. In the future, in exchange for such assistance the government must insist on specific integration/conversion plans and actions from the industry, lest the industry become more and more defense dependent and fail to take the lead in bringing about the desired restructured industrial base.

America's labor unions also have a leading role to play in pushing for new training and education of the labor force, not in lobbying for subsidies to maintain the current structure. The major responsibility of the federal government is to create an overall environment favorable to long-term national economic growth. It must create incentives for long-term investments (by firms, pension funds, and individuals); reduce the national deficit; and redraft current industrial policies. A reallocation of resources is required, from subsidies to agriculture, home building, small restaurants, and similar areas to sectors with the potential opportunity for rapid economic growth, increased exports, and the creation of whole new industries. Obviously, this shift is made far more difficult by the fact that new industries have very few voters, while old and decaying industries have enormous political power. Thus the restructuring strategy must explicitly address the issue of work force transition to the new structure.

Improved management of existing resources includes improved management of people. Since the growth industries are clearly going to be information intensive, a high-skill domestic work force is required. If resources are not spent on training local labor, U.S. industry will be forced to move offshore to find its workers.

The most immediate, government actions, however, relate to removing existing barriers to civil/military integration. As noted, between 60 and 75 percent[2] of the current barriers can be removed by the executive branch (largely the DoD) without legislative changes, although many require at least the passive cooperation of the Congress. The remaining barriers are primarily driven by legislation—and must be addressed by the Congress. The two most difficult obstacles to transition are the cost-based contracting process and the procurement process (both made worse by the DoD's often extreme interpretations and applications of the laws in these areas). In the future, the Congress must be willing to step down from its position of imperial rule maker, in which any legislator—without study or advice—can simply implement a bill that he or she feels will improve ("reform") the defense procurement system. It will be necessary for the Congress to allow defense procurement to be done in a fashion similar to that of the commercial world. For this to be achieved, each proposed piece of legislation must be subjected to independent analysis of its likely cost and structural impact. The same procedure of course must apply to executive branch regulations.

To better understand the reason for study and negotiation prior to implementation, consider the following example:[3] On April 17, 1992, the government's Cost Accounting Standards (CAS) Board published a "Recodification of Cost Accounting Standards Board Rules and Regulations" in the Federal Register. The board issued the recodification even though, at that time, there was a presidentially directed federal government moratorium on new regulations. The announced logic was that, "The economic impact on contracts resulting from this recodification is expected to be minor . . . [and] regulatory impact analysis is not required."

Commenting on this, the accounting firm Arthur Anderson stated: "In our view, the recodification is probably the most significant piece of regulation to impact non-DoD contractors in the last 20 years or more. We believe that the government made a serious error in extending full CAS coverage to non-defense contracts. It will result in fewer suppliers willing to do business with the government and then only at higher prices."

Thus a seemingly minor regulatory change intended only to "recodify," resulted in significantly higher prices and less competition for government business. But the regulator never analyzed the cost impacts prior to the action.

Congress will have to have better control over its own actions. A major boost toward these required changes was provided in 1993 by Vice President Gore's task force on "reinventing government." Its highest priority government procurement recommendation was to "shift from a set of rigid rules to a set of guiding principles"[4]—supplying detailed explanations and guidance but allowing government procurement personnel and program managers to be empowered to make management decisions in the government's best interest—the same concept that is applied in the commercial sector with the Uniform Commercial Code.

Sixteen Specific Government Actions

The restructuring of the defense industrial base is, above all, a cultural change, in many ways similar to that which U.S. and foreign companies have been forced to go through in order to remain competitive. From them, there are useful lessons to be learned.[5]

1. The first step in successful transformations has been a clear "vision statement"—in this case, of an integrated defense industrial base. This must be accompanied by a strategy for achieving that vision—in this case, technological leadership, human resource development, and removal of the barriers to integration. It is essential that these objectives be reinforced repeatedly—by the president as well as by the leaders of Congress—and eventually elaborated on. For example, one elaboration would be a clear statement of the strong American preference for private sector operations whenever possible.

In the same way, it will be necessary to continuously emphasize the three aspects of civil/military integration that have been highlighted throughout this book: dual-use R & D; integrated facilities; and the purchase of commercial parts, subsystems, and equipment. It is important to counter the tendency to simply say "we'll buy a few commercial items and that will take care of integrating the industrial base." Rather, what is needed is a full transformation that must focus on dual-use R & D and factory-floor integration.

2. Once the vision and strategy are set—and continuously repeated—the second step is to achieve some early successes. The best way is to build on initiatives that have already been started, for example, by recognizing the positive contribution of an individual weapon system program manager who took bold steps to streamline operations.

Another initiative that can be expanded immediately is to dramatically increase the DoD's purchases of commercial items. With the passage of the National Defense Authorization Act for FY91, Congress declared that the time had come to start the process of rationalizing, codifying, and streamlining the defense acquisition process. An advisory panel was established that made recommendations[6] for consolidating and simplifying current laws and, particularly, for allowing the government to buy commercial items. But even these changes immediately ran into special-interest barriers, for example, the long-standing requirement that all small items (anything under $25,000) be "set aside" for procurement from small businesses. This restriction on size immediately limits procurement and takes a purchase out of the normal commercial world and puts it back into the tortuous world of defense-unique procurements.

To prevent this, greater rationalization of procurement guidelines and an expanded definition of what encompasses commercial items (for example, modifications of commercial items and items intended for commercial use but not yet sold to the general public) are needed. The procurement reforms approved by Congress in 1994 move in this direction.

3. Then the definition of "commercial" needs to be expanded still further, specifically to encompass commercial facilities—as an important step toward integration. Initially, one could define a defense-unique item that came from a largely commercial facility (one with 80 percent of its sales going to commercial markets) as being a "commercial item." Then one could waive all of the special provisions that would otherwise apply to the defense-unique item. Public trust would be assured by the normal market forces that drive the operation of that commercial facility in terms of product cost and quality. Trust could be further increased by government-performed, independent market (price) analyses of the value of the DoD goods being purchased.

4. An expanded definition of "commercial" would still not include the major weapon systems area, where the overwhelming majority of defense dollars are spent. Here it is essential to make a weapon's price a part of the military requirement—similar to a weapon's performance. This single step would explicitly create the incentives for introducing all of the other efficiency-oriented changes. It would force economic considerations to take an equal priority with the historic, cultural/political/operational considerations that have almost exclusively driven both domestic and international defense programs in the past.

The impact of price considerations can be most easily seen in the case of future joint international weapons development. In the past, each country insisted on its own technology developments and production lines, regardless of duplication. Each country also insisted on its "just return" (getting back the share of the business that it invested in the program), rather than having the design or production work go to the country that is most competitive on a given product. Using cost as a driving consideration on these multinational programs would have enormous economic benefits for each of the countries involved. However, it would require an approach based on affordability, rather than on politics.

Affordability and effectiveness must similarly be put ahead of special interests in the United States. Consistent with making costs—specifically future production and support costs—a weapon's requirement would be to evaluate the adverse cost impacts of each and every law, regulation, specification, and standard currently imposed on a weapon's program— as well as those proposed in the future.

5. The next step is to recognize that each sector of the defense industrial base (ships, aircraft, electronics, munitions, vehicles, services, etc.) is dramatically different. Detailed sectoral analyses are therefore required, matching likely DoD demands in each sector (for R & D, production, and logistics support) against existing private and public capacities and capabilities. In some sectors, significant downsizing will occur; in others, preservation, or even initiation of new efforts, will be required. For example, the next tank and its engine may be made from materials like composite armor and a ceramic engine, so new facilities may be needed—and they should be planned as dual-use facilities.

An essential requirement of these sectoral analyses will be determining the desired structure in each sector, not picking winning and losing firms but deciding how many plants should remain in the XYZ sector, what the mix of private and public plants should be, and so on. The desired results will be achieved through the use of competitive market forces—assuming competition is present or can be created—and implemented through DoD contract awards. In the future, industrial base considerations will have to be a significant element in DoD's resource allocations and program decisions.[7]

6. The next step is that the DoD must establish a true preference for commercial specifications and standards in all DoD designs and manufacturing operations. Initial steps in this direction were taken—through Defense Secretary Perry's leadership—in 1994.[8] To implement this change the Defense Department would have to redirect its normal military specification and standards writers to either find equivalent commercial specs and standards or, together with the relevant industrial representatives, establish new ones. Maintenance of these dual-use specs and standards should be handled by national and preferably international standards groups that exist in the private sector—the DoD would simply be one of the organizations represented.

7. Since over 50 percent of the cost of defense weapon systems is at the lower tiers of the defense industry (supplier and parts) where transition to commercial items is most easily accomplished, there must be an immediate prohibition against passing down defense-unique rules to these suppliers. Today the prime contractor must pass down over eighty specific clauses to its suppliers,[9] and the primes often choose to add many more of their own. In a few cases, stopping this pass-down practice will require some legislative changes; in most cases, it will simply require the DoD to do some greater risk sharing with its prime contractors. They will be reluctant since the primes have the responsibility of meeting the government's unique requirements. The long-term solution is to remove defense-unique requirements from prime contractors as well.

8. Then there will have to be significant changes in the DoD's research and development practices, specifically, providing manufacturing-oriented efforts far greater resource support. Existing programs, such as

the manufacturing technology (ManTech) program, help stimulate process design and lower-cost technology development, but the greatest impact comes from actual weapon systems' lower-cost manufacturing and support. The R & D resources must be particularly shifted toward design-for-manufacturing and support (on weapons development programs). Thus a key element of the new R & D practices must involve a requirement for, and the funding of, the use of concurrent engineering on all new programs and major system modifications.

In addition, it is important that all production planning be done with the assumption of small-quantity production, which will most likely lead to the requirement for flexible manufacturing and multiproduct production on a common line. Ideally, this would mean all defense products integrated with commercial items, but—in the few cases where this is not possible—a least multiple defense products on the same production lines.

As with many of the other proposed changes, not all of the critical R & D changes require legislative revisions for their achievement. Nonetheless, they will be difficult cultural changes—requiring strong and sustained DoD leadership.

9. The next change would require that contractor support of logistics activities (sparing, repairs, and upgrades) should be assumed as the norm. Organic capability by the DoD should only be justified under special circumstances—such as on the front lines. Contractors should be given incentives to continuously redesign and upgrade their equipment for improved reliability. If firms chose to stop production of an old item, the drawings should go to the government to ensure a life-long supply of the item.

The move from organic maintenance to contractor maintenance would result in the reduction of large numbers of government civilian workers and large inventories of spare parts. It would shift DoD logistics support to the modern, "lean" approach, where the parts would almost all come directly from the factory, and where maintenance would be done largely at the contractor's expense, thereby ensuring greater initial reliability and continued product improvements. With modern communications and transportation techniques, inventories could be greatly reduced and parts could arrive "just-in-time."

10. Defense industry overheads must be dramatically reduced, probably through the use of activities-based costing. This modern management approach provides detailed visibility into the resources and time devoted to each activity within an industrial facility and highlights non-value-added functions. Thus the data for more efficient management would be immediately available, so the defense industry could direct its attention to reducing costs instead of simply justifying them. This should also reduce the need for excessive auditing and oversight by the government.

If activities-based costing is used in a dual-use facility, it will make the added costs associated with defense-unique requirements and their impact on each activity immediately clear. Where uniqueness is necessary, it will result in proper allocation of those costs. Thus a commercial item in an integrated plant will not be unduly burdened by the additional defense requirements as is often the case today.

11. Incentives must be created for firms to move to integrated facilities. For example, once activities-based costing has been introduced into integrated (largely commercial) facilities, these companies should be excluded from any unique defense procurement laws. This step would create an enormous incentive for defense plants to move in the direction of dual use, since all they would need to achieve "commercial" status would be to generate (for example) 20 percent of commercial sales out of the integrated facility, in return for which they would receive waivers from all of the unique requirements they previously struggled to live with. Public trust would be maintained through the management visibility provided by activities-based costing.

A complement to this, and an added incentive for factory integration, would be for the DoD to examine the quality of a manufacturing process, instead of exclusively the quality of the product produced. The modern factory management concept is to control the production process to remove all variability. When this is achieved, the process is responsive to any changing set of conditions and continuously yields high quality products. A supplier certification process can be set up to identify these world-class vendors, all of which can then be suppliers to the DoD.

It is important to emphasize that these processes will not be identical from firm to firm. Nor does the certification process become a fairness constraint on who can be a DoD supplier; it is totally open to anyone who can qualify. But it does restrict suppliers to only those who are quality producers. In 1986 the Presidential Blue Ribbon Commission on Acquisition (known as the Packard Commission) attempted to introduce statistical quality control as a requirement for achieving high quality in the semiconductor manufacturing process. Many DoD suppliers objected that this would be an "unfair" practice, even though it was common practice in most commercial semiconductor firms. Such hurdles will have to be overcome this time.

12. It is necessary to revise many of the Justice Department and Federal Trade Commission antitrust rules if the downsizing process is to be rational. As noted, there will be instances in which only two facilities in any given sector are all that are affordable, and yet provide adequate competition. Current antitrust laws would greatly discourage such consolidation if there were only three or four firms in that sector today. In some sectors it may be necessary to allow consolidation even below two, but here great effort should be made by the DoD to assure an expanded market definition—to include firms in related businesses that could potentially enter the market and to encourage firms that are not already making products in that area, but that have competitive technologies to consider developing their capabilities in the needed military arena.[10] Perhaps small DoD R & D contracts to these new defense suppliers would provide sufficient incentives to bring them in, once the current barriers to integration have been removed.

A related area in the antitrust regime is to encourage R & D consortia and other cooperative ventures. Industry (both defense and commercial), government laboratories, and universities should be allowed to work together, especially in the early development of new products that have market potential (the so-called precompetitive phases). The participants would share risks, costs, and know-how. Industry gains access to government technology and talent, and the government gains a better sense of market needs.

13. Advanced capital equipment, including information technology, is extremely expensive, particularly for small and medium-sized firms. The government therefore must give some consideration to the special financial problems associated with the capital investment situation in the de-

fense industrial base. As a result of the large investments in new plant and equipment made in the 1980s, many defense firms are saddled with a heavy burden. Since they are required by DoD accounting rules to charge off this equipment on any commercial work they might do (as well as on their defense business), it gives them a very severe competitive handicap— in fact, creating a significant disincentive to plant integration. Many small and medium-sized defense firms simply do not have the resources to invest in the equipment needed to be competitive in the commercial world. Thus the government must find a means to encourage conversion by these firms, either through rapid write-offs on current and new equipment, or through the availability of long-term, low-cost capital. One recommendation[11] is to set up a private-sector bank (one proponent called it the "Corporation for Defense Conversion") for investments in firms that need help in making the transition. The condition for receiving funds would be that the only constraint on the firm's success was a lack of capital. Other options, including government-guaranteed loans or even government-furnished equipment, are also possible.

14. There must be a widespread shift from today's lengthy and cumbersome government contract award process to a modern, electronic-data-exchange procurement system. This "lean" system would shorten a process that now takes nine to eighteen months (or longer for major weapon systems) to one that takes a few months or less. It is a necessary move toward facilitating increased efficiency and effectiveness in performing government business.

15. There must be a government civilian manpower reduction plan for the DoD. This would include reduced government oversight, management, and acquisition people, as well as the government (and quasi-government) workers in the depots, labs, arsenals, and federally funded research and development centers. Fewer workers will be needed to staff and supervise the few remaining unique government requirements. But to assure a smooth downsizing, there needs to be a specific manpower phase-down plan. Part of this could be satisfied through base closures, attrition, and other such techniques; but the overall master plan needs to be made explicit and then to be monitored on a quarterly basis. Without the deliberate removal of government people who are no longer required, there will simply be a shifting of personnel from one function to another; where

regulation and excessive oversight is removed in one area it will increase someplace else. Thus the only way to assure successful implementation is to reduce in-house staffing, thereby decreasing the civilian work force by 30 percent to 50 percent.

Vice President Gore's 1993 task force on "reinventing government" recommended an overall civilian government work force reduction of 252,000 people over a five-year period.[12] (President Clinton had run on a platform of at least a 100,000 cut.) Were this reduction to be achieved and the process continued as changes evolved, there would clearly be a significant gain in government efficiency.

16. The last and perhaps most critical of the actions—besides the need for establishing a clear vision and strategy—is to have explicit institutional mechanisms to monitor the progress of the cultural transformation. A system based on output measures has to be established to evaluate all aspects of integration—facilities, operations, costs, shorter development and production cycles, higher reliability, and so on. There will be a need for flexibility and mid-course corrections but not for alterations in the objectives.

A senior, independent group of outsiders (former congressional leaders and defense industry executives, academics, etc.) should be set up by DoD officials to help them monitor progress. Because many of the transition issues necessarily involve other departments of the executive branch (Treasury, Commerce) it may be useful to also have a separate interagency organization assisting with the implementation (discussed below). The outside advisory group could help them too. But this outside group should not have an authority of its own (such as a congressional or a presidential commission) to avoid the danger of developing two sets of initiatives (one from the DoD leadership and one from the commission). All prior successful cultural transformations have clearly shown the need for a single coherent leadership and direction.

Two suggestions that have considerable merit relate to the issue of how to get congressional support for the required cutbacks and essential legislative changes. The public sector of the defense industry (depots, labs, arsenals) have such strong congressional influence that it may be impossible to close them down one-by-one. Thus it has been proposed[13] that a "Commission on Rational Downsizing of the Public Sector of the Defense

Industry" be established. Modeled on the independence of the Base Closure Commission and chartered by the Congress, its objective would be privatizing the defense industrial base in all areas except for those functions that are inherently governmental. It would periodically submit an all-or-nothing list of balanced cutbacks for administration and congressional approvals, as the Base Closure Commission now does. (Or, as an alternative, the Base Closure Commission itself could be used to achieve this objective.)

Similarly, it may be necessary to approach many of the required legislative changes in an all-or-nothing fashion. This is a recommendation that was explicitly endorsed in an independent Carnegie Commission study[14] on defense acquisition reform. Some such technique may be required simply to get the Congress to do what they know is necessary, but that they cannot bring themselves to do on their own.

One way to greatly speed up the transformation process is to take maximum advantage of existing legislation wherever it can be used—and thus avoid going through the Congress to begin the changes. As can be seen from table 12.1, many of the proposed sixteen changes do not require congressional action. In fact, on a number of them, the DoD has already begun to take initial steps.

The Defense Production Act

One law that was explicitly set up for strengthening the defense industrial base and moving it toward a dual-use model was the Defense Production Act (DPA); specifically, the 1992 Reauthorization of the Defense Production Act.

In the past, Title III of this act was used chiefly to create incentives to spur domestic development of new capacity for advanced materials required by the DoD, but only available offshore. In most cases, government help was required to overcome industry reluctance to invest because of the uncertainty of the demand and/or the threat of foreign competition entering the market. To counter this concern, a two-phase program was established. The first phase typically gives a contractor a fixed sum to produce small quantities of material and make it available for compliance testing. In the second phase, the contractor reaches quantity production

Table 12.1
Sixteen specific government actions

---

1. Issue and continuously reiterate a strong statement of the new vision and strategy, that is, civil/military integration and the three-part strategy;

2. Encourage the buying of commercial items; specifically, fully implement the Panel 800 recommendations;

3. Immediately expand the definition of "commercial" to include defense-unique items produced in a largely commercial facility;

4. Make costs (production and support) an essential requirement for weapons' design—at a level comparable to performance;

5. Perform sector-by-sector analyses of the desired future structures—both private and public—of each critical defense industrial sector, and identify the paths and actions leading to achievement of the new structures;

6. Require the use of commercial/industrial specifications and standards—unless written waivers are obtained;

7. Prohibit flow-down of any defense-unique requirements to the lower tiers—unless written waivers are obtained;

8. Shift R & D resources—generic and, particularly, programmatic—to focus on process technologies, concurrent engineering, and dual-use applicability;

9. Shift logistics support to industry (from organic), and use "lean" (just-in-time) concepts;

10. Shift to activities-based costing to reduce industry overheads and, correspondingly, government oversight and auditing;

11. Create incentives for defense plants to move to dual-use operations—for example, by providing waivers from defense-unique requirements if a plant achieves 20 percent commercial sales and gets its quality and activities-based costing processes certified;

12. Revise antitrust rules to allow efficient and effective defense industry downsizing;

13. Explicitly address defense firms' capital needs—especially the small and medium-sized firms—for low-cost capital and rapid write-offs;

14. Rapidly shift the defense procurement process to a "lean," electronic system, to reduce the procurement period from many months to weeks, but still preserve public trust;

15. Implement and monitor a government (civilian) work force reduction plan to reduce government overhead and assure acquisition process streamlining; and

16. Establish an outside senior advisory group to help the DoD leadership (and perhaps other executive departments) monitor implementation and assure achievement of the envisioned changes.

under a purchase commitment that establishes the government as the buyer of last resort, with the expectation that there will actually be an adequate commercial market to absorb the production.

Today the Title III program's mission is changing rapidly. The reductions in DoD's procurement budget and Congress's 1992 decision to give the program an explicit mandate to foster civil/military integration has shifted its emphasis to dual-use products. Thus Title III could become an important tool in the conversion efforts. For example, as an alternative and/or addition to its prior focus, Title III funds may be used for product development, testing, and qualification without continuing on to production. This approach was recently used for open architecture, numerically controlled, machine tool controllers. The government supported the development of an "industry standard" prototype by a joint venture of controls manufacturers and ensured that the system would be fully tested, and the results made available for use in future product marketing. The actual production and marketing of the controllers are the responsibility of the individual firms that will compete for the business.

The Title III program has historically been limited by administrative action to purchases and purchase commitments. But grants, loans, and loan guarantees are also authorized and could provide a broader range of conversion assistance. Since the current prohibition is based on an interagency agreement between the Office of Management and Budget and the DoD, it could easily be changed to meet conversion objectives.

The overall purpose of Title III of the DPA is to ensure the viability of an industrial source that is critical to DoD, while increasing that company's ability to operate profitably in the commercial marketplace. This objective is obviously closely aligned with the conversion needs of the defense industry, as well as with the objectives of the DoD's required future defense industrial base.

Complementary Broad Government Actions

There are a few significant areas in which the government could facilitate a more rapid evolution to a new defense industrial structure. One of these is for the Congress to shift to a multiyear resource allocation process. The current one-year fiscal cycle—and often even less than that, since continuing resolutions are frequently used—greatly hampers efficiency.

No other developed country operates on a one-year fiscal plan. Most of them use a rolling five-year plan, where they annually debate the sixth year and simply approve a budget for the current year based on the first year of the prior multiyear plan. The United States could move to a rolling three-year budget; the current congressional budget process is geared to that.[15] A simple two-year budget would not likely achieve the required stability because of the uncertainty at the end of the second year, including the significant incremental changes that would likely occur at that time.

Another area in which the government can have a significant impact is in its international dealings, particularly with Japan and Europe. The United States must take a far more integrated view, linking its trade policies, export-control policies, joint-development programs, and others to the objectives for a restructured defense industrial base.

The export control of critical defense technologies has traditionally been under government management. In the future, the list of items that are controlled can be greatly reduced because in most cases economic competitiveness is more of a concern than national security. What needs to be done is to develop a very limited list of items that are critical for both commercial and military reasons. For example, the DoD for years has successfully controlled foreign access to the design of advanced versions of the critical hot-section of aircraft jet engines—an obvious dual-use product. A short list of controlled exports—that will vary from sector to sector—will also provide the required guidance to industry.

Critical technologies management should be expanded to include the gathering and dissemination of information from other countries. Since the United States is no longer the leader in many critical areas, it is essential to take advantage of the available data, often in foreign languages. Historically the United States has taken a very narrow view of such international data gathering—primarily because America was usually ahead—so the only interest was in intelligence gathering on potential military adversaries. Unlike most U.S. economic competitors, American engineers do not take full advantage of what is available from foreign sources. The U.S. government must help sponsor foreign study, foreign data gathering, foreign language programs, exchange programs with foreign industry, etc., to improve the data gathering and benchmarking on international competitors in areas of critical technology. Again, tracking of such data can be part of the required sectoral analyses.

The government can also greatly facilitate the conversion effort by encouraging high-technology civilian investments, primarily in R & D. There are enormous overlaps with defense technology in such areas as information, communications, transportation, law enforcement, domestic security, medicine, health care, energy, education and training, environment, civilian space applications, and manufacturing technologies. In areas where there are mission applications that are controlled by other government agencies (e.g., transportation, energy, environment), it is up to the government to stimulate the long-term, high-risk research and development; in some cases, this may mean becoming the guaranteed first production purchaser. The government must actively create an attractive nondefense market for many defense firms.

Finally, the government can make significant investments in public sector infrastructure that can have a dramatic impact on economic growth, as well as help in defense conversion. For example, investments in the infrastructure associated with air traffic management, national information networks, and smart highways could stimulate new markets and new domestic industries. At the same time, they would provide business opportunities for high-tech defense firms.

Overcoming the Resistance to Change

This book could not possibly end without addressing the obvious question of "why is this defense procurement reform likely to succeed when all of the other attempts over the past decades have failed?"

The first, and easiest, answer to this question is that, today, things are different. In the past, no matter what people said, there was always the firm conviction that the defense budget would remain high—because the communist threat was still there and growing. In the post–cold war era, there is a general acknowledgment that the world has changed. There is no question that defense dollars will stay down for some time. Yet there is still the need to maintain a strong defense posture—especially in view of the worldwide instabilities, conflicts, and spread of arms. So, with high and rising weapon system costs, a declining defense budget, an inefficient and rapidly deteriorating defense industry, and a requirement for new weapons, a Defense Department crisis is at hand!

Prior successful cultural changes—such as those in some state and local government agencies, as well as those in U.S. industry—all began with the recognition of a crisis. This is a necessary, but not sufficient, condition for achieving a cultural change of the magnitude being considered here.

The defense industry recognizes a crisis. With its market disappearing and the current isolation of the industry, there are few directions for the vast majority of the defense industrial managers to turn. A few will choose to dramatically shrink down and form the basis of the remaining defense-unique facilities. But the overwhelming majority will either diversify or disappear. This recognition of the industrial crisis is different today than it was in the past, when most firms felt they could simply weather the storm.

Another reason for believing that it might be possible to make the change this time is that many of the nation's leaders—in both the executive and legislative branches—recognize the need for this change and are in agreement about the direction in which it should go. In the Defense Department (initially led by Clinton appointee William Perry, as deputy secretary of defense and then as secretary), the integrated, civil/military industrial base model is increasingly being accepted as the desired future direction. It is also being accepted throughout other major portions of the government. President Clinton, Vice President Gore, and many other members of the first post–cold war administration (from the Commerce Department, the Labor Department, and, particularly, the new National Economic Council) have all advocated a similar direction. Naturally, there is still strong opposition—both in portions of the executive branch and particularly on Capitol Hill from those representing the various special interests that would be affected by such a change. Nonetheless, the leadership is sufficiently aligned and motivated to achieve dramatic changes. This is a condition that has not been true in the past when many in the DoD and in the White House argued that things were fine as is.

Some important lessons can be learned from looking at specific reasons why prior major recommendations for change in the DoD have failed.[16] Specifically, there were seven principal impediments:

1. The goal of the recommendation was not fully accepted by the implementing organization and/or by the top-level management.

2. There were threats to jobs, and/or a perceived conflict of interest in implementing the recommendation.

3. There was poor communication of the intent of the recommendation.

4. There were no incentives to change, and change represented a risk to a basically risk-adverse group.

5. Inadequate resources were provided to make the change. Savings were projected and people were told to reduce the resources and implement change—but there was no recognition that the change costs money and that it would take time to realize the eventual benefits.

6. There was no sustained supported for the change from the leadership, and often not even sustained leadership. The time required for full and effective implementation was often longer than the time that political appointees were in their jobs.

7. In all cases there were no output measures of improvement.

Each of these issues must be addressed in attempting to change the way the DoD does business. Actions taken to start an effort—a reorganization or the issuance of a directive—cannot be considered the measure of accomplishment. The improvements required must be viewed as a process change, not just as a rewriting of rules or a redirection of programs. And the implementations must be carried through until they produce the intended results. This is a particularly critical point; the type of change recommended here will take at least five years, and perhaps three years to even begin to see the impact in any measurably significant way. There will be visible qualitative changes along the way, however, and these must be highlighted and built upon.

To overcome the anticipated resistance to change, there must be an excess of communication. A coherent and simple message, easily understood, must be reiterated again and again. People must be assured that their concerns have been addressed and that they are being dealt with fairly.

Because of the relatively short time that most political appointees are in office—typically an average of two and one-half years or less—it is essential that an institutional mechanism be established for helping to make defense conversion happen, to measure its progress, and to make midcourse changes as needed. At the beginning of the Clinton administration, an Interagency Conversion Committee was set up, co-chaired by the deputy director of the National Economic Council and the under secretary of defense for acquisition. It included representatives of all of the relevant agencies. This committee could serve as the basis for such a more permanent interagency institution.

One of the main functions of both the interagency committee and the external advisory board will be to help establish output measures of effectiveness (of the change) and to report on them over time. These obviously include longer-term cost and schedule trends in weapon system developments, as well as some intermediate measures affecting the transformation of various systems (specifications and standards, cost accounting, auditing, procurement) and, from the industrial side, the actual achievement of plant integration, commercial component, subsystem and system acquisitions, and the implementation of modern electronic information technology within the industrial structure.

Other functions of an advisory committee can include:

• identification of the critical product and process technologies that will provide long-term technological leadership for security and economic growth;
• adequate, efficient, and effective government and industry stimulation of research, engineering, and manufacturing efforts in the identified critical areas;
• assurance of coordinated civil/military integration of both government efforts and particularly domestic industrial activities;
• adequate consideration of public trust and fairness issues;
• necessary antitrust revisions to allow appropriate downsizing and consortia in both the engineering and manufacturing areas;
• incentives for the stimulation of capital investments by industry;
• assistance in access to foreign technology;
• export control over critical dual-use technologies;
• support for the necessary infrastructures; and
• assurance of adequate international benchmarking data on critical technology areas.

Conclusion

By the mid-1990s, U.S. commercial industry was starting to turn the corner, significantly enhancing its productivity in many sectors. The macroeconomic conditions were not yet favorable for greater gains, however, and many in the Congress had not yet recognized the need for introducing serious institutional changes. Certainly, the United States was not well on its way to restructuring its defense industrial base or the DoD weapons acquisition process. On the positive side, a number of lower-level organizations within the DoD were initiating changes in the desired direction, and numerous top-level policy changes were being instituted. Yet policy changes are not enough—careful attention must be paid to the details of implementation.

Successful change of the magnitude envisioned here requires a six-step process:[17]

1. Preparation: establish the vision and the strategy;
2. Commitment: high priority of leadership time and team-building;
3. Deployment: communication and training to gain widespread alignment;
4. Action: slow at first, but accelerating as it spreads;
5. Reinforcement: team rewards and widespread recognition of successes; and,
6. Results measurement and feedback: output measures and adjustments as required.

The benefits of the proposed change can be extremely significant. Literally, tens of *billions* of dollars of increased efficiency and effectiveness can be realized in the defense weapons acquisition arena alone. The United States will have a defense industrial base capable of providing for its peacetime and crisis demands at a dramatically lower cost. And, U.S. economic growth and international industrial competitiveness will be aided by the large defense R & D and production investments that will, and must, be made for the nation's long-term security.

The alternative is to continue on the present path and end up with a small, highly subsidized, inefficient, ineffective, noncompetitive, and technologically obsolete defense industrial base, with an absence of either a surge capability for crisis demands or any civilian benefits to the nation from defense R & D and procurement expenditures.

Notes

Chapter 1

1. *Business Week,* August 7, 1989, p. 5. See also: Los Angeles Times-Mirror poll and Yankelovich poll for *Time* and CNN as reported in A. Pine and T. Redbum, "U.S. Sounds an Economic Call to Arms," *Los Angeles Times,* August 6, 1989.

2. John Truman, "Less is More," *Boston Globe,* May 9, 1993.

3. For example, see the report by the Committee on Science, Space, and Technology, U.S. House of Representatives, February 1992.

4. See figure 11.1 (Source: U.S. Department of Labor Statistics).

5. The actual multiplier effect, that is, the number of indirect workers affected by a cut in direct employment, is estimated to be an added 50 percent (a factor of 1.5) by the end of the first year and a factor of 2.5 by the end of three years, with some estimates reaching 3.5. For these three estimates, see Leon Taub, "The Macroeconomic Impact of Increased Defense Spending," Chase Econometrics (Wharton Forecasting Model), Occasional Papers, 1983, p. A-8; Albert A. Hirsch, "Policy Multipliers in the BEA Quarterly Econometric Model," U.S. Department of Commerce, *Survey of Current Business,* June 1977, p. 63; and the 3.5 ratio is suggested by Terleckyj in Gene Koretz, "Defense Cuts Could Wound the Economy for a Decade," *Business Week,* October 5, 1992, p. 30.

6. After the Korean War peak of 12 percent, defense expenditures fell to 6 percent of GDP; from Vietnam the fall was from around 8.5 percent to 5 percent; and the Reagan peak reached around 6.5 percent. Source: Budget of the U.S. Government, FY93, Supplement, February 1992 (Washington, DC: Government Printing Office), pp. 82–88.

7. Jay Mathews, "IBM Plans to Cut 35,000 More Jobs, Reports $8 Billion Quarterly Loss," *Washington Post,* July 28, 1993.

8. Boyce Rensberger and Daniel Southerland, "National Science Board Warns U.S. Must Beef Up R & D," *Washington Post,* August 13, 1992.

9. Lois Lembo, "Lessons from the Past: Mitigating the Effects of Military Cutbacks on Defense Workers," in *Military Cutbacks and the Expanding Role of*

Education, Nevzer Stacey, ed., Office of Educational Research and Improvement, Department of Education, Washington, DC, October 1992.

10. "Adjusting to the Drawdown," report of the Defense Conversion Commission, Department of Defense, Washington, DC, December 31, 1992, Annex B.

11. J. S. Gansler, *Affording Defense* (Cambridge, MA: MIT Press, 1989), p. 53.

12. Ibid., p. 175.

13. This concept has been evolving over the last few years and is the working title of a forthcoming book by the futurist Alvin Toffler. It was also independently suggested by Andrew Marshal of the Office of the Secretary of Defense.

14. "Acquisition Streamlining," Defense Science Board, unpublished study, Washington, DC, 1992.

15. A. Carter, W. Perry, and J. Steinbrunner, "A New Concept of Cooperative Security," (Washington, DC: Brookings Institution, 1992), pp. 29, 30. In addition, the 1994 Defense Science Board summer study on "Information Systems Architecture" (final report, August 1994, Washington, DC) drew an interesting distinction between information used *in* warfare and information warfare itself (where the latter focuses on deception or destruction of enemy information systems). The term "information-based warfare" used here is intended to include both types.

16. Statement by Les Aspin, Chairman of the House Armed Services Committee, April 23, 1992, office press release, p. 3 (also in Congressional Record for that day).

17. "A Trial of Strength" *The Economist,* April 3, 1993, p. 31.

18. Rep. Les Aspin, "The Use and Usefulness of Military Forces in the Post-Cold War, Post-Soviet Worlds," office press release, Washington, DC, September 21, 1992.

19. Richard Bitzinger, Defense Budget Project, Washington, DC, February 26, 1993.

20. As so brilliantly described by Elting Morison in *Men, Machines, and Modern Times* (Cambridge, MA: MIT Press, 1966), and by Robert O'Connell in *Of Arms and Men: A History of War, Weapons, and Aggression* (New York: Oxford University Press, 1989).

21. "A Persistently Nuclear Nightmare," *The Economist,* April 3, 1993. p. 52.

22. *London Observer,* May 9, 1993.

23. Barton Gellman, "U.S. Sought Saudi Aid to Block Sale of Russian Submarines to Iran," *The Washington Post,* October 30, 1992.

24. Brian Bremner and Amy Borrus, "Get Yer Red Hot Bombers, Tanks, & Missiles" *Business Week,* September 21, 1992, p. 44.

25. *International Herald Tribune,* London, May 5, 1993.

26. "Arms Sales Boom," *The Economist,* August 13, 1994, pp. 24–28.

27. "Asia Unleashed," *The Economist,* April 3, 1993, p. 15.

28. "A New Wolf in South-East Asia," *The Economist*, March 21, 1992, p. 37.

29. P. Choate and J. Linger, *The High Flex Society: Shaping America's Economic Future* (New York: Alfred Knopf, 1986).

Chapter 2

1. K. Adelman and N. Augustine, *The Defense Revolution* (San Francisco, CA: ICS Press, 1990), p. 130.

2. *New York Times*, September 20, 1992.

3. Laura D'Andrea Tyson, "Ask the Right Questions About America's Strategic Industries," *Harvard Business Review*, November-December 1988, pp. 103–107.

4. For a detailed discussion of this dual economy, see chapter 6 of J. S. Gansler, *The Defense Industry* (Cambridge, MA: MIT Press, 1980), pp. 128–161.

5. Defense Conversion Commission, Logistics Management Institute, "Impacts of Defense Spending Cuts on Industry Sectors, Occupational Groups, and Localities," report Annex F, Bethesda, MD, p. iv.

6. *Richmond Times Dispatch*, September 12, 1993.

7. A 1987 Massachusetts government study found a 23 percent higher average pay for defense workers. As quoted in the *New York Times*, April 15, 1990.

8. Department of Defense, "100 Companies Receiving the Largest Dollar Volume of Prime Contract Awards," FY 1991, Washington, DC, 1992.

9. Richard Bitzinger, Defense Budget Project, Washington, DC, 1993.

10. Martin Bollinger, Booz-Allen and Hamilton, Washington, DC, April 23, 1993.

11. For a detailed discussion of these unique practices, see Gansler, *Affording Defense*, pp. 141–215.

12. This was the position taken explicitly by the Bush administration, as frequently stated by Chief of Staff John Sununu and many others. For a good discussion of this (with specific quotations), see Kennedy School of Government case (C16–90–942.0) "DARPA and High Definition Systems: For Home or For War?" (Harvard University, Cambridge, MA, 1990).

13. Gansler, *The Defense Industry*, pp. 9–12.

14. Bruce Scott, "Competitiveness: Self Help for a Worsening Problem," *Harvard Business Review*, July-August 1989, p. 120.

15. Choate and Linger, *High Flex Society*, p. 651.

16. Testimony of Clyde Prestowitz to the Joint Economic Committee, Washington, DC, December 3, 1991.

17. T. Misa, "Military Needs, Commercial Realities, and the Development of the Transistor, 1948–1958," in M. Smith, ed., *Military Enterprise and Technological*

Change: Perspectives on the American Experience (Cambridge, MA: MIT Press, 1985), pp. 276–287.

18. D. Noble, "Social Choice in Machine Design," in A. Zimbalist, ed., *Studies in Labor Process* (Monthly Review Press, 1979), pp. 25–26.

19. As quoted by John Mintz in "For U.S. Shipbuilders, a Perilous Passage to 'Conversion'," *Washington Post,* August 30, 1993.

20. A detailed analysis of the firm type, revenue size, and defense dependency has been done by Richard Bitzinger, "Adjusting to the Drawdown: The Transition in the Defense Industry," Defense Budget Project, Washington, DC, 1993.

21. The basic idea is to have an objective commission review a set of base closures recommended by the DoD, and then to submit a single, inclusive list to the Congress. The law requires that the Congress cannot change any item on the list. They must either accept the full list or reject it totally.

22. Aerospace Industries Association, "Year-End Review and Forecast—An Analysis," Washington, DC, December 1992.

23. National Research Council, *High Stakes Aviation: U.S.-Japanese Technology Linkages in Transport Aircraft* (Washington, DC: National Academy Press, 1994).

24. Laura D'Andrea Tyson, *Who's Bashing Whom?: Trade Conflict in High Technology Industries* (Washington, DC: Institute for International Economics, 1992), pp. 214–215.

25. Statement by President Clinton as reported in the *Washington Post,* October 27, 1993.

26. Memo from Leon Panetta, director of the Office of Management and Budget, to Agencies, Washington, DC, March 1993.

27. This observation comes from: J. DiIulio, G. Garvey, and D. Kettl, *Improving Government Performance: An Owner's Manual* (Washington, DC: Brookings Institution, 1993).

Chapter 3

1. U.S. Congress, Office of Technology Assessment, *Global Arms Trade: Commerce in Advanced Military Technology and Weapons* (Washington, DC: Government Printing Office, 1991).

2. Akio Morita and Shintaro Ishihara, *The Japan That Can Say No: The New U.S.-Japan Relations Card,* (Washington, DC: Government Printing Office, 1989), p. 4.

3. Theodore Moran, "The Globalization of America's Defense Industries: Managing the Threat of Foreign Dependence," *International Security* (Summer 1990), p. 69.

4. David Leech, "Conversion, Integration and Foreign Dependency: Prelude to a New Economic Security Strategy," *GeoJournal* 31.2 (October 1993), pp. 193–206.

5. Congressional Budget Office, Fiscal Analysis Division, Washington, DC, 1991.

6. David E. Sanger, ".Japanese Busy Seeking Superconductive Products; Though Success Is Seen as Far Off, Many Work to Apply Technology," *New York Times*, January 29, 1989.

7. R. Fof and N. Gross, "Silicon Valley Is Watching Its Worst Nightmare Unfold," *Business Week*, September 4, 1989, pp. 63, 67.

8. Stan Hinden, "Taking Their Orders from Tokyo," *Washington Post*, November 8, 1992.

9. Clyde Prestowitz, "Giving Japan a Handout: Why Fork Over $7 Billion in Aircraft Technology" (General Dynamics Corp signs agreement to help develop Japan's FSX fighter jet), *Washington Post*, January 29, 1989.

10. Paul Blustein and John Burgess, "High-Tech's Global Links: Costs Unite Former Rivals" (international partnerships), *Washington Post*, July 16, 1992.

11. Evelyn Richards, "ATT, NEC Join Forces on Chips" (joint development of advanced microchip technology), *Washington Post*, April 23, 1991.

12. Martin and Susan Tolchin, *Selling Our Security: The Erosion of America's Assets* (New York: Alfred Knopf, 1992), p. 220.

13. Testimony by John Wilson of the National Academy of Sciences, July 21, 1992, based on the report "The Government Role in Civilian Technology: Building a New Alliance," National Academy of Engineering, Washington, DC, 1992.

Chapter 4

1. Federal Procurement Data Center, as contained in Richard Bitzinger, Defense Budget Project, "Adjusting to the Drawdown," Washington, DC, 1993.

2. "Still Waiting for the Bang," *The Economist*, October 2, 1993, p. 70.

3. Defense Budget Project, "Adjusting to the Drawdown," Washington, DC, 1993, pp. 15–16.

4. Offsets are arrangements whereby the seller agrees to let the buyer perform some assembly or manufacture of a weapon system as a condition of the sale, or else the seller agrees to make reciprocal purchases of some other goods the buyer produces.

5. Informal speech by William Anders, Washington, DC, April 7, 1993.

6. Amy Borrus, et al., "From Bullets to Bullet Trains: It Won't Be Easy," *Business Week*, April 20, 1992, p. 110.

7. John Lancaster, "Defense Bill Includes Soviet Aid," *Washington Post*, November 2, 1991.

8. Steven Pearlstein, "Putting Off Tough Choices on Weapons" (White House and Congress delay decisions on which weapons programs to cut), *Washington Post*, October 7, 1992.

9. Steven Pearlstein, "FTC Seeks to Block Merger of Defense Firms," *Washington Post,* November 7, 1992.

10. Gansler, *Affording Defense,* pp. 183–84.

11. *Defense News,* April 15, 1991, p. 3.

12. Martin and Susan Tolchin, *Selling Our Security,* pp. 231–232.

13. From 1991 to 1993, an index of defense stocks created by Jack Modzelewski of Paine Weber (and reported in *Business Week,* September 20, 1993, p. 88) rose 140 percent, while the Standard and Poor's 500 index rose only 38 percent. And this was in a time of plummeting defense budgets, with no expectation of future increases.

14. David Ravenscroft and Frederick M. Scherer, *Mergers, Sell-offs, and Economic Efficiency* (Washington, DC: Brookings Institution, 1988).

15. *Washington Post,* September 28, 1992.

16. "Arms Sales Monitor," *Federation of American Scientists* 21 (July 1993), p. 16; also see: "Arms Sales Boom," *The Economist,* August 13, 1994, pp. 24–28.

17. *Washington Post,* October 4, 1992.

18. Ibid.

19. Martin and Susan Tolchin, *Selling Our Security,* p. 149.

20. Richard Stevenson, "No Longer the Only Game in Town," *New York Times,* December 4, 1988.

21. R. Forsberg and J. Cohen, "The Global Arms Market: Prospects for the Coming Decade," Institute for Defense and Disarmament Studies, Cambridge, MA, 1993.

22. Some argued that Congress was structurally unable to take the difficult but required actions. See "Beyond Distrust: Building Bridges Between Congress and the Executive," National Academy of Public Administration, Washington, DC, January 1992.

23. Stevenson-Wydler Technology Innovation Act (P.L. 96–480), which in 1980 sought to expand technology transfer of federal research efforts to industry; amendments to Patent and Trademark Act (P.L. 96–517), which in 1980 gave title to inventions arising from federal funding to businesses, universities, and non-profit institutions; the Federal Technology Transfer Act (P.L. 99–502), which gives (1986) title to authorized activities designed to encourage government, industry, and universities to perform cooperative research; and the Omnibus Trade and Competitiveness Act (P.L. 100–418), which created (1988) the Advanced Technology Program at the Department of Commerce and established the Regional Centers for the Transfer of Manufacturing Technology (also funded by the Department of Commerce).

24. John Burgess, "U.S. Awards Grants to Aid Technology," *Washington Post,* March 6, 1991.

25. Jane Rottenbach, "Technology Transfer Works on a Regional Level," *Managing Automation,* May 1991, pp. 50–52.

26. Christopher Farrell, et al., "Industrial Policy," *Business Week,* April 6, 1992, p. 73.

27. Ibid.

28. "Compendium of Programs to Assist the Transition," Annex G to "Adjusting to the Drawdown," report of the Defense Conversion Commission, Washington, DC, February 1993.

29. General Accounting Office, *Multiple Employment Programs* (Washington, DC: Government Printing Office, GAO/HRD-92–39R, 1992). Also, see *Nations Business,* March 1993, p. 25.

Chapter 5

1. Michael Porter, "From Competitive Advantage to Corporate Strategy," *Harvard Business Review,* May-June 1987, p. 43.

2. T. Dunne, et al., "Patterns of Firm Entry and Exit in U.S. Manufacturing Industries," RAND *Journal of Economics,* Winter 1988.

3. Ravenscroft and Scherer, "Mergers, Sell-offs and Economic Efficiency."

4. Paul Healy, Finance and Service Industry Seminar, Sloan School, Industrial Liaison Program, MIT, Cambridge, MA, October 27, 1989.

5. T. Michael Nevens, et al., "Commercializing Technology: What the Best Companies Do," *Harvard Business Review,* May-June 1990, pp. 154–163.

6. For example, see Ann Markusan, "Dismantling the Cold War Economy," *World Policy Journal,* vol. 9, no. 3, Summer 1992, p. 389ff.

7. Steven Elliott and Regis Schultis reported a 70 percent failure rate for venture startups.

8. Paul Blumhardt of Martin Marietta reported a 32 percent success rate from data over the 1973–93 time period. "Defense Conversion," Naval Research Advisory Committee report, Washington, DC, November 1993, p. 55, while a 1991 survey of 148 firms reported a success rate of 36 percent. The Wiabridge Group, DRI/McGraw-Hill, The Fraser Group, "The Commercialization of Defense Technology: A Survey of Industry Experience," Lexington, MA, November 1991, p. 2.

9. Blumhardt's data showed that firms that converted into closely related areas had much higher success rates, for example, commercial aerostructure subcontracting (71 percent), and civil government information systems (67 percent).

10. J. Lundquist, "The False Promise of Defense Conversion," *Wall Street Journal,* March 18, 1993.

11. 1972 National Science Foundation Study, "The Western European Experience," Washington, DC.

12. Seymour Melman, *The Permanent War Economy* (New York: Simon and Schuster, 1974), p. 243.

13. "Economic Adjust/Conversion," report by the President's Economic Adjustment Commission, Washington, DC, 1985, p. 43.

14. Seymour Melman, *Profits Without Production* (New York: Alfred Knopf, 1983). See also Melman, *Permanent War Economy*, p. 85.

15. Ibid.

16. Ibid.

17. Richard Nelson, "High Technology Policies: A Five Nation Comparison," American Enterprise Institute, Washington, DC, 1984, p. 73.

18. B. Udis, "Adjustment of High Technology Organizations," National Science Foundation, Washington, DC, October 1974.

19. C. A. Montgomery and B. Wernerflet, "Diversification, Ricardian Rents, and Tobin's," RAND *Journal of Economics*, Winter 1988, pp. 623–632.

20. This was the case found in Swedish defense industry diversification. See N. Ball, "Converting the Workforce," *International Labor Review*, July-August 1986, p. 412.

21. S. Gordon and D. McFadden, *Economic Conversion: Revitalizing America's Economy* (Cambridge, MA: Ballinger, 1984), p. 112.

22. Murray Weidenbaum, *Small Wars, Big Defense: Paying for the Military After the Cold War* (New York: The Twentieth Century Fund, 1992), p. 47.

23. Ball, "Converting the Workforce," p. 410.

24. Ibid.

25. Ibid.

26. David Leech, "Conversion, Integration and Foreign Dependency," *GeoJournal*, October 1993, pp. 193–206. The SIC code information is based on unpublished work by Brian Dickson of TASC (for the Department of Defense) and reported to the Defense Conversion Commission, October 30, 1992, Washington, DC.

27. C. K. Prahala and Gary Hamel, "The Core Competence of the Corporation," *Harvard Business Review*, May-June, 1990, pp. 79–91.

28. Melman, *Permanent War Economy*, p. 230.

29. Malcolm S. Salter and Wolf A. Weinhold, "Diversification via Acquisition: Creating Value," *Harvard Business Review*, July-August 1978, p. 176.

30. Eric Schine, et al., "The Defense Whizzes Making It in Civvies," *Business Week*, September 7, 1992, p. 90.

31. "Export-led Growth Strategy for Israel," Jerusalem Institute of Management, Tel Aviv, Israel, February 1987, p. 56.

32. Dunne et al., "Patterns of Firm Entry and Exit in U.S. Manufacturing Industries," RAND *Journal of Economics*, pp. 503–513.

33. W. Claiborne, "Surviving a Base Closure: Isolated Town Shows How Conversion Works," *Washington Post,* July 13, 1993.

34. Gordon and McFadden, *Economic Conversion.*

Chapter 6

1. The broad models noted here are based on Adams and Brock, *The Bigness Complex,* p. 345. Also, see Gansler, *Affording Defense,* pp. 283–284.

2. Many others have since made similar proposals. For example, Rep. Clyde Tavenner proposed it in 1914 to "prevent profiteering, fraud, and false patriotism," and Bernard Baruch in 1931 to "tak[e] the profits out of war." For a more extensive discussion of some of these proposals, see E. Molander, "Historical Antecedents of Military Industrial Criticism," *Military Affairs,* April 1976, pp. 60–61.

3. J. K. Galbraith, "The Big Defense Firms Are Really Public Firms and Should Be Nationalized," *New York Times Magazine,* November 16, 1979.

4. For a discussion of this approach, see G. Hall, "Defense Procurement and Public Utility Regulation," Rand Corporation report, 1968.

5. Joseph Bower, *When Markets Quake: The Management Challenge of Restructuring Industry* (Boston, MA: Harvard Business School Press, 1986), p. 90.

6. Richard W. Nelson, *High Technology Policies: A Five Nation Comparison* (Washington, DC: American Enterprise Institute, 1984), pp. 85–86.

7. The benefits of this to the U.S. economy are described in S. Cohen and J. Zysman, *Manufacturing Matters: The Myth of the Post-Industrial Economy* (New York: Basic Books, 1987).

8. "A Radical Reform of the Defense Acquisition System," Carnegie Commission on Science, Technology, and Government, New York, December 1, 1992.

9. Gansler, *Affording Defense,* pp. 183–189.

10. This can be clearly seen by comparing the biannually published DoD's Critical Technologies list, the Department of Commerce's Critical Emerging Technologies list, and the White House Office of Science and Technology Policy's National Critical Technologies list.

11. In this particular case, the machine was put into Watervliet Arsenal, which was built in the Civil War era, in upstate New York, and sits idle waiting for a demand for more cannons. Obviously, the small demand will not result in much modernization or even trained operator usage.

12. Ralph Nash and John Cibinic, "Nash & Cibinic Report," Washington, DC, May 1989, pp. 72–77.

13. A. Markusen and C. Hill, "Converting the Cold War Economy: Prospects for Industry, Workers and Communities," unpublished paper, Rutgers University, New Brunswick, NJ, March 1992.

14. This is the position taken by some leaders of the defense industry, such as William Anders, when he was chief executive officer of General Dynamics.

15. Gerald Lundquist, "The False Promise of Defense Conversion," *Wall Street Journal*, March 18, 1993, and Gerald Lundquist, "Shrinking Fast and Smart in the Defense Industry," *Harvard Business Review*, November-December 1992, p. 74. See also rebuttal by J. S. Gansler, "Smart Defense," a letter to the editor, *Harvard Business Review*, March-April 1993, p. 143.

16. *Foreign Affairs*, Fall 1991, as quoted in John Tirman, "Less is More," *Boston Globe*, May 9, 1993.

17. Malcolm Chalmers and Owen Green, "The United Nations Register of Conventional Arms," an initial examination of the first report, "Bradford Arms Register Studies, no. 2," and updates, Department of Peace Studies, Bradford University, West Yorkshire, U.K., October 1993.

18. These include controls on the board of directors of these firms, and the prohibition on all but financial data being exchanged.

19. Raimo Väyrynen, "Military Industrialization and Economic Development: Theory and Historical Case Studies," United Nations Institute for Disarmament Research, Dartmouth College, Hanover, N.H., 1992, p. 41.

20. *U.S. Military Coproduction Programs Assist Japan in Developing Its Civil Aircraft Industry* (Washington, DC: General Accounting Office, 1982); see also "Technology Transfer: Japanese Firms Involved in F-15 Coproduction and Civil Aircraft Programs" (Washington, DC: General Accounting Office, 1992).

21. M. W. Chinworth and D. C. Mowery, "Cross-Border Linkages and the U.S. Defense Industry: Outlook and Policy Changes," March 1993, to be published.

22. Originally published in July 1970. See *Defense and Foreign Affairs*, July 1983, p. 25.

23. Malcolm McIntosh, *Japan Rearmed* (New York: St. Martins Press, 1986), p. 25. The remark was made in 1984.

24. "The Sincerest Form of Flattery; Japanese Companies Plan to Break into the Commercial Aircraft Market," *The Economist*, November 11, 1989, p. 79.

25. *Newsweek*, January 9, 1985.

26. McIntosh, *Japan Rearmed*, p. 55.

27. "Defence R & D: A National Resource," Cabinet Office Advisory Council on Science and Technology, London, Her Majesty's Stationery Office, London, 1989.

28. "Lessons in Restructuring Defense Industry: The French Experience," Office of Technology Assessment, Washington, DC, 1992.

29. Ibid., p. 32.

Chapter 7

1. Louis Uchitelle, "Economy Expected to Absorb Effects of Military Cuts," *New York Times,* April 15, 1990.

2. One suggestion has been to simply make this facility subsidy a line item in the budget, rather than charge it to a very small quantity of a specific weapon. This was tried by the air force in 1976, when it funded about $12 million for the annual "maintenance of vital capacity: at Air Force Plant 4 (General Dynamics) and Plant 6 (Lockheed)."

3. Gansler, *Affording Defense,* pp. 181–188.

4. Arthur Alexander, *Conversion Lessons From Declining Industries in Japan* (Japan Economic Institute of America, Washington, DC, November 1990).

5. UN Center on Transnational Corporations, Risson Foundation, as shown in *The Economist,* August 21, 1993, p. 19.

6. The legislative basis in the U.S. Army is the Army Arsenal Act of 1853, which has a public sector bias, while the U.S. Air Force uses the Air Force Arsenal Act of 1951, which leaves the choice up to the Secretary of the Air Force. The Defense Industrial Reserve Act of 1973 maintains the congressional policy ambiguity with regard to the public/private issue.

7. U.S. Congress, OTA, "Building Future Security," June 1992, p. 119, gives a breakdown of the approximately $14 billion cost of annual depot maintenance.

8. Another independent study of actual public versus private operation—this one, of an air force base in Oklahoma—found a private sector cost advantage of 26 percent (for work that ranged from aircraft maintenance to base operation). *Wall Street Journal,* December 26, 1978, p. 24.

9. John Carey, et al., "Firefight Over the Weapons Labs: Can Uncle Sam's Massive R & D Machine Really Help Industry?" *Business Week,* June 7, 1993, p. 105.

10. Paul Dickson, *Think Tanks* (New York: Atheum, 1971).

11. Office of the Comptroller of the Department of Defense, "National Defense Budget Estimates for FY 1994," Washington, DC, May 1993.

12. John Deutch, Under Secretary of Defense (Acquisition), speech in Washington, DC, April 7, 1993.

13. Department of Defense, "Manpower Requirements Report FY 1994," Washington, DC, June 1993.

14. J. Mintz, "Hill Battle Expected Over Military Repairs," *Washington Post,* September 2, 1993.

15. Section 2466 of Title 10, U.S. Code.

16. "National Defense Authorization Act for FY 1994," House and Senate Bills, House Section 343, 345, 346; Senate Section 334, 335 (Washington, DC: Government Printing Office).

17. Thomas Ricks, "With Cold War Over, the Military Industrial Complex Is Dissolving," *Wall Street Journal*, May 20, 1993.

18. Subsequently, on a sale of 520 tanks to Egypt, the government proposed making all of the gun mounts themselves.

19. "Escaping the Heavy Hand of the State," *The Economist*, June 13, 1992, pp. 73–74.

20. In 1906 Congress provided funds for the army to build a small plant to make gunpowder, since DuPont had a monopoly on military powder. A. D. Chandler, *Strategy and Structure: Chapters in the History of Industrial Enterprise* (Cambridge, MA: MIT Press, 1962). As F. M. Scherer notes in *Industrial Market Structure and Economic Performance* (Chicago: Rand-McNally, 1970), this competition between the public and private sector may be the "second best" solution under some circumstances.

Chapter 8

1. "Streamlining Defense Acquisition Law," report of the DoD Acquisition Law Advisory Panel known as the "Panel 800" (Washington, DC: Government Printing Office, 1993).

2. Ray Huang, *1587 a Year of No Significance: The Ming Dynasty in Decline* (New Haven, CT: Yale University Press, 1981), p. 177.

3. U.S. General Accounting Office, *Competition Act: Defense Science Board Recommended Changes to the Act*, GAO-NSIAF-89–48, November 1988, pp. 2–5.

4. Quotations by Chairman Brooks are from "GAO Criticizes Defense Science Board Attack on Competition," news release, Committee on Government Operations, U.S. Congress, Washington, DC, November 10, 1988.

5. "Demand Side Barriers: An Agenda for Change," CSIS Working Group on Specifications and Standards, Center for Strategic and International Studies, Washington, DC, April 2, 1993, p. 4.

6. B. Dickson and L. Sullivan, "A Comparative Assessment of the Defense and Commercial Sectors," unpublished study by TASC, for the Department of Defense, March 31, 1993.

7. "Integrating Civilian and Military Technologies: An Industry Survey," interim report from the CSIS Integrating Commercial and Military Technologies for National Strength Project, Debra van Opstal, Center for Strategic and International Studies, Washington, DC, April 1993.

8. George Krikorian, "DoD's 'Cost Premium' 30 to 50 Percent," *National Defense*, Washington, DC, September 1992, pp. 12–14.

9. "Functional Performance Requirements," Defense Science Board, 1986; "Use of Commercial Components in Military Equipment," Defense Science Board, 1989.

10. Bill McAllister, "Procurement Procedures Overwhelming, Study Says; Officers 'Basically Qualified' but 'Rule Bound'" (Merit Systems Protection Board survey), *Washington Post,* July 21, 1992.

11. Andy Plattner, "Crusading for Kids on the Hostings" (Democratic presidential candidates focus on children's issues), *US News and World Report,* Sept. 14, 1987, p. 29.

12. Gansler, *Affording Defense,* p. 196.

13. "Integrating Civilian and Military Technologies," an industry survey, Center for Strategic and International Studies, Washington, DC, April 1993.

14. "Integrating Commercial and Military Technologies for National Strength," report of the CSIS Steering Committee on Security and Technology, Center for Strategic and International Studies, Washington, DC, March 1991. Co-chaired by Senator J. Bingaman, Dr. J. S. Gansler, and Dr. R. Kupperman.

15. "Integrating Civilian and Military Technologies."

16. Gansler, *Affording Defense,* pp. 174–175.

17. Department of Defense, Office of Assistant Secretary for Installations and Logistics, "Profit '76, Summary Report," Washington, DC, December 1976.

18. "Integrating Commercial and Military Technologies for National Strength."

19. Ibid., pp. 19–20.

20. Ibid., p. 24.

21. *The Economist,* July 17, 1993, p. 24. For example, in Los Angeles County, a company wanting to plant a tree has to get permission from eight different agencies and to chop one down requires forty-seven more permits.

22. "Demand Side Barriers: An Agenda for Change," CSIS Working Group on Specs and Standards, April 1993. The other 17,000 documents in the Index include commercial item descriptions, federal standards, and nongovernmental standards (such as commercial or international standards).

23. For an excellent recent report on the specifications and standards issue, see "Road Map for MILSPEC Reform: Integrating Commercial and Military Manufacturing," Center for Strategic and International Studies, Washington, DC, 1993.

24. Ibid.

25. Ibid., Appendix 1.

26. Discussion with Robert Trimble, director of contracts at Martin Marietta, Washington, DC, June 7, 1989.

27. Vice President Al Gore, "National Performance Review: Creating a Government That Works Better and Costs Less" (Washington, DC: Government Printing Office, September 7, 1993), Appendix C, p. 164.

28. J. S. Gansler, "Reforming the Defense Budget Process," *The Public Interest,* no. 75, Spring 1984, pp. 62–75.

29. J. S. Gansler, "National Security and T & E at the Beginning of the 21st Century," presented at the 1992 Annual Symposium International Test and Evaluation Association, Albuquerque, New Mexico, October 12–15, 1992.

30. Michael D. Rich, "Toward a New Government-Industry Partnership in Aerospace," Rand Corp., Santa Monica, CA. Speech delivered in Orlando, FL, February 24, 1993, p. 6.

31. Ibid.

32. A briefing by Bert Fowler, independent consultant, Washington, DC, June 2, 1993.

Chapter 9

1. Barry Bosworth, Brookings Institution, at a Capitol Hill forum arranged by the Economic Strategy Institute, titled "Economics as Strategy: America's Goals for the 21st Century," Washington, DC, March 10, 1992.

2. John P. Kotter, A Force for Change: How Leadership Differs from Management (New York: The Free Press, 1990).

3. Gansler, Affording Defense, pp. 285–286.

4. At the start of the Clinton administration, a new position (assistant secretary for economic security) was created, with the intent that it specifically be given this responsibility. The position remained unfilled for the first eighteen months after the election. In June 1994, however, it was filled and had this as its intended objective.

5. Based on an interview by noted OECD economist Henry Ergas, Washington, DC, July 1993.

6. This specific suggestion has been pushed strongly by George Heilmeier, president and chief executive officer of Bellcore (New Jersey).

7. This is from the "Panel 800" Group that was set up at the end of the Bush administration to evaluate how the government could buy more commercial equipment. They made numerous recommendations which were similar to those contained in this book and these particular quotations come from their final report "Streamlining Defense Acquisition Law," report of the DoD Acquisition Law Advisory Panel, March 1993, pp. 1–140.

8. This methodology and the data provided here was generated by the author along with Phil Odeen, Joan Habermann, and Bob Cattoi in connection with a Defense Science Board Task Force in July 1993 (chaired by Bob Hermann). It has been reported in "Report of the Defense Science Board Task Force on Defense Acquisition Reform," Office of the Under Secretary of Defense for Acquisition, Washington, DC, July 1993.

9. Amy Borrus, "The Godfather of Stealth Won't Slip This One By," Business Week, September 6, 1993, p. 60.

10. "A Quest for Excellence," Final Report to the President by the President's Blue Ribbon Commission on Defense Management, Washington, DC, June 1986.

11. "The DoD Regulatory Cost Premium: A Quantitative Assessment," Coopers and Lybrand and TASC study prepared for the Under Secretary of Defense, Acquisition and Technology, Washington, DC, December 1994.

Chapter 10

1. Christopher Farrell et al., "Industrial Policy," *Business Week,* April 6, 1992, p. 72.

2. Comment made (not for attribution) by a French government official (and senior economist) during a talk in Washington, DC, in 1991.

3. Cohen and Zysman, *Manufacturing Matters.*

4. National Science Foundation, 1992; approximately the same numbers were reported by *The Economist,* February 16, 1991.

5. Eric Block, "Toward a U.S.-Technology Strategy," National Academy of Science, Washington, DC, February 1991.

6. This is an appointed advisory board made up of senior industry, academic, and former government experts who meet frequently to advise the secretary and his staff on R & D issues. While its name is based on Science, its role has evolved toward technology (including manufacturing) and public policy, as the needs of the Department have evolved.

7. M. Scully, "Science and Technology Panel Promoted," *Washington Technology,* December 2, 1992.

8. Choate and Linger, *High Flex Society,* p. 110.

9. Bill Gertz, "Japan's Network Rated Best at Reaping Intelligence Data," *Washington Times,* July 14, 1989; also see "Trends and Future Tasks in Industrial Technology: Summary of White Paper on Industrial Technology," Ministry of International Trade and Industry, Tokyo, September 1988.

10. Statement at a conference at Harvard University by Professor Frederick M. Scherer, September 14, 1992.

11. Raymond Vernon in *Technology and Global Industry: Companies and Nations in the World Economy,* eds. B. Guile, H. Brooks (Washington, DC: National Academy Press, 1987), p. 184.

12. *U.S. News and World Report,* July 10, 1989, p. 43.

13. M. Schrage, "Software Research Groups Set," *Washington Post,* October 10, 1984.

14. National Academy of Engineering, study of microelectronic consortia, Washington, DC, 1992.

15. For an excellent and full discussion of this whole issue of technology transfer and dual-use R & D, see Alic, Branscomb, Brooks, Carter, and Epstein, *Beyond Spinoff: Military and Commercial Technologies in a Changing World* (Boston, MA: Harvard Business School Press, 1992).

16. Public Law 96–480, "Stevenson-Wydler Technology Innovation Act of 1980," October 26, 1980, Section 11(a).

17. National Competitiveness Technology Transfer Act of 1989, Public Law 101-189, Part C, Sections 3131–3133.

18. Norman Augustine, chairman of Martin Marietta, Testimony U.S. Congress, Washington, DC, August 5, 1992.

19. Through Public Law 85-325, February 1958.

20. Defense Science Board Task Force Report, "Engineering in the Manufacturing Process," March 1993, Office of the Under Secretary of Defense for Acquisition, Washington, DC; also see "The Role of Concurrent Engineering in Weapon System Acquisition," Institute for Defense Analyses Report R-338, Washington, DC, December 1988.

21. Presentation by William Reid, director of the Defense Contracts Audit Agency, Washington, DC, June 1, 1993.

22. Edwin Mansfield, "R & D in Japan and the U.S.," *American Economic Association Proceedings*, May 1988, p. 301.

23. Hobart Rowen, "Exposing Trade Curbs' Real Costs," *Washington Post*, August 22, 1993.

24. *Datamation*, December 1989, p. 44.

25. Michael E. Knell "DARPA Funds Research Yielding High-Tech Results," *Boston Herald*, June 10, 1992.

26. Neil Gross, "A Japanese 'Flop' That Became a Launching Pad," *Business Week*, June 8, 1992, p. 103.

27. Joseph Schumpeter, "Capitalism, Socialism, and Democracy," 1992.

28. Christopher Farrell, et al., "Industrial Policy," *Business Week*, April 6, 1992, p. 72.

29. It might be noted here that industrial "teaming" is not a form of competition, so that if teaming is present, there must be multiple teams.

30. Carnegie Commission on Science, Technology, and Government, January 29, 1992.

31. R. Reich, "The Quiet Path to Technology of Preeminence," *Scientific American*, October 1989, p. 47.

Chapter 11

1. *Business Week*, July 27, 1992, p. 14.

2. See U.S. Department of Labor Statistics, "Employment and Earnings," various issues.

3. National Center for Education Statistics, "Assessing Literacy: The Framework for the National Adult Literacy Survey," U.S. Department of Education, Washington, DC, 1992.

4. D. Yankelovich and J. Immerwaki, "Putting the Work Ethic to Work: A Public Agenda Report on Restoring America's Competitive Vitality," Public Agenda Foundation, New York, NY, 1983.

5. "Adult Literacy in America: A First Look at the Results of the National Adult Literacy Survey," National Center for Education Statistics, Washington, DC, September 1993.

6. Tsicho Okno, "Toyota Production System: Beyond Large-Scale Production," Production Press, 1988, p. 4.

7. Choate and Linger, *High Flex Society,* p. 196.

8. Robert Heibroner "Rust into Gold," CEO International Strategies, March/ April 1991, p. 38.

9. "Workforce 2000: Work and Workers for the 21st Century," Hudson Institute, Indianapolis, 1987, p. 102 (based on a U.S. Department of Education assessment among 21–25-year-olds).

10. William H. Kolberg, "Rebuilding America's Workforce: Business Strategies to Close the Competitiveness Gap," Irwin Professional Publications, 1991.

11. U.S. Chamber of Commerce, National Business Agenda, 1992.

12. *The Futurist,* July–August 1988.

13. "Training in America," American Society of Training and Development, 1989.

14. Based on data by Cornell labor economist John Bishop; as published in *Fortune,* August 9, 1993, p. 24.

15. Ibid.

16. Ray Marshall and Marc Tucker, *Thinking for a Living* (New York: Basic Books, 1992).

17. "Training in America," American Society of Training and Development, 1989. Based on work by Jacob Mincer, "Job Training, Wage Growth, and Labor Turnover," NCEE Background Paper, 1988.

18. Ibid.

19. *Business Week,* October 17, 1994, p. 85.

20. P. J. Hills, "Will Bush Pay Attention to Science?" *Washington Post,* November 20, 1988.

21. Lloyd Reuss, president of General Motors, at the Economic Club of Detroit, April 15, 1991.

22. Ruth Davis, Pymatuming Corp. report, Washington, DC, 1988.

23. The study was done by economists Andrei Shleifer, Keven Murphy, and Robert Vishney and reported in *Business Week,* April 6, 1992, p. 74.

24. Reuss, Economic Club of Detroit, April 15, 1991.

25. Paper by Rep. Frank Wolf (R-Va.) at a conference in Washington, DC, March 10, 1992.

26. J. Havermann, "Profiles of a Shifting U.S. Work Force," *Washington Post,* August 17, 1989.

27. *The Economist,* March 27, 1993, p. 17.

28. Cornelli Barnett, "The Collapse of British Power" (Atlantic Highlands, NJ: Humanities Press International, 1972).

29. Perversely, in 1994 Congress began passing laws to limit defense industry executives salaries (Defense Appropriations Act for FY95).

30. Author's personal experiences in touring plants in Japan and Europe. See also *Business Week,* October 23, 1989, p. 142FF.

31. Carolyn Duffy, "Lack of Technicians Threatens Workforce," *Washington Technology,* September 28, 1989.

32. Ibid.

33. *The Economist,* September 7, 1991, p. 32.

34. K. Adelman and N. Augustine, *The Defense Revolution* (San Francisco, CA: ICS Press, 1990) p. 119.

35. *The Economist,* February 25, 1989, p. 25.

36. *Washington Post,* May 3, 1992.

37. American Society for Training and Development, National Center on Education and the Economy; also, *The Economist,* August 22, 1992.

38. *U.S. News and World Report,* September 21, 1992.

39. Tyson, *Who's Bashing Whom?*

40. *The Economist,* November 13, 1993, p. 30.

41. Based on data from Brian Turner, AFL/CIO Industrial Union, Washington, DC, 1993.

42. Brian Dickson and David Leech (TASC) "Critical Defense Occupations," briefing to Defense Conversion Commission, Washington, DC, October 30, 1992.

43. *The Economist,* August 22, 1992.

44. Bill McAllister, "Quality of Work Force Seen as Not in Decline," *Washington Post,* August 13, 1992.

45. Choate and Linger, *High Flex Society,* p. 172.

46. *The Economist,* August 22, 1992.

47. *Business Week,* September 14, 1992.

48. Teledyne Brown Engineering briefing on "Employee Involvement," Washington, DC, 1992.

49. Professor Daniel Roos, MIT, Briefing to Defense Science Board, Washington, DC, July 14–15, 1993.

50. Charles Ferguson "America's High-Tech Decline," *Foreign Policy,* Spring 1989, p. 144.

51. R. Reich "The Quiet Path to Technological Preeminence," *Scientific American,* October 1989, p. 43.

52. Richard Samuel (MIT), National Research Council Meeting in Washington, DC, July 8, 1993.

53. U.S. Chamber of Commerce, *Nations Business,* Washington, DC, 1993.

54. M. J. Cetron, W. Rocha, and R. Luckins, "Into the 21st Century: Long Term Trends Affecting the United States;" *The Futurist,* July–August 1988, p. 29.

55. "Workforce 2000: Work and Workers for the 21st Century," Hudson Institute, Indianapolis, 1987.

Chapter 12

1. Niccolo Machiavelli, "On Introducing Change in Government," in *The Prince.*

2. "Engineering in the Manufacturing Process," Defense Science Board Task Force Summer 1992, Department of Defense, Washington, DC, March 1993.

3. *Government Contract Accounting,* Arthur Anderson, Spring/Summer 1992.

4. Vice President Gore, "National Performance Review: Creating a Government that Works Better and Costs Less," Government Printing Office, Washington, DC, September 7, 1993, Appendix C, p. 164.

5. For example, refer to John P. Kotter, *A Force for Change* (New York: The Free Press, 1990) for the private sector lessons; and to *Reinventing Government* (Reading, MA: Addison-Wesley, 1992) for the public sector lessons. Also see National Research Council report "Breaking the Mold" (National Academy Press, Washington, DC, 1993) for a description of the change process itself.

6. "Streamlining Defense Acquisition Law," Report of the DoD Acquisition Law Advisory Panel, Washington, DC, March 1993.

7. It is assumed that this will be the responsibility of the Assistant Secretary of Defense for Economic Security—a position established in the Clinton administration in recognition of this need.

8. A directive implementing this action was signed by secretary of defense Perry in June 1994. Its implementation will be resisted and must be aggressively pursued to have a chance for success.

9. Leslee A. Ellenson, "Flow-Down Clauses in Subcontracts," *Contract Management,* November 1993, p. 11ff.

10. For a more extensive discussion of the antitrust issue in the defense area, see Gansler, *Affording Defense,* pp. 183–184.

11. This idea was floated by Bernard Schwartz, chairman and CEO of Loral Corporation, as well as by Dale Church (a former Defense Department official). The concept is covered in an article by Lucy Reily, "Defense Conversion Loans," *Washington Technology,* July 15, 1993.

12. Vice President Gore, "National Performance Review."

13. "Engineering in the Manufacturing Process," Defense Science Board, Washington, DC, March 1993.

14. Carnegie Commission on Science, Technology, and Government, "A Science and Technology Agenda for the Nation," December 1992, p. 15.

15. Gansler, "Reforming the Defense Budget Process," pp. 62–75.

16. A Defense Science Board study, chaired by the author and reported on in "Acquisition Streamlining: Barriers to Implementation of Prior Recommendations, A Report to the Defense Science Board's Acquisition Streamlining Task Force from Team 3," (Report RE001R1, Logistics Management Institute, Bethesda, Maryland, January 1991, Volumes I and II) covered some of the older sets of recommendations (such as the Hoover Commissions of 1949 and 1955, the Fitzhugh Blue Ribbon Commission of 1970, and the Government Procurement Commission of 1972), but focuses on many of the independent study recommendations in the latter half of the 1980s and the early 1990s (with particular emphasis on those that came from the Packard Commission of 1986 and a series of Defense Science Board studies during the subsequent years). It identifies some of the fundamental obstacles and disincentives to implementation that have deterred these prior recommendations. In all cases, there were serious DoD attempts made to implement the majority of the recommendations.

17. National Research Council, *Breaking the Mold: Forging a Common Defense Manufacturing Vision* (Washington, DC: National Academy Press, 1993).

Index

About the Author

Since 1977 Jacques Gansler has been Senior Vice President and Director, TASC (an applied information technology company). Formerly he was Deputy Assistant Secretary of Defense (Materiel Acquisition); Assistant Director of Defense Research and Engineering (Electronics); Vice President, I.T.T.; Program Manager, Singer Corporation; and Engineering Section Manager, Raytheon Corporation.

He is also currently a Visiting Scholar at the Kennedy School of Government, Harvard University (where, since 1984, he has lectured on government acquisition management). He is the author of *Affording Defense* (MIT Press, 1989) and *The Defense Industry* (MIT Press, 1980). He has been a member of numerous special committees and advisory boards on defense management and government R & D policy. He is currently vice chairman of the Defense Science Board.

He holds a B.E., Yale University (Electrical Engineering); M.S., Northeastern University (Electrical Engineering); M.A., New School for Social Research (Political Economy); and Ph.D., American University (Economics).